Themes of the Qur'an

What does Qur'an say to us ?

Dr. S. Saleem MBBS

Ta-Ha Publishers Ltd.
1 Wynne Road,
London SW9 0BB
UK

Copyright © Dr. S. Saleem

Published Rabi' ath-Thani 1424/June 2003 by:
Ta-Ha Publishers Ltd.
1 Wynne Road
London SW9 0BB
Website: http://www.taha.co.uk
Email: sales@taha.co.uk

All rights reserved. No part of this publication may be reproduced, stored in any retrieval system, or transmitted in any form or by any means, electronic or otherwise, without written permission of the publishers.

By: Dr. S. Saleem
General Editor: Afsar Siddiqui
Edited by: Abdassamad Clarke

British Library Cataloguing in Publication Data
Saleem, Dr. S.
Themes of the Qur'an
I. Title

ISBN 1 842000 50 0

Typeset by: Bookwright
Website: http://www.bogvaerker.dk/Bookwright
Email: bookwright@bogvaerker.dk

Printed and bound by: Deluxe Printers, London.

Email: deluxeprinters@aol.com

Contents

Foreword	viii
Preface	x
Iman	1
One and Single	1
Light	8
Allah – Friend And Helper	9
Allah's Grace & Guidance	11
All-Knowing	16
Kind and Forgiving	19
The Messenger of Allah ﷺ	24
The Last Hour and the Day Of Judgement	29
Rewards for Right Action	44
Wrong Actions and Punishments	49
Allah's Signs	51
Qur'an	53
Shaytan	67
The Fire of Hell	71
Description of the Garden	75
Islam	83
Iman and Action	83
Doing as One Says	89
Salat and Zakat	90
Salat – prayer	93
Zakat and Spending in the Way of Allah ﷺ	97
Wastefulness and profligacy	105
Fasting	106
Hajj	106
Mosques	110
Praying At Night	111
Hijra – Emigration for the sake of Allah	112
Jihad – fighting for the sake of Allah	114

Themes of the Qur'an

- Ihsan 119
  - Nearness of Allah ﷻ 119
  - Remembering Allah ﷻ (Dhikr) 120
  - Tawba – Turning to Allah in Repentance 123
  - Praise 126
  - Gratitude and Ingratitude 130
  - Sabr – Steadfastness 134
  - Taqwa and Fear of Allah ﷻ 136
  - Tawakkul – Trust In Allah ﷻ and Reliance upon Him 142
- The Creation and Allah's Swearing Oaths by His Creations 145
  - Creation of the Human Being 161
  - Human Nature 165
  - Death 167
- People 171
  - Friends 171
  - Mumin and Kafir 173
  - The Muminun 183
  - The People of the Book 188
  - Parents 189
  - Relatives 190
  - Orphans 191
  - Differences and Disagreements 192
- Good and Bad Behaviour 195
  - One's Own Deeds 195
  - Obedience 197
  - Shirk – association of partners with Allah 200
  - Right action 207
  - Tolerance And Forgiveness 210
  - Kindness and Good Counsel 211
  - Pride And Arrogance 212
  - Humility 216
  - Respect 217
  - Backbiting 217
  - Mischief Making and Corruption 218
  - Worldly Attractions 219
  - Sustenance and provision 226
  - Testing, Trials and Calamities 228
  - Courtesy 232
  - Accusations and Slander 234
  - Promises, Trusts and Oaths 235

Contents

Shari'ah 238
    Justice 238
    Permissible and Impermissible 239
    Debts and writing them down 242
    Retaliation 243
    Marriage 244
    Divorce 245
    Inheritance 252
    Weights and Measures 253
    Riba – Usury 254
Miscellanous 256
    Dress 256
    Travel 257
    Bequests 258
    The Ummah and Islam 258
Du'a – Supplication 260
Glossary of Terms 267

بسم الله الرحمن الرحيم

Foreword

Here we have before us a book deriving from the Book of Allah and indeed consisting entirely of quotations from the Divine Book, the Qur'an, the last revelation to mankind from the One Who has no likeness.

Dr. Saleem's work here has been to extract certain themes which have always been understood by knowledgeable Muslims to be key themes of the revelation, although for the reader new to the Qur'an and reading it for the first time, they are often not immediately aware of the significance of the repeated and yet subtly varied statements that thread their ways through the text. Thus although it is now almost universally known even to non-Muslims that establishment of the prayer is one of the essential five pillars of Islam, it is not at all well known – sometimes even to contemporary Muslims – that the life-transaction of Muslims itself comprises not just Islam, but also Iman and Ihsan,[1] nor in what they comprise. Thus this book[2] will, in particular, introduce the person new to the Qur'an to some – not necessarily all – of the key themes of the revelation in a systematic way, and hopefully lead them to read the entire Qur'an as it is meant to be read, from beginning to end and back to the beginning again. Perhaps then he or she might also advance to being one of those who when they have finished set out upon another reading, not merely from a sense of religious duty but because of the inexhaustible fascination of the Book itself from which people in each age, while benefitting from the generations of scholarship

---

[1] As explained by the Messenger of Allah Muhammad ﷺ in hadith number two of the Forty Hadith of Imam an-Nawawi. (See *The Complete Forty Hadith*, Imam an-Nawawi, Ta-Ha, London, UK.)

[2] We have used throughout *The Noble Qur'an: a translation of its meanings*, by Abdalhaqq and Aisha Bewley, Bookwork, Norwich, UK. We have chosen this translation, the result of twenty-five years work, because of its marriage of impeccable scholarship in its drawing upon the most universally acknowledged of the literature of Qur'anic commentary and Arabic linguistic usages with an extremely felicitous use of a contemporary literate English.

and wisdom derived from the Qur'an, draw out new and fascinating insights pertinent to their age, their lives and the future they face, most significantly our own inevitable deaths and return to the One Who brought us all into being.

Although it might appear self-evident, yet this matter of reading is not all that it appears to be. The Qur'an is The Reading, but it is necessary to grasp something of what the nature of reading is in order to be able to approach the Book, for in this apparently most literate of ages, increasing numbers of people are only able to read what they already conceive to be there in the text, and when confronted with anything even slightly different from their preconceptions, are simply unable to comprehend it.

Thus the first task of the reader is to open him- or her-self – whether Muslim or non-Muslim – to listening in order to try and hear what the Lord of the Universe is saying to us. There is simply no other starting point that is of any use to the reader than understanding that this Book, although revealed over a thousand four hundred years ago to the Messenger of Allah ﷺ, is from one's own Lord directly to oneself. It is only reading with that alertness to hear what Allah is saying to one that can begin to allow one to see beyond the thick mass of prejudices that are the consequence of living in this deeply programmed society. Then sometimes one is just able to grasp some of the astonishing statements that are so liable to slip past one's everyday consciousness.

Although it is widely acknowledged that a knowledge of Arabic and the sciences of Qur'anic commentary – shari'ah, hadith, the abrogating and abrogated ayat, the Makkan and Madinan Surahs, Arabic rhetoric, tasawwuf, etc., – are vital for a deep understanding of Qur'an, yet a great deal can be gleaned from a competent translation, and we hope that the reader will find Dr. Saleem's arrangement of some of the ayats of the Qur'an according to their thematic content useful in his or her study.

Abdassamad Clarke

Preface

This is not the "Meaning of the Qur'an" nor is it tafsir of Qur'an. This is only an everyday reminder on topics in our lives as to how we should live, how we should behave and what we should all do according to the message and guidance Allah ﷻ has sent for us through His and our beloved Prophet ﷺ.

Verses mentioned are only for reference. The translation is taken from Abdalhaqq and Aisha Bewley's *The Noble Qur'an: a new rendering of its meaning in English*.

In order to reach the spirit of the revelation, it would be necessary to go to the Book for the ayah mentioned and go into it deeply in its context. Occasionally, quoting the Ayat alone misses some of this.

Often one ayah contains more than one subject resulting either in its repetition under different topics or its being split to go under the relevant headings, and sometimes there are overlaps. So, it is even more important to go through the entire passage and its proper explanation. That may be difficult but the life we are living is very short, even if we live a hundred years or more, and the life after death is forever and ever.

Once our granddaughter Maryam, then aged six, said: "It is hard to be a Muslim." So true – so very true. But this hardship is only for a short time in return for eternal happiness and the good pleasure of our Creator Who has promised all the comfort for which one could wish, and all of it everlasting!

Even here in this world, if we do every thing to please our Lord, it all becomes so easy.

In this life, so often we go endure hard work and difficulties to achieve good results; so why not endeavour for perpetual good results?

This is a humble effort to remind ourselves in many fields to stay on the track and not fall into the dark, fathomless pit Shaytan, our enemy, is constantly preparing for us.

May Allah ﷻ help us all, Ameen.

Iman

One and Single

1. Your God is One God. There is no god but Him, the All-Merciful, the Most Merciful. Al-Baqara 162
2. ...Say: 'He is only One God, and I am free of all you associate with Him.' Al-An'am 20
3. Say: 'What do you think? If Allah took away your hearing and your sight and sealed up your hearts, what god is there, other than Allah, who could give them back to you...?' Al-An'am 47
4. Mankind! I am the Messenger of Allah to you all, of Him to whom the kingdom of the heavens and earth belongs. There is no god but Him. He gives life and causes to die.' So have iman in Allah and His Messenger, the Unlettered Prophet, who has iman in Allah and His words, and follow him so that hopefully you will be guided. Al-A'raf 158
5. Allah is He to whom the kingdom of the heavens and earth belongs. He gives life and causes to die. You have no protector or helper besides Allah. At-Tawba 117
6. Do you not see how your Lord stretches out shadows? If He had wished He could have made them stationary. Then We appoint the sun to be the pointer to them. Then We draw them back to Ourselves in gradual steps. It is He who made the night a cloak for you and sleep a rest, and He made the day a time for rising. It is He who sends out the winds, bringing advance news of His mercy. And We send down from heaven pure water so that by it We can bring a dead land to life and give drink to many of the animals and people We created. Al-Furqan 45-49
7. He is Allah. There is no god but Him. Praise be to Him in the dunya and the akhira. Judgement belongs to Him. You will be returned to Him. Al-Qasas 70
8. Say: 'What do you think? If Allah made it permanent night for you till the Day of Rising, what god is there other than Allah to bring you light? Do you not then hear?' Say: 'What do you think? If Allah made it permanent day for you till the Day of Rising, what

god is there other than Allah to bring you night to rest in? Do you not then see?' Al-Qasas 71-72

9. Do not call on any other god along with Allah. There is no god but Him. All things are passing except His Face. Judgement belongs to Him. You will be returned to Him. Al-Qasas 88

10. So seek your provision from Allah and worship Him and give thanks to Him. It is to Him you will be returned.' Al-'Ankabut 17

11. It is Allah who made the earth a stable home for you and the sky a dome, and formed you, giving you the best of forms, and provided you with good and wholesome things. That is Allah, your Lord. Blessed be Allah, the Lord of all the worlds. Al-Mumin 64

12. That is Allah, your Lord. There is no god but Him, the Creator of everything. So worship Him. He is responsible for everything. Al-An'am 103

13. Nay, He Who created the heavens and the earth, and sent down for your water from the cloud; then We cause to grow thereby beautiful gardens; it is not possible for you that you should make the trees thereof to grow. Is there a god with Allah? Nay! They are a people who deviate. Or, Who made the earth a resting place and made in it rivers, and raised on it mountains, and placed between the two seas a barrier. Is there a god with Allah? Nay! Most of them do not know! Or, Who answers the distress one when he calls upon Him and removes the evil, and He will make you successors in the earth. Is there a god with Allah? Little is it that you mind! Or, Who guides you in utter darkness of the land and the sea, and Who sends the winds as good news before His mercy. Is there a god with Allah? Exalted be Allah above what they associate (with Him). Or, who originates the creation, then reproduces it, and Who gives you sustenance from the heaven and the earth. Is there a god with Allah? Say: Bring your proof if you are truthful. Say: No one in the heavens and the earth knows the unseen but Allah; and they do not know when they shall be raised. An-Naml 60-65

14. Your God is One God. As for those who do not have iman in the akhira, their hearts are in denial and they are puffed up with pride. An-Nahl 22

15. My slaves, you who have iman, My earth is wide, so worship Me alone! Al-'Ankabut 56
16. ...So worship Allah, making your deen sincerely His. Indeed is the sincere deen not Allah's alone? Az-Zumar 2-3
17. Say: 'I am commanded to worship Allah, making my deen sincerely His.' Az-Zumar 12
18. No! Worship Allah and be among the thankful. Az-Zumar 63
19. So call upon Allah, making your deen sincerely His, even though the kafirun detest it. Al-Mumin 13
20. I only created jinn and man to worship Me. Adh-Dhariyat 56
21. Allah is my Lord and your Lord so worship Him. This is a straight path.' Az-Zukhruf 64
22. So do not call on any other god along with Allah or you will be among those who will be punished. Ash-Shu'ara 212
23. You God is one God. Ha-Mim 6
24. That is Allah, your Lord, the Creator of everything. There is no god but Him – so how have you been perverted? Al-Mumin 62
25. If Allah had desired to have a son He would have chosen whatever He wished from what He has created. Glory be to Him! He is Allah, the One, the All-Conquering. Az-Zumar 5
26. Allah, there is no god but Him, the Living, the Self-Sustaining. He is not subject to drowsiness or sleep. Everything in the heavens and the earth belongs to Him. Who can intercede with Him except by His permission? He knows what is before them and what is behind them but they cannot grasp any of His knowledge save what He wills. His Footstool encompasses the heavens and the earth and their preservation does not tire Him. He is the Most High, the Magnificent. Al-Baqara 253-4
27. Allah bears witness that there is no god but Him, as do the angels and the people of knowledge, upholding justice. There is no god but Him, the Almighty, the All-Wise. Al 'Imran 18
28. This is the true account: there is no other god besides Allah. Allah – He is the Almighty, the All-Wise. Al 'Imran 61
29. Allah, there is no god but Him. He will gather you to the Day of Rising about which there is no doubt. And whose speech could be truer than Allah's? An-Nisa 86

30. What is in the heavens and in the earth belongs to Allah. Allah encompasses all things. An-Nisa 125
31. What is in the heavens and in the earth belongs to Allah. Allah suffices as a Guardian. An-Nisa 131
32. The kingdom of the heavens and the earth and everything in them belongs to Allah. He has power over all things. Al-Ma'ida 122
33. Allah is He to Whom everything in the heavens and everything in the earth belongs... Ibrahim 3
34. ...'Give warning that there is no god but Me, so have taqwa of Me!' An-Nahl 2
35. Allah says, 'Do not take two gods. He is only One God. So dread Me alone.' Everything in the heavens and earth belongs to Him, and the deen belongs to Him, firmly and for ever. So why do you fear anyone other than Allah? Any blessing you have is from Allah. Then when harm touches you, it is to Him you cry for help. But when He removes the harm from you, a group of you associate others with their Lord, ungrateful for what We have given them. Enjoy yourselves. You will soon know! An-Nahl 51-55
36. Say: 'If there had, as you say, been other gods together with Him, they would have sought a way to the Master of the Throne.' Glory be to Him! He is exalted above what they say in Greatness and Sublimity! The seven heavens and the earth and everyone in them glorify Him. There is nothing which does not glorify Him with praise but you do not understand their glorification. He is All-Forbearing, Ever-Forgiving. Bani Isra'il 42-44
37. ...your god is One God. Al-Kahf 105
38. ...Everything in front of us, and everything behind us, and everything in between belongs to Him. Your Lord does not forget.'
He is Lord of the heavens and the earth and everything in between them, so worship Him and persevere in His worship. Do you know of any other with His Name? Maryam 64-65
39. ...the All-Merciful, established firmly upon the Throne. Everything in the heavens and everything on the earth and everything in between them and everything under the ground belongs to Him. Though you speak out loud, He knows your secrets and what is even more concealed. Allah, there is no god but Him. The Most

Beautiful Names are His. Ta Ha 4-7

40. Your God is only Allah, there is no god but He; He comprehends all things in His knowledge. Ta Ha 98

41. …Your Lord is the Lord of the heavens and the earth, He who brought them into being… Al-Anbiya 56

42. Say: 'It is revealed to me that your god is One God. So are you Muslims?' Al-Anbiya 107

43. That is because Allah is the Real and gives life to the dead and has power over all things. Al-Hajj 6

44. …Allah merges night into day and merges day into night and because Allah is All-Hearing, All-Seeing. That is because Allah is the Real and what you call on apart from Him is false. Allah is the All-High, the Most Great. Do you not see that Allah sends down water from the sky and then in the morning the earth is covered in green? Allah is All-Subtle, All-Aware. Everything in the heavens and everything in the earth belongs to Him. Allah is the Rich Beyond Need, the Praiseworthy. Al-Hajj 59-62

45. …'My people, worship Allah. You have no god other than Him. So will you not have taqwa?' Al-Muminun 23

46. It is He who gives life and causes to die and His is the alternation of the night and day. So will you not use your intellect? Al-Muminun 81

47. Allah has no son and there is no other god accompanying Him, for then each god would have gone off with what he created and one of them would have been exalted above the other. Glory be to Allah above what they describe, Knower of the Unseen and the Visible! May He be exalted above all they associate with Him! Al-Muminun 92-93

48. Exalted be Allah, the King, the Real. There is no god but Him, Lord of the Noble Throne. Al-Muminun 117

49. Everything in the heavens and the earth belongs to Allah. An-Nur 62

50. He who created the heavens and the earth and everything in between them in six days, and then established Himself firmly on the Throne; the All-Merciful – ask anyone who is informed about Him. Al-Furqan 59

51. Say: Tell me, if Allah were to make the night to continue indefinitely on you till the day of resurrections, who is the god besides Allah that could bring you light? Al-Qasas 71
52. Alif Lam Mim Allah, there is no god but Him, the Living, the Self-Sustaining. Al 'Imran 1
53. ...your God is One: Lord of the heavens and the earth and everything between them; Lord of the Easts. As-Saffat 4-5
54. Lord of the heavens and the earth and everything between them, the Almighty, the Endlessly Forgiving.' Sad 65
55. He is the Raiser of ranks, the Possessor of the Throne, He sends the Ruh by His command to whichever of His slaves He wills so that he may warn mankind about the Day of Meeting: Al-Mumin 14
56. It is He who gives life and causes to die. When He decides on something, He just says to it, 'Be!' and it is. Al-Mumin 68
57. The Path of Allah to Whom everything in the heavens and everything on the earth belongs. Indeed all matters return eventually to Allah. Ash-Shura 50
58. It is He who is God in heaven and God on earth. He is the All-Wise, the All-Knowing. Blessed be Him to whom belongs the sovereignty of the heavens and the earth and everything in between them. The knowledge of the Hour is with Him. You will be returned to Him. Az-Zukhruf 84-85
59. The Lord of the heavens and the earth and everything in between them, if you are people with certainty. There is no god but Him – He gives life and causes to die – your Lord and the Lord of your forefathers, the previous peoples. Ad-Dukhan 6-7
60. ...that it is He Who brings about both laughter and tears; that it is He Who brings about both death and life; An-Najm 42-43
61. Blessed be the name of your Lord, Master of Majesty and Generosity. Ar-Rahman 77
62. The Lord of the two Easts and the Lord of the two Wests. Ar-Rahman 15
63. He is Allah – there is no god but Him. He is the Knower of the Unseen and the Visible. He is the All-Merciful, the Most Merciful. He is Allah – there is no god but Him. He is the King, the

Most Pure, the Perfect Peace, the Trustworthy, the Safeguarder, the Almighty, the Compeller, the Supremely Great. Glory be to Allah above all they associate with Him. He is Allah – the Creator, the Maker, the Giver of Form. To Him belong the Most Beautiful Names. Everything in the heavens and earth glorifies Him. He is the Almighty, the All-Wise. Al-Hashr 22-24

64. He – exalted be the Majesty of our Lord ! – has neither wife nor son. Al-Jinn 3

65. Lord of the East and West – there is no god but Him – so take Him as your Guardian. Al-Muzzammil 9

66. Your Lord's Assault is very fierce indeed. He originates and regenerates. He is the Ever-Forgiving, the All-Loving, the Possessor of the Throne, the All-Glorious, the Doer of whatever He desires. Al-Buruj 12-16

67. ...the Almighty, the All-Praiseworthy – Him to whom the Kingdom of the heavens and the earth belongs. Allah is Witness of all things. Al-Buruj 8-9

68. Recite: And your Lord is the Most Generous, He who taught by the pen, taught man what he did not know. Al-'Alaq 3-5

69. In the name of Allah, All-Merciful, Most Merciful Say: He is Allah, Absolute Oneness, Allah, the Everlasting Sustainer of all. He has not given birth and was not born. And no one is comparable to Him. Al-Ikhlas 1-4

70. Everything in the heavens and everything in the earth belongs to Allah. Whether you divulge what is in yourselves or keep it hidden, Allah will still call you to account for it. He forgives whoever He wills and He punishes whoever He wills. Allah has power over all things. Al-Baqara 283

71. Allah – Him from Whom nothing is hidden, either on earth or in heaven. It is He who forms you in the womb however He wills. There is no god but Him, the Almighty, the All-Wise. Al 'Imran 5-6

72. Say, 'O Allah! Master of the Kingdom! You give sovereignty to whoever You will You take sovereignty from whoever You will. You exalt whoever You will You abase whoever You will. All good is in Your hands. You have power over all things. You

merge the night into the day. You merge the day into the night. You bring out the living from the dead. You bring out the dead from the living. You provide for whoever You will without any reckoning.' Al 'Imran 26-27

73. Everything in the heavens and everything in the earth belongs to Allah. He forgives whoever He wills and punishes whoever He wills. Allah is Ever-Forgiving, Most Merciful. Al 'Imran 129

74. Allah is only One God. He is too Glorious to have a son! Everything in the heavens and in the earth belongs to Him. Allah suffices as a Guardian. An-Nisa 170

75. 'The kingdom of the heavens and the earth and everything between them belongs to Allah. He is our final destination.' Al-Ma'idah 18

76. That is because Allah merges night into day and merges day into night and because Allah is All-Hearing, All-Seeing. That is because Allah is the Real and what you call on apart from Him is false. Allah is the All-High, the Most Great. Al-Hajj 59-60

77. Say: 'Who is the Lord of the Seven Heavens and the Lord of the Mighty Throne?' They will say: 'Allah.' Say: 'So will you not have taqwa?' Al-Muminun 87

78. Say: 'In whose hand is the dominion over everything, He who gives protection and from whom no protection can be given, if you have any knowledge?' Al-Muminun 89

79. There is no changing the words of Allah. Yunus 64

80. Shall man then have whatever he covets? The last and the first belong to Allah. An-Najm 24-25

Light

1. They desire to extinguish Allah's Light with their mouths. But Allah refuses to do other than perfect His Light, even though the kafirun detest it. At-Tawba 32

2. Allah is the Light of the heavens and the earth. The metaphor of His Light is that of a niche in which there is a lamp, the lamp inside a glass, the glass like a brilliant star, lit from a blessed tree, an olive, neither of the east nor of the west, its oil all but giving off light even if no fire touches it. Light upon Light. Allah

guides to His Light whoever He wills and Allah makes metaphors for mankind and Allah has knowledge of all things. In houses which Allah has permitted to be built and in which His name is remembered, there are men who proclaim His glory morning and evening, not distracted by trade or commerce from the remembrance of Allah and the establishment of salat and the payment of zakat… An-Nur 35-36

3. And the earth will shine with the Pure Light of its Lord; the Book will be put in place; the Prophets and witnesses will be brought; it will be decided between them with the truth; and they will not be wronged. Az-Zumar 66

4. They desire to extinguish Allah's Light with their mouths but Allah will perfect His Light, though the kafirun hate it. As-Saff 8

5. Mankind! a clear proof has come to you from your Lord. We have sent down a Clear Light to you. An-Nisa 173

6. It is He Who calls down blessing on you, as do His angels, to bring you out of the darkness into the light. He is Most Merciful to the muminun. Al-Ahzab 43

Allah – Friend And Helper

1. Allah loves good-doers. Al 'Imran 148 & 134, Al-Ma'ida 13
2. Allah loves those who purify themselves. At-Tawba 108
3. He loves those who purify themselves. Al-Baqara 222
4. Yes, the friends of Allah will feel no fear and will know no sorrow: those who have iman and show taqwa. Yunus 62-63
5. If Allah afflicts you with harm, no one can remove it except Him. If He desires good for you, no one can avert His favour. He bestows it on whichever of His slaves He wills. He is Ever-Forgiving, Most Merciful. Yunus 107
6. No, Allah is your Protector. And He is the best of helpers. Al 'Imran 150
7. If Allah touches you with harm, none can remove it but Him. If He touches you with good, He has power over all things. Al-An'am 18
8. Say: 'What do you think? If Allah took away your hearing and your sight and sealed up your hearts, what god is there, other than

Allah, who could give them back to you?' Al-An'am 47

9. ...know that Allah is your Master, the Best of Masters, and the Best of Helpers! Al-Anfal 40

10. The successful outcome is for those who have taqwa. Anyone who does a good action will get something better. Al-Qasas 83-84

11. ...hold fast to Allah. He is your Protector – the Best Protector, the Best Helper. Al-Hajj 76

12. When harm touches people they call on their Lord, making tawba to Him. But then, when He gives them a taste of mercy from Him, a group of them immediately associate others with their Lord. Ar-Rum 32

13. Say: 'Who is going to shield you from Allah if He desires evil for you or desires mercy for you?' They will find no one to protect or help them besides Allah. Al-Ahzab 17

14. Have they then taken others besides Him as protectors? But Allah is the Protector. Ash-Shura 7

15. You will not be able to thwart Him on the earth and you have no protector or helper besides Allah. Ash-Shura 29

16. Whoever Allah misguides has no one to protect them after that. Ash-Shura 41

17. They have no one to protect or help them apart from Allah. There is no way out for anyone Allah misguides. Ash-Shura 43

18. You who have iman! if you help Allah, He will help you and make your feet firm. Muhammad 8

19. If Allah helps you, no one can vanquish you. If He forsakes you, who can help you after that? So the muminun should put their trust in Allah. Al 'Imran 160

20. ...And if anyone inflicts an injury the same as the one done to him and then is again oppressed, Allah will come to his aid. Allah is All-Pardoning, Ever-Forgiving. Al-Hajj 58

21. ...'Seek help in Allah and be steadfast. The earth belongs to Allah. He bequeathes it to any of His slaves He wills. The successful outcome is for those who have taqwa.' Al-A'raf 128

22. My Protector is Allah who sent down the Book. He takes care of the salihun.' Al-A'raf 196

23. We will certainly help Our Messengers and those who have iman both in the life of the dunya and on the Day the witnesses appear, Al-Mumin 51

24. It is He who sent down serenity into the hearts of the muminun thereby increasing their iman with more iman – the legions of the heavens and the earth belong to Allah. Allah is All-Knowing, All Wise - Al-Fath 4

25. Everyone in the heavens and earth requests His aid. Every day He is engaged in some affair. Ar-Rahman 27

26. Allah suffices as a Protector; Allah suffices as a Helper. An-Nisa 44

27. Our Lord is the All-Merciful, the One whose help is sought in the face of what you describe.' Al-Anbiya 111

28. Anyone who thinks that Allah will not help him in the dunya and the akhira should stretch a rope up to the ceiling and then hang himself. Let him see whether his stratagem gets rid of what enrages him! Al-Hajj 15

29. Remember when you called on your Lord for help and He responded to you: 'I will reinforce you with a thousand angels riding rank after rank.' Allah only did this to give you good news and that so your hearts would be at rest. Al-Anfal 9-10

30. Then Allah sent down His serenity on His Messenger and on the muminun, and sent down troops you could not see,... At-Tawba 26

31. ...Then Allah sent down His serenity upon him and reinforced him with troops you could not see... At-Tawba 40

Allah's Grace & Guidance

1. Say, 'Allah's guidance is true guidance. ... Say, 'All favour is in Allah's Hand and He gives it to whoever He wills. Allah is All-Encompassing, All-Knowing. He picks out for His mercy whoever He wills. Allah's favour is indeed immense.' Al 'Imran 72-73

2. Allah showed great kindness to the muminun when He sent a Messenger to them from among themselves to recite His Signs to them and purify them and teach them the Book and Wisdom, even though before that they were clearly misguided. Al 'Imran 164

3. Allah desires to make things clear to you and to guide you to the correct practices of those before you and to turn towards you. Allah is All-Knowing, All-Wise.
4. Allah desires to turn towards you, but those who pursue their lower appetites desire to make you deviate completely.
5. Allah desires to make things lighter for you. Man was created weak. An-Nisa 26-27-28
6. Whoever obeys Allah and the Messenger will be with those whom Allah has blessed: the Prophets and the siddiqun, the martyrs and the salihun. What excellent company such people are! That is favour from Allah. Allah suffices as a Knower. An-Nisa 68-69
7. Allah has sent down the Book and Wisdom to you and taught you what you did not know before. Allah's favour to you is indeed immense. An-Nisa 112
8. He has made mercy incumbent on Himself. Al-An'am 12
9. Your Lord is the Rich Beyond Need, the Possessor of Mercy. If He wanted, He could remove you and replace you with anything else He wanted to, just as He produced you from the descendants of another people. Al-An'am 134
10. We have brought them a Book elucidating everything with knowledge, as guidance and a mercy for people who have iman. Al-A'raf 51
11. He said, 'As for My punishment, I strike with it anyone I will. My mercy extends to all things but I will prescribe it for those who have taqwa and pay zakat, and those who believe in Our Signs... Al-A'raf 156
12. And among the desert arabs there are some who have iman in Allah and the Last Day and regard what they give as something which will bring them nearer to Allah and to the prayers of the Messenger. It does indeed bring them near. Allah will admit them into His mercy. Allah is Ever-Forgiving, Most Merciful. Al-Tawba 100
13. Allah is All-Compassionate to mankind, Most Merciful. Al-Hajj 63
14. Among His Signs is that He sends the winds bearing good news, to give you a taste of His mercy, and to make the ships run by His command, and to enable you to seek His bounty so that hopefully you will be thankful. Ar-Rum 45

15. Whoever holds fast to Allah has been guided to a straight path. Al 'Imran 101
16. When Allah desires to guide someone, He expands his breast to Islam. When He desires to misguide someone, He makes his breast narrow and constricted as if he were climbing up into the sky. Al-An'am 126
17. Say: 'Allah's is the conclusive argument. If He had willed He could have guided every one of you.' Al-An'am 150
18. Whoever Allah guides is truly guided; but those He misguides are the lost. Al-A'raf 178
19. Allah does not guide wrongdoing people. At-Tawba 19
20. Allah does not guide people who are deviators. At-Tawba 24
21. Allah misguides whoever He wills and guides to Himself all who turn to Him. Ar-Ra'd 28
22. If Allah had willed He would have made you one community. However, He misguides anyone He wills and guides anyone He wills. You will be questioned about what you did. An-Nahl 93
23. Allah augments those who are guided by giving them greater guidance. Maryam 77
24. ... so that those who have been given knowledge will know it is the truth from their Lord and have iman in it and their hearts will be humbled to Him. Allah guides those who have iman to a straight path. Al-Hajj 52
25. We have sent down Signs making things clear. Allah guides whoever He wills to a straight path. An-Nur 44
26. Allah misguides whoever He wills and guides whoever He wills. Fatir 8
27. The skins of those who fear their Lord tremble at it [the Qur'an] and then their skins and hearts yield softly to the remembrance of Allah. That is Allah's guidance by which He guides whoever He wills. And no one can guide those whom Allah misguides. Az-Zumar 22
28. If Allah misguides someone, he has no guide and if Allah guides someone, he cannot be misguided. Az-Zumar 35
29. Allah chooses for Himself anyone He wills and guides to Himself those who turn to Him. Ash-Shura 11

30. He increases in guidance those who are already guided and gives them their taqwa. Muhammad 18
31. You did not expect to be given the Book. It is nothing but a mercy from your Lord... Al-Qasas 86
32. ...proclaim Allah's greatness for the way that He has guided you... Al-Hajj 35
33. Your Lord is the Rich Beyond Need, the Possessor of Mercy. Al-An'am 134
34. Prescribe good for us in the dunya and the akhira. We have truly turned to You.' He said, 'As for My punishment, I strike with it anyone I will. My mercy extends to all things but I will prescribe it for those who have taqwa and pay zakat, and those who believe in Our Signs. Al-A'raf 156
35. But Allah selects for His mercy whomever He wills. Allah's favour is truly vast. Al-Baqara 104
36. How can Allah guide a people who have become kafir after having had iman? They bore witness that the Messenger was true and that the Clear Signs had come to them. Allah does not guide people who are wrongdoers. Al 'Imran 85
37. Allah does not guide deviant people. Al-Ma'ida 108
38. ...Their bad actions are made to seem good to them. Allah does not guide kafir people. At-Tawba 37
39. Allah does not guide deviant people. At-Tawba 81
40. It is not right for the Prophet and those who have iman to ask forgiveness for the mushrikun – even if they are close relatives – after it has become clear to them... At-Tawba 114
41. Allah calls to the Abode of Peace and He guides whom He wills to a straight path. Yunus 25
42. Say: 'Can any of your partner-gods guide to the truth?' Say: 'Allah guides to the truth. Who has more right to be followed – He who guides to the truth, or he who cannot guide unless he is guided? What is the matter with you? How do you reach your judgement?' Yunus 35
43. ...Allah misguides anyone He wills and guides anyone He wills. He is the Almighty, the All-Wise. Ibrahim 5
44. ...Whoever Allah guides is truly guided. But if He misguides

someone, you will find no protector for them to guide them rightly. Al-Kahf 17

45. But when guidance comes to you from Me, all those who follow My guidance will not go astray and will not be miserable. Ta Ha 120-1

46. ...your Lord is a sufficient guide and helper. Al-Furqan 31

47. You cannot guide those you would like to but Allah guides those He wills. He has best knowledge of the guided. Al-Qasas 56

48. However, those who do wrong pursue their whims and desires without any knowledge. Who can guide those whom Allah has led astray? They will have no helpers. Ar-Rum 28

49. You will not make dead men hear; you will not make deaf men hear the call, when they turn their backs in flight. You will not guide blind men from their misguidance. You will not make anyone hear except for those who have iman in Our Signs and so are Muslims. Ar-Rum 51-52

50. They think they have done you a favour by becoming Muslims! Say: 'Do not consider your Islam a favour to me. No indeed! It is Allah who has favoured you by guiding you to iman if you are telling the truth.' Al–Hujurat 17

51. ...Allah does not guide people who are deviators. As-Saff 5

52. Who could do greater wrong than someone who invents a lie against Allah when he has been called to Islam? Allah does not guide wrongdoing people. As-Saff 7

53. It is He who sent His Messenger with guidance and the Deen of Truth to exalt it over every other deen, though the mushrikun hate it. As-Saff 9

54. Allah does not guide ungrateful (kafir) people. Al-Baqara 264

55. He gives wisdom to whoever He wills and he who has been given wisdom has been given great good. But no one pays heed but people of intelligence. Al-Baqara 269

56. Allah guides whoever He wills. Al-Baqara 271

57. Allah does not guide any unbridled inveterate liar. Al-Mumin 28

58. When Allah misguides someone, you will find no way for him. An-Nisa 87. See also an-Nisa 143

59. If Allah knew of any good in them, He would have made

them able to hear. But even if He had made them able to hear, they would still have turned away. Al-Anfal 23
60. Whoever holds fast to Allah has been guided to a straight path. Al 'Imran 101
61. Say, 'Both East and West belong to Allah. He guides whoever He wills to a straight path.' Al-Baqara 141

All-Knowing

1. He is Allah in the heavens and in the earth. He knows what you keep secret and what you make public and He knows what you earn. Al-An'am 4
2. They will ask you about the Hour: when is it due? Say: 'Knowledge of it rests with my Lord alone. He alone will reveal it at its proper time...' Al-A'raf 187
3. Allah is All-Knowing, All-Wise. At-Tawba 107
4. The keys of the Unseen are in His possession. No one knows them but Him. He knows everything in the land and sea. No leaf falls without His knowing it. There is no seed in the darkness of the earth, and nothing moist or dry which is not in a Clear Book. Al-An'am 60
5. You do not engage in any matter or recite any of the Qur'an or do any action without Our witnessing you while you are occupied with it. Not even the smallest speck eludes your Lord, either on earth or in heaven. Nor is there anything smaller than that, or larger, which is not in a Clear Book. Yunus 61
6. See how they wrap themselves round trying to conceal their feelings from Him! No, indeed! When they wrap their garments round themselves, He knows what they keep secret and what they make public. He knows what their hearts contain. Hud 5
7. Your Lord is not unaware of what you do. Hud 123
8. The Unseen of the heavens and earth belongs to Allah. The matter of the Hour is only the blink of an eye away, or even nearer. Allah has power over all things. An-Nahl 77
9. Do you not know that Allah knows everything in heaven and earth? That is in a Book. That is easy for Allah. Al-Hajj 68
10. Allah is All-Knowing, All-Forbearing. Al-Hajj 57

11. Allah knows everything in the heavens and in the earth. Al-'Ankabut 52
12. Truly Allah has knowledge of the Hour and sends down abundant rain and knows what is in the womb. And no self knows what it will earn tomorrow and no self knows in what land it will die. Allah is All-Knowing, All-Aware. Luqman 33
13. Whether you divulge a thing or conceal it, Allah has knowledge of all things. Al-Ahzab 54
14. No female becomes pregnant or gives birth except with His knowledge. Fatir 11
15. Allah knows the Unseen of the heavens and earth. Allah knows what the heart contains. Fatir 38
16. 'Our Lord, You encompass everything in mercy and knowledge! Al-Mumin 6
17. He (Allah) knows what the heart contains. Ash-Shura 22
18. He is the First and the Last, the Outward and the Inward. He has knowledge of all things. Al-Hadid 3
19. Allah knows what you keep secret and what you make public. An-Nahl 19
20. Allah knows what you were doing. An-Nahl 28
21. [He is] the Knower of the Unseen and the Visible, the Most Great, the High-Exalted. Ar-Ra'd 10
22. He knows what is said openly and He knows what you hide. Al-Anbiya 110
23. Say, 'Whether you conceal what is in your breasts or make it known, Allah knows it. He knows what is in the heavens and what is on earth. Allah has power over all things.' Al 'Imran 29
24. Allah knows the contents of your hearts. Al 'Imran 154, (See also Bani Isra'il 25 and Ash-Shura 24)
25. Most of them follow nothing but conjecture. Conjecture is of no use whatsoever against the truth. Allah most certainly knows what they are doing. Yunus 36
26. The Unseen of the heavens and the earth belongs to Him. How perfectly He sees, how well He hears! Al-Kahf 26
27. He knows what is before them and what is behind them. All matters return to Allah. Al-Hajj 74

28. Your Lord knows what their hearts conceal and what they divulge. Al-Qasas 69

29. He knows what goes into the earth and what comes out of it, and what comes down from heaven and what goes up into it. And He is the Most Merciful, the Ever-Forgiving. Those who are kafir say, 'The Hour will never come.' Say: 'Yes, by my Lord, it certainly will come!' He is the Knower of the Unseen, Whom not even the weight of the smallest particle eludes, either in the heavens or in the earth; nor is there anything smaller or larger than that which is not in a Clear Book. Saba' 2-3

30. Knowledge of the Hour is referred to Him. And no fruit emerges from its husk, nor does any female get pregnant or give birth, without His knowledge... Fussilat 46

31. Your Lord knows best those who are misguided from His Way and He knows best those who are guided. An-Najm 29

32. He has most knowledge of you when He first produced you from the earth, and when you were embryos in your mothers' wombs. So do not claim purity for yourselves. He knows best those who have taqwa. An-Najm 31

33. Do you not see that Allah knows what is in the heavens and on the earth? Three men cannot confer together secretly without Him being the fourth of them, or five without Him being the sixth of them, or fewer than that or more without Him being with them wherever they are. Then He will inform them on the Day of Rising of what they did. Allah has knowledge of all things. Al-Mujadila 7

34. Whether you keep your words secret or say them out loud He knows what the heart contains. Does He who created not then know? He is the All-Pervading, the All-Aware. Al-Mulk 13-14

35. He is the Knower of the Unseen, and does not divulge His Unseen to anyone – except a Messenger with whom He is well pleased, and then He posts sentinels before him and behind him, so that He may know that they have indeed transmitted the Messages of their Lord. He encompasses what is in their hands and has counted the exact number of everything. Al-Jinn 26-28

36. He is with them when they spend the night saying things

which are not pleasing to Him. Allah encompasses everything they do. An-Nisa 107

37. Eyesight cannot perceive Him but He perceives eyesight. He is the All-Penetrating, the All-Aware. Al-An'am 104

38. The Words of your Lord are perfect in truthfulness and justice. No one can change His Words. He is the All-Hearing, the All-Knowing. Al-An'am 116

39. Your Lord knows best who is misguided from His Way and He knows best those who are guided. Al-An'am 118

40. Our Lord! You know what we keep hidden and what we divulge. Nothing is hidden from Allah either on the earth or in heaven. Ibrahim 40

41. Surely Allah knows whatever thing they call upon besides Him, and He is the Mighty, the Wise. Al-'Ankabut 42

42. Say: 'It is He who scattered you about the earth and you will be gathered to Him.' They say, 'When will this promise come about if you are telling the truth?' Say: 'The knowledge is with Allah alone and I am only a clear warner.' Al-Mulk 24-26

Kind and Forgiving

1. Allah shows favour to the muminun. Al 'Imran 152 (see also 174)

2. ...your Lord is Ever-Forgiving, Most Merciful. At-Tawba 100 and see also an-Nahl 119

3. Your Lord knows best what is in your selves. If you are salihun, He is Ever-Forgiving to the remorseful. Bani Isra'il 25

4. The seven heavens and the earth and everyone in them glorify Him. There is nothing which does not glorify Him with praise but you do not understand their glorification. He is All-Forbearing, Ever-Forgiving. Bani Isra'il 44

5. Allah is All-Pardoning, Ever-Forgiving. Al-Hajj 58

6. Truly your Lord is the Almighty, the Most Merciful. Ash-Shu'ara 191

7. Allah is Ever-Forgiving, Most Merciful. Al-Ahzab 24,

8. Allah is Ever-Forgiving, Most Merciful. At-Tawba 100

9. When We let people taste mercy after hardship has afflicted them,

immediately they plot against Our Signs. Say: 'Allah is swifter at plotting.' Your plotting is recorded by Our Messengers. Yunus 21

10. He has given you everything you have asked Him for. If you tried to number Allah's blessings, you could never count them. Man is indeed wrongdoing, ungrateful. Ibrahim 36

11. We have honoured the sons of Adam and conveyed them on land and sea and provided them with good things and favoured them greatly over many We have created. Bani Isra'il 70

12. We send down in the Qur'an that which is a healing and a mercy to the muminun... Bani Isra'il 82

13. If We wished We could take away what We have revealed to you and then you would not find any to guard you from Us – but for a mercy from your Lord. His favour to you is indeed immense. Bani Isra'il 86-87

14. Allah is All-Compassionate to mankind, Most Merciful. Al-Hajj 63

15. ...it is Our duty to help the muminun. Ar-Rum 46

16. Give good news to the muminun that they will receive immense favour from Allah. Al-Ahzab 47

17. Any mercy Allah opens up to people, no one can withhold, and any He withholds, no one can afterwards release. He is the Almighty, the All-Wise. Fatir 2

18. Those who recite the Book of Allah and establish salat and give of what We have provided for them, secretly and openly, hope for a transaction which will not prove profitless: that He will pay them their wages in full and give them more from His unbounded favour. He is Ever-Forgiving, Ever-Thankful. Fatir 29-30

19. Say: 'My slaves, you who have transgressed against yourselves, do not despair of the mercy of Allah. Truly Allah forgives all wrong actions. He is the Ever-Forgiving, the Most Merciful.' Az-Zumar 50

20. Those who bear the Throne, and all those around it, glorify their Lord with praise and believe in Him and ask forgiveness for those who have iman: 'Our Lord, You encompass everything in mercy and knowledge! Forgive those who turn to You and who follow Your Way and safeguard them from the punishment of the Blazing Fire. Al-Mumin 6

Iman

21. You who have iman! have taqwa of Allah and iman in His Messenger. He will give you a double portion of His mercy and grant you a Light by which to walk and forgive you. Allah is Ever-Forgiving, Most Merciful. So that the People of the Book may know that they have no power at all over any of Allah's favour and that all favour is in the Hand of Allah. He gives it to anyone He wills. Allah's favour is indeed immense. Al-Hadid 27-28

22. ...And seek forgiveness from Allah. Allah is Ever-Forgiving, Most Merciful. Al-Muzzammil 18

23. If you avoid the serious wrong actions you have been forbidden, We will erase your bad actions from you and admit you by a Gate of Honour. An-Nisa 31

24. And ask Allah's forgiveness. Allah is Ever-Forgiving, Most Merciful. An-Nisa 105

25. But if anyone opposes the Messenger after the guidance has become clear to him, and follows other than the path of the muminun, We will hand him over to whatever he has turned to. An-Nisa 114

26. If Allah misguides people, no one can guide them. We will abandon them to wander blindly in their excessive insolence. Al-A'raf 186

27. Mankind! admonition has come to you from your Lord and also healing for what is in the breasts and guidance and mercy for the muminun. Yunus 57

28. The Best of Guardians is Allah. He is the Most Merciful of the merciful. Yusuf 64

29. However, those who do wrong pursue their whims and desires without any knowledge. Who can guide those whom Allah has led astray? They will have no helpers. When harm touches people they call on their Lord, making tawba to Him. But then, when He gives them a taste of mercy from Him, a group of them immediately associate others with their Lord to show ingratitude for what We have given them. Ar-Rum 32-33

30. But others have acknowledged their wrong actions and mixed a right action with another which is wrong. It may well be that Allah will turn towards them. Allah is Ever-Forgiving, Most Merciful. At-Tawba 103

31. 'My Lord, I seek refuge with You from asking You for anything about which I have no knowledge. If You do not forgive me and have mercy on me, I will be among the lost.' Hud 47

32. He said, 'My Lord, I have wronged myself. Forgive me.' So He forgave him. He is the Ever-Forgiving, the Most Merciful. Al-Qasas 15

33. Any disaster that strikes you is through what your own hands have earned and He pardons much. Ash-Shura 28

34. It is He who sends down Clear Signs to His slave to bring you out of the darkness to the light. Allah is All-Gentle with you, Most Merciful. Al-Hadid 9

35. I do not say my self was free from blame. The self indeed commands to evil acts – except for those my Lord has mercy on. My Lord, He is Forgiving, Merciful.' Yusuf 53

36. It is He who sends down abundant rain, after they have lost all hope, and unfolds His mercy. He is the Protector, the Praiseworthy. Ash-Shura 26

37. 'Who despairs of the mercy of his Lord except for misguided people?' Al-Hijr 56

38. [Ibrahim said] 'They are all my enemies – except for the Lord of all the worlds: He who created me and guides me; He who gives me food and gives me drink; and when I am ill, it is He who heals me; He who will cause my death, then give me life; He who I sincerely hope will forgive my mistakes on the Day of Reckoning.' Ash-Shu'ara 77-82

39. He will put your actions right for you and forgive you your wrong deeds... Al-Ahzab 71

40. ...and (Allah) turn towards the men and women of the muminun. Allah is Ever-Forgiving, Most Merciful. Al-Ahzab 73

41. And as for those who strive hard for Us, We will most certainly guide them to Our ways; and Allah is most surely with the doers of good. Al-'Ankabut 69

42. Among His Signs is your sleep by night and day and your seeking after His bounty. There are certainly Signs in that for people who hear. Ar-Rum 22

43. Have you seen him who takes his whims and desires to be his god – whom Allah has misguided knowingly, sealing up his

hearing and his heart and placing a blindfold over his eyes? Who then will guide him after Allah? So will you not pay heed? Al-Jathiya 23

44 Our people, respond to Allah's caller and believe in Him. He will forgive you some of your wrong actions and save you from a painful punishment. Al-Ahqaf 30

45. Know then that there is no god except Allah and ask forgiveness for your wrongdoing, and for the men and women who have iman. Allah knows both your activity and your repose. Muhammad 20

46. Know that the Messenger of Allah is among you. If he were to obey you in many things, you would suffer for it. However, Allah has given you love of iman and made it pleasing to your hearts, and has made kufr, deviance and disobedience hateful to you. People such as these are rightly guided. Al-Hujurat 7

47. If they call you a liar, say: 'Your Lord possesses boundless mercy, but His violent force cannot be averted from the people of the evildoers.' Al-An'am 148

48. Allah would not punish them while you (the prophet) were among them. Allah would not punish them as long as they sought forgiveness. Al-Anfal 33

49. If Allah afflicts you with harm, no one can remove it except Him. If He desires good for you, no one can avert His favour. He bestows it on whichever of His slaves He wills. He is Ever-Forgiving, Most Merciful. Yunus 107

50. Your Lord has forgiveness for people for their wrongdoing; but your Lord is also severe in retribution. Ar-Ra'd 7

51. Allah, the Maker of the heavens and the earth, invites you to forgive you your faults and to respite you till an appointed term. Ibrahim 10

52. ...and then they would not be saved – except as an act of mercy from Us, to give them enjoyment for a time. Ya Sin 42-43

53. To whoever avoids the major wrong actions and indecencies – except for minor lapses – truly your Lord is vast in forgiveness. An-Najm 31

54. I said, "Ask forgiveness of your Lord. Truly He is Endlessly

Forgiving. He will send heaven down on you in abundant rain and reinforce you with more wealth and sons, and grant you gardens and grant you waterways. Nuh 10-12

55. Allah is Ever-Gentle with His slaves. Al 'Imran 30

56. Tell My slaves that I am the Ever-Forgiving, the Most Merciful. Al-Hijr 49

57. ...It may well be that, in calling on my Lord, I will not be disappointed.' Maryam 48

58. O Prophet! When women who have iman come to you pledging allegiance to you on the grounds that they will not associate anything with Allah or steal or fornicate or kill their children or give a false ascription of paternity – making up lies about their bodies – or disobey you in respect of anything right, then accept their pledge and ask forgiveness for them. Allah is Ever-Forgiving, Most Merciful. Al-Mumtahana 12

59. Our Lord is the All-Merciful, the One whose help is sought in the face of what you describe.' Al-Anbiya 111

60. Anyone who thinks that Allah will not help him in the dunya and the akhira should stretch a rope up to the ceiling and then hang himself. Let him see whether his stratagem gets rid of what enrages him! Al-Hajj 15

The Messenger of Allah ﷺ

1. Among them are some who insult the Prophet... As for those who insult the Messenger of Allah, they will have a painful punishment. At-Tawba 61

2. A Messenger has come to you from among yourselves. Your suffering is distressing to him; he is deeply concerned for you; he is gentle and merciful to the muminun. At-Tawba 129

3. We have only sent you [The Prophet Muhammad] as a mercy to all the worlds. Al-Anbiya 106

4. You [Muhammad] never recited any Book before it nor did you write one down with your right hand. If you had, the purveyors of falsehood would have voiced their doubts. Al-'Ankabut 48

5. We sent no Messenger except to be obeyed by Allah's permission. If only when they wronged themselves they had come to

Iman

you and asked Allah's forgiveness and the Messenger had asked forgiveness for them they would have found Allah Ever-Returning, Most Merciful. An-Nisa 63

6. Then We will rescue Our Messengers and those who have iman as well. It is incumbent upon Us to rescue the muminun. Yunus 103

7. Your Lord knows you best. If He wills, He will have mercy on you, and, if He wills, He will punish you. We did not send you to be their guardian. Bani Isra'il 54

8. We favoured some of the Prophets over others. Bani Isra'il 55

9. Warn your near relatives, and take the muminun who follow you under your wing. If they disobey you, say, 'I am free of what you do.' Ash-Shu'ara 213-215

10. The prophet has a greater claim on the faithful than they have on themselves, and his wives are as their mothers.

11. You have an excellent model in the Messenger of Allah, for all who put their hope in Allah and the Last Day and remember Allah much. Al-Ahzab 21 12. When Allah and His Messenger have decided something it is not for any mumin man or woman to have a choice about it. Anyone who disobeys Allah and His Messenger is clearly misguided. Al-Ahzab 36

12. Muhammad is not the father of any of your men, but the Messenger of Allah and the Seal of the Prophets. Allah has knowledge of all things.. Al-Ahzab 40

13. Allah and His angels call down blessings on the Prophet. You who have iman, call down blessings on him and ask for complete peace and safety for him. As for those who abuse Allah and His Messenger, Allah's curse is on them in the dunya and the akhira. He has prepared a humiliating punishment for them. Al-Ahzab 56-57

14. People of the Book! Our Messenger has come to you, making clear to you much of the Book that you have kept concealed, and passing over a lot. A Light has come to you from Allah and a Clear Book. Al-Ma'ida 15

15. We have sent you with the Truth, bringing good news and giving warning. Do not ask about the inhabitants of the Blazing Fire. Al-Baqara 118

16. People of the Book! Our Messenger has come to you, making

things clear to you, after a period with no Messengers, lest you should say, 'No one came to us bringing good news or warning.' Someone has come to you bringing good news and a warning. Allah has power over all things. Al-Ma'ida 19

17. Messengers before you were also mocked, but those who jeered were engulfed by what they mocked. Al-An'am 11

18. Every nation has a Messenger and when their Messenger comes everything is decided between them justly. They are not wronged. Yunus 47

19. My people! I do not ask you for any wage for it. My wage is the responsibility of Him who brought me into being. So will you not use your intellect? Hud 51

20. (O' Muhammad!) ...You are only a warner. Every people has a guide. Ar-Ra'd 8

21. We sent Messengers before you and gave them wives and children. Nor was any Messenger able to bring a Sign except by Allah's permission. There is a prescribed limit to every term. Ar-Ra'd 39

22. We have not sent any Messenger except with the language of his people so he can make things clear to them. Allah misguides anyone He wills and guides anyone He wills. He is the Almighty, the All-Wise. Ibrahim 5

23. Has news not reached you of those who came before you [Muhammad], the peoples of Nuh and 'Ad and Thamud, and those who came after them who are known to no one but Allah? Ibrahim 11-12

24. We only send the Messengers to bring good news and to give warning. Al-Kahf 55

25. We have only ever sent before you men who were given Revelation. Ask the People of the Reminder if you do not know. Al-Anbiya 7

26. Messengers, eat of the good things and act rightly. I most certainly know what you do. Al-Muminun 52

27. We sent you only to bring good news and to give warning. Al-Furqan 56

28. We only sent you for the whole of mankind, bringing good news and giving warning. But most of mankind do not know it. Saba 28

29. You are only a warner. We have sent you with the truth bringing good news and giving warning. There is no community to which a warner has not come. If they deny you, those before them also denied the truth. Their Messengers came to them with Clear Signs, and psalms and the Illuminating Book. Fatir 23-25
30. Truly you are one of the Messengers on a Straight Path. Ya Sin 2-3
31. We have sent you bearing witness, bringing good news and giving warning Al-Fath 8
32. It is He who sent His Messenger with the Guidance and the Deen of Truth to exalt it over every other deen and Allah suffices as a witness. Al-Fath 28
33. Muhammad is the Messenger of Allah… Al-Fath 29
34. Your companion is not misguided or misled; nor does he speak from whim. An-Najm 2-3
35. And when 'Isa son of Maryam said, 'Tribe of Israel, I am the Messenger of Allah to you, confirming the Torah which came before me and giving you the good news of a Messenger after me whose name is Ahmad.' When he brought them the Clear Signs, they said, 'This is downright magic.' As-Saff 6
36. It is He who raised up among the unlettered people a Messenger from them to recite His Signs to them and purify them and teach them the Book and Wisdom, even though before that they were clearly misguided. And others of them who have not yet joined them. He is the Almighty, the All-Wise. That is Allah's favour which He gives to whoever He wills. Allah's favour is indeed immense. Al-Jumu'a 2-4
37. If the two of you would only turn to Allah, for your hearts clearly deviated. . . But if you support one another against him, Allah is his Protector and so are Jibril and every right-acting man of the muminun and, furthermore, the angels too will come to his support. At-Tahrim 4
38. O Prophet! do jihad against the kafirun and munafiqun and be harsh with them. Their refuge is Hell. What an evil destination! At-Tahrim 9
39. Indeed you are truly vast in character. Al-Qalam 4

40. We will cause you to recite so that you do not forget – except what Allah wills. He knows what is voiced out loud and what is hidden. We will ease you to the Easy Way. Remind, then, if the reminder benefits. He who has fear will be reminded; but the most miserable will shun it. Al-A'la 6-11

41. So remind them! You are only a reminder. You are not in control of them. Al-Ghashiya 21-22

42. Your Lord has not abandoned you nor does He hate you. The Last will be better for you than the First. Your Lord will soon give to you and you will be satisfied. Did He not find you orphaned and shelter you? Did He not find you wandering and guide you? Did He not find you impoverished and enrich you? Ad-Duha 3-8

43. Did We not expand your breast for you and remove from you your load which weighed down your back? Did We not raise high your renown? Al-Inshirah 1-4

44. For this We sent a Messenger to you from among you to recite Our Signs to you and purify you and teach you the Book and Wisdom and teach you things you did not know before. Al-Baqara 150

45. These Messengers: We favoured some of them over others. Allah spoke directly to some of them and raised up some of them in rank. Al-Baqara 251

46. The Messenger has iman in what has been sent down to him from his Lord, and so do the muminun. Each one has iman in Allah and His angels and His Books and His Messengers. We do not differentiate between any of His Messengers. They say, 'We hear and we obey. Forgive us, our Lord! You are our journey's end.' Al-Baqara 284

47. Muhammad is only a Messenger and he has been preceded by other Messengers. If he were to die or be killed, would you turn on your heels? Those who turn on their heels do not harm Allah in any way. Allah will recompense the thankful. Al 'Imran 144

48. Say: 'I possess no power to help or harm myself, except as Allah wills. If I had had knowledge of the Unseen, I would have sought to gain much good and no evil would have touched me. I am only a warner and a bringer of good news to people who have iman.' Al-A'raf 188

49. Do not move your tongue trying to hasten it. Its collection and recitation are Our affair. So when We recite it, follow its recitation. Then its explanation is Our concern. Al-Qiyama 16-18

50. [Ibrahim ï prayed] 'Our Lord, raise up among them a Messenger from them to recite Your Signs to them and teach them the Book and Wisdom and purify them. You are the Almighty, the All-Wise.' Al-Baqara 128

[So, the Prophet Muhammad @ was the fulfilment of the prayer of Ibrahim ï and the good tidings of Isa ï and the dream of Amina according to one hadith].

51. We do not send the Messengers except to bring good news and to give warning. As for those who have iman and put things right, they will feel no fear and will know no sorrow. Al-An'am 49

52. Those who follow the Messenger, the Unlettered Prophet, whom they find written down with them in the Torah and the Gospel, commanding them to do right and forbidding them to do wrong, making good things halal for them and bad things haram for them, relieving them of their heavy loads and the chains which were around them. Those who have iman in him and honour him and help him, and follow the Light that has been sent down with him, they are the ones who are successful. Al-A'raf 157

The Last Hour and the Day Of Judgement

1. They will ask you about the Hour: when is it due? Say: 'Knowledge of it rests with my Lord alone. He alone will reveal it at its proper time. It hangs heavy in the heavens and the earth. It will not come upon you except suddenly.' They will ask you as if you had full knowledge of it. Say: 'Knowledge of it rests with Allah alone. But most people do not know that.' Al-A'raf 187

2. On the day when every soul will find itself confronted with all that it has done of good and all that it has done of evil, every soul will long that there might be a mighty space of distance between it and that evil. Allah asks you to beware of Him. Allah is full of mercy for you. Al 'Imran 30

3. The Unseen of the heavens and earth belongs to Allah. The matter of the Hour is only the blink of an eye away, or even nearer.

Allah has power over all things. An-Nahl 77

4. The quaking of the Hour is a terrible thing. Al-Hajj 1

5. ...fearing a day when all hearts and eyes will be in turmoil – An-Nur 36

6. People will ask you about the Last Hour. Say: 'Only Allah has knowledge of it. What will make you understand? It may be that the Last Hour is very near.' Al-Ahzab 63

7. On the Day of Rising you will see those who lied against Allah with their faces blackened. Do not the arrogant have a dwelling place in Hell? Az-Zumar 57

8. The Trumpet will be blown and those in the heavens and those in the earth will all lose consciousness, except those Allah wills. Then it will be blown a second time and at once they will be standing upright, looking on. Az-Zumar 65

9. When the stars are extinguished, when heaven is split open, when the mountains are pulverised, when the Messengers' time is appointed – until what day is that deferred? Until the Day of Decision. And what will teach you what the Day of Decision is? Al-Mursalat 8-14

10. The Day of Decision is a fixed appointment: the Day the Trumpet is blown and you come in droves, and heaven is opened and becomes doorways, and the mountains are shifted and become a mirage. An-Naba' 17-20

11. He will say, 'Just as Our Signs came to you and you forgot them, in the same way you too are forgotten today.' Ta Ha 124

12. When Yajuj and Majuj are let loose and rush down from every slope. Al-Anbiya 95

13. Before them there is an interspace until the Day they are raised up. Al-Muminun 101

14. [Follow the best that has been sent down to you from your Lord] ...lest anyone should say, 'Alas for me for neglecting what Allah was due, and being one of the scoffers!' or lest they should say, 'If only Allah had guided me, I would have had taqwa,' or lest he should say, when he sees the punishment, 'If only I could have another chance so that I could be a good-doer!' Az-Zumar 53-55

15. Have fear of a Day when no self will be able to compensate for

another in any way. No intercession will be accepted from it, no ransom taken from it, and they will not be helped. Al-Baqara 47

16. Have fear of a Day when no self will be able to compensate for another in any way, and no ransom will be accepted from it, and no intercession benefit it, and they will not be helped. Al-Baqara 122

17. As for those who reject Allah's Signs, and kill the Prophets without any right to do so, and kill those who command justice, give them news of a painful punishment. They are the ones whose actions come to nothing in the dunya or the akhira. They will have no helpers. Al 'Imran 21-22

18. On the day Allah gathers the Messengers together and says, 'What response did you receive?' they will say, 'We do not know. You are the Knower of unseen things.' Al-Ma'ida 109

19. The weighing that Day will be the truth. As for those whose scales are heavy, they are the successful. As for those whose scales are light, they are the ones who have lost their own selves because they wrongfully rejected Our Signs. Al-A'raf 7-8

20. ...the Day its fulfilment occurs, those who forgot it before will say, 'The Messengers of our Lord came with the Truth. Are there any intercessors to intercede for us, or can we be sent back so that we can do something other than what we did?' They have lost their own selves and what they invented has forsaken them. Al-A'raf 52

21. On the Day We gather them all together, We will say then to those who associated others with Allah, 'To your place, you and your partner-gods!' Then We will sift them out, and their partner-gods will say, 'It was not us you worshipped. Allah is a sufficient witness between us and you. We were unaware of your worship.' Then and there every self will be tried for what it did before. They will be returned to Allah, their Master, the Real, and what they invented will abandon them. Yunus 28-30

22. On the day We gather them together – when it will seem if they had tarried no more than an hour of a single day – they will recognise one another. Those who denied the meeting with Allah will have lost. They were not guided. Yunus 45

23. There is certainly a Sign in that for anyone who fears the punishment of the akhira. That is a Day to which mankind will all be gathered. That is a Day which will be witnessed by everyone. We will only postpone it until a predetermined time. On the Day it comes, no self will speak except by His permission. Some of them will be wretched and others glad. As for those who are wretched, they will be in the Fire, where they will sigh and gasp, remaining in it timelessly, for ever, as long as the heavens and earth endure, except as your Lord wills. Your Lord is the Doer of what He wills. As for those who are glad, they will be in the Garden, remaining in it timelessly, for ever, as long as the heavens and earth endure, except as your Lord wills: an uninterrupted gift. Hud 103-108

24. On that Day every self will come to argue for itself and every self will be paid in full for what it did. They will not be wronged. An-Nahl 111

25. We have fastened the destiny of every man about his neck and on the Day of Rising We will bring out a Book for him which he will find spread open in front of him. 'Read your Book! Today your own self is reckoner enough against you!' Bani Isra'il 13-14

26. On the Day We summon every people with their records, those who are given their Book in their right hand will read their Book and they will not be wronged by even the smallest speck. Bani Isra'il 71

27. Whoever Allah guides is truly guided. But as for those He leads astray, you will not find any protectors for them apart from Him. We will gather them on the Day of Rising, flat on their faces, blind, dumb and deaf. Their shelter will be Hell... Bani Isra'il 97

28. On the Day We make the mountains move and you see the earth laid bare and We gather them together, not leaving out a single one of them, they will be paraded before your Lord in ranks: 'You have come to Us just as We created you at first. Yes indeed! Even though you claimed that We would not fix a time with you.' The Book will be set in place and you will see the evildoers fearful of what is in it. They will say, 'Alas for us! What is this Book which does not pass over any action, small or great, without recording it?' They will find there

everything they did and your Lord will not wrong anyone at all. Al-Kahf 46-48

29. By your Lord, We will collect them and the shaytans together. Then We will assemble them around Hell on their knees. Then We will drag out from every sect the one among them most insolent towards the All-Merciful. Then it is We who will know best those most deserving to roast in it. There is not one of you who will not come to it. That is the final decision of your Lord. Then We will rescue those who had taqwa and We will leave the wrongdoers in it on their knees. Maryam 68-72

30. We will set up the Just Balance on the Day of Rising and no self will be wronged in any way. Even if it is no more than the weight of a grain of mustard-seed, We will produce it. We are sufficient as a Reckoner. Al-Anbiya 47

31. On the Day the Last Hour arrives the evildoers will swear they have not even tarried for an hour. That is the extent to which they are deceived. Those who have been given knowledge and iman will say, 'You tarried in accordance with Allah's Decree until the Day of Rising. And this is the Day of Rising, but you did not know it.' On that Day the excuses of those who did wrong will not help them nor will they be able to appease Allah. Ar-Rum 54-56

32. And do not let the kufr of those who are kafir sadden you. They will return to Us and We will inform them about the things they did. Allah knows what the heart contains. Luqman 22

33. Today We seal up their mouths and their hands speak to us, and their feet bear witness to what they have earned. Ya Sin 64

34. They do not measure Allah with His true measure. The whole earth will be a mere handful for Him on the Day of Rising, the heavens folded up in His right hand. Glory be to Him! He is exalted above the partners they ascribe! Az-Zumar 64

35. ... the Day when they will issue forth and when not one thing about them will be hidden from Allah. 'To whom does the kingdom belong today? To Allah, the One, the Conqueror! Every self will be repaid today for what it earned. Today there will be no injustice. Allah is swift at reckoning.' And warn them of the Day of Immediacy when hearts rise choking to the throat. The

wrongdoers will have no close friend nor any intercessor who might be heard. Al-Mumin 15-18

36. The Hour is coming – there is no doubt about it. But most of mankind have no iman. Al-Mumin 59

37. On that Day the closest friends will be enemies to one another – except for those who have taqwa. Az-Zukhruf 67

38. So be on the watch for a day when heaven brings forth a distinctive smoke, which enshrouds mankind. 'This is a painful punishment! Our Lord, remove the punishment from us. We are really muminun.' Ad-Dukhan 9-11

39. The Day of Decision will be their appointment all together:the Day when friends will be of no use at all to one another,and they will not be helped – except for those Allah has mercy on. He is the Almighty, the Most Merciful. Ad-Dukhan 38-40

40. Say:'Allah gives you life, then causes you to die, and then will gather you together for the Day of Rising about which there is no doubt. But most people do not know it.' The kingdom of the heavens and earth belongs to Allah and, on the Day that the Hour arrives,that Day the liars will be lost. You will see every nation on its knees, every nation summoned to its Book:'Today you will be repaid for what you did. This is Our Book speaking against you with the truth. We have been recording everything you did.' As for those who had iman and did right actions,their Lord will admit them into His mercy. That is the Clear Victory. Al-Jathiya 25-29

41. But as for those who were kafir:'Were My Signs not recited to you and yet you proved arrogant; you were a people of evil-doers? When you were told, "Allah's promise is true and so is the Hour, of which there is no doubt," you said, "We have no idea what the Hour is. We have only been conjecturing. We are by no means certain."' The evil deeds they did will appear before them and the things they mocked at will engulf them. They will be told, 'Today We have forgotten you as you forgot the meeting of this your Day. Your refuge is the Fire and you have no helpers. Al-Jathiya 29-33

42. The Trumpet will be blown. That is the Day of the Threat. Every self will come together with a driver and a witness: 'You

were heedless of this so We have stripped you of your covering and today your sight is sharp.' His inseparable comrade will say, 'This is what I have ready for you.' 'Hurl into Hell every obdurate kafir, impeder of good, doubt-causing aggressor, who set up another god together with Allah. Hurl him into the terrible punishment.' His inseparable comrade will say, 'Our Lord, I did not make him overstep the limits. He was, in any case, far astray.' He will say, 'Do not argue in My presence when I gave you advance warning of the Threat. My Word, once given, is not subject to change and I do not wrong My slaves.' On the Day He says to Hell, 'Are you full?' it will ask, 'Are there no more to come?' And the Garden will be brought up close to those with taqwa, not far away: 'This is what you were promised. It is for every careful penitent: those who fear the All-Merciful in the Unseen and come with a contrite heart. Qaf 20-33

43. Listen out for the Day when the Summoner shall call out from a nearby place. The Day they hear the Blast in truth, that is the Day of Emergence. It is We who give life and cause to die and We are their final destination. The Day the earth splits open all around them as they come rushing forth, that is a gathering, easy for Us to accomplish. Qaf 41-44

44. What you are promised is certainly true – the Judgement will certainly take place! Adh-Dhariyat 5-6

45. On the Day when heaven sways to and fro and the mountains shift about, woe that Day to the deniers. At-Tur 8-10

46. And how many angels there are in the heavens whose intercession is of no benefit at all until Allah has authorised those He wills and is pleased with them! An-Najm 26

47. The Imminent is imminent! No one besides Allah can unveil it. An-Najm 56-57

48. The Hour has drawn near and the moon has split. Al-Qamar 1

49. When heaven is split apart and goes red like dregs of oil. So which of your Lord's blessings do you both then deny? That Day no man or jinn will be asked about his sin. So which of your Lord's blessings do you both then deny? The evildoers will be recognised by their mark and seized by their forelocks and their

feet. So which of your Lord's blessings do you both then deny? Ar-Rahman 36-41

50. When the Great Event occurs, none will deny its occurrence; bringing low, raising high. When the earth is convulsed and the mountains are crushed and become scattered dust in the air. And you will be classed into three: the Companions of the Right: what of the Companions of the Right? the Companions of the Left: what of the Companions of the Left? and the Forerunners, the Forerunners. Al-Waqi'a 1-12

51. Neither your blood relations nor your children will be of any use to you. On the Day of Rising He will differentiate between you. Allah sees what you do. Al-Mumtahana 3

52. On the Day He gathers you for the Day of Gathering – that is the Day of Profit and Loss. As for those who have iman in Allah and act rightly, We will erase their bad actions from them and admit them into Gardens with rivers flowing under them, remaining in them timelessly, for ever and ever. That is the Great Victory! At-Taghabun 9

53. ... on the Day the earth and mountains shake and the mountains become like shifting dunes. Al-Muzzammil 13

54. How will you safeguard yourselves, if you are kafir, against a Day which will turn children grey, by which heaven will be split apart? His promise will be fulfilled. Al-Muzzammil 16

55. For when the Trumpet is blown, that Day will be a difficult day, not easy for the kafirun. Al-Muddaththir 8-10

56. Yet man still wants to deny what is ahead of him, asking, 'So when is the Day of Rising?' But when the eyesight is dazzled, and the moon is eclipsed, and the sun and moon are fused together, on that Day man will say, 'Where can I run?' No indeed! There will be no safe place. That Day the only resting place will be your Lord. That Day man will be told what he did and failed to do. In fact, man will be clear proof against himself in spite of any excuses he might offer. Al-Qiyama 5-15

57. Faces that Day will be radiant, gazing at their Lord. And faces that Day will be glowering, realising that a back-breaking blow has fallen. Al-Qiyama 21-24

58. What you are promised will certainly happen. When the stars

are extinguished, when heaven is split open, when the mountains are pulverised, when the Messengers' time is appointed – until what day is that deferred? Until the Day of Decision. And what will teach you what the Day of Decision is? On that Day, woe to the deniers! Al-Mursalat 7-15

59. On the Day when the Spirit and the angels stand in ranks, no one will speak, except for him who is authorised by the All-Merciful and says what is right. That will be the True Day. So whoever wills should take the way back to his Lord. We have warned you of an imminent punishment on the Day when a man will see what he has done, and the kafir will say, 'Oh, if only I were dust!' An-Naba' 38-40

60. On the Day the first blast shudders, and the second blast follows it, hearts that Day will be pounding and eyes will be cast down. An-Nazi'at 6-9

61. There will be but one Great Blast, and at once they will be on the surface, wide awake! An-Nazi'at 13-14

62. When the Deafening Blast comes, the Day a man will flee from his brother and his mother and his father, and his wife and his children: on that Day every man among them will have concerns enough of his own. That Day some faces will be radiant, laughing, rejoicing. That Day some faces will be dust-covered, overcast with gloom. Those are the dissolute kafirun. 'Abasa 33-42

63. When the sun is compacted in blackness, when the stars fall in rapid succession, when the mountains are set in motion, when the camels in foal are neglected, when the wild beasts are all herded together, when the oceans surge into each other, when the selves are arranged into classes, when the baby girl buried alive is asked for what crime she was killed, when the Pages are opened up, when the Heaven is peeled away, when the Fire is set ablaze, when the Garden is brought up close: then will each self know what it has done. At-Takwir 1-14

64. When the sky is split apart, when the stars are strewn about, when the seas flood and overflow, when the graves are emptied out, each self will know what it has sent ahead and left behind. Al-Infitar 1-5

65. What will convey to you what the Day of Judgement is? Again! What will convey to you what the Day of Judgement is? It is the Day when a self will have no power to help any other self in any way. The command that Day will be Allah's alone. Al-Infitar 17-19

66. When the sky bursts open, hearkening to its Lord as it is bound to do! When the earth is flattened out and disgorges what is inside it and empties out, hearkening to its Lord as it is bound to do! Al-Inshiqaq 1-5

67. As for him who is given his Book in his right hand, he will be given an easy reckoning and return to his family joyfully. But as for him who is given his Book behind his back, he will cry out for destruction but will be roasted in a Searing Blaze. He used to be joyful in his family. He thought that he was never going to return. But in fact his Lord was always watching him! Al-Inshiqaq 7-15

68. When the earth is convulsed with its quaking and the earth then disgorges its charges and man asks, 'What is wrong with it?', on that Day it will impart all its news because your Lord has inspired it. That Day people will emerge segregated to see the results of their actions. Whoever does an atom's weight of good will see it. Whoever does an atom's weight of evil will see it. Az-Zilzala 1-9

69. Does he not know that when the graves are emptied out, and the heart's contents are brought into the open, that Day their Lord will certainly be aware of them. Al-'Adiyat 9-11

70. The Crashing Blow! What is the Crashing Blow? What will convey to you what the Crashing Blow is? It is the Day when mankind will be like scattered moths and the mountains like tufts of coloured wool. As for him whose balance is heavy, he will have a most pleasant life. But as for him whose balance is light, his motherland is Hawiya. And what will convey to you what that is? A raging Fire! Al-Qari'a 1-10

71. ...on the Day when the secrets are sought out and man will have no strength or helper. At-Tariq 9-10

72. Woe that Day to the deniers: those who deny the Day of Reckoning. No one denies it except for every evil aggressor. Al-Mutaffifin 10-12

73. No indeed! Rather that Day they will be veiled from their Lord. Al-Mutaffifin 15

74. No indeed! When the earth is crushed and ground to dust and your Lord arrives with the angels rank upon rank and that Day Hell is produced, that Day man will remember; but how will the remembrance help him? He will say, 'Oh! If only I had prepared in advance for this life of mine!' Al-Fajr 23-27

75. Has news of the Overwhelmer reached you? Some faces on that Day will be downcast, labouring, toiling endlessly, roasting in a red-hot Fire. Al-Ghashiya 1-4

76. Then you will be asked that Day about the pleasures you enjoyed. At-Takathur 8

77. 'Our Lord, You are the Gatherer of mankind to a Day of which there is no doubt. Allah will not break His promise.' As for those who are kafir, their wealth and children will not help them against Allah in any way. They are fuel for the Fire. Al 'Imran 9-10

78. Do not consider Allah to be unaware of what the wrongdoers perpetrate. He is merely deferring them to a Day on which their sight will be transfixed, rushing headlong – heads back, eyes vacant, hearts hollow. Warn mankind of the Day when the punishment will reach them. Those who did wrong will say, 'Our Lord, reprieve us for a short time. We will respond to Your call and follow the Messengers.'... Ibrahim 44-46

79. On the Day the earth is changed to other than the earth, and the heavens likewise, and they parade before Allah, the One, the Conquering, that Day you will see the evildoers yoked together in chains, wearing shirts of tar, their faces enveloped in the Fire. Ibrahim 50-52

80. On the Day We raise up a witness from every nation, those who were kafir will not be excused nor will they be able to appease Allah. When those who did wrong see the punishment, it will not be lightened for them. They will be granted no reprieve. When those who associated others with Allah see those they associated, they will say, 'Our Lord, these are our partner gods, the ones we called upon apart from You.' But they will fling their words back in their faces: 'You are truly liars!' On that Day they

will offer their submission to Allah and the things they invented will abandon them. As for those who were kafir and barred access to the way of Allah, We will heap punishment on top of their punishment because of the corruption they brought about. On that Day We will raise up among every community a witness against them from amongst themselves, and bring you as a witness against them. We have sent down the Book to you making all things clear and as guidance and mercy and good news for the Muslims. An-Nahl 84-89

81. On the Day the Trumpet is blown – and We will gather the evildoers sightless on that Day – they will whisper secretly to one other, 'You only stayed for ten.' We know best what they will say when the most correct of them will say, 'You only stayed a day.'

They will ask you about the mountains. Say: 'My Lord will scatter them as dust. He will leave them as a barren, level plain on which you will see no dip or gradient.' On that day they will follow the Summoner who has no crookedness in him at all. Voices will be humbled before the All-Merciful and nothing but a whisper will be heard. On that Day intercession will not be of any use except for him whom the All-Merciful has authorised and with whose speech He is well-pleased. He knows what is in front of them and behind them. But their knowledge does not encompass Him. Faces will be humbled to the Living, the All-Sustaining. and anyone weighed down with wrongdoing will have failed. Ta Ha 100-108

82. But if anyone turns away from My reminder, his life will be a dark and narrow one and on the Day of Rising We will gather him blind.' He will say, 'My Lord, why have you gathered me blind when before I was able to see?' He will say, 'Just as Our Signs came to you and you forgot them, in the same way you too are forgotten today.' Ta Ha 122-124

83. That Day We will fold up heaven like folding up the pages of a book. As We originated the first creation so We will regenerate it. It is a promise binding on Us. That is what We will do. Al-Anbiya 103

84. On the day they see it, every nursing woman will be oblivious

of the baby at her breast, and every pregnant woman will abort the contents of her womb, and you will think people drunk when they are not drunk; it is just that the punishment of Allah is so severe. Al-Hajj 2

85. ...Before them there is an interspace until the Day they are raised up. Then when the Trumpet is blown, that Day there will be no family ties between them; they will not be able to question one another. Those whose scales are heavy, they are the successful. Those whose scales are light, they are the losers of their selves, remaining in Hell timelessly, for ever. Al-Muminun 101-104

86. On the Day the Trumpet is blown and everyone in the heavens and everyone on the earth is terrified – except those Allah wills, everyone will come to Him abject. You will see the mountains you reckoned to be solid going past like clouds – the handiwork of Allah who gives to everything its solidity. He is aware of what you do. An-Naml 89-90

87. On the Day you see the men and women of the muminun, with their light streaming out in front of them, and to their right: 'Good news for you today of Gardens with rivers flowing under them, remaining in them timelessly, for ever. That is the Great Victory.' That Day the men and women of the munafiqun will say to those who have iman, 'Wait for us so that we can borrow some of your light.' They will be told, 'Go back and look for light!' And a wall will be erected between them with a gate in it, on the inside of which there will be mercy but before whose exterior lies the punishment. They will call out to them, 'Were we not with you?' They will reply, 'Indeed you were. But you made trouble for yourselves and hung back and doubted and false hopes deluded you until Allah's command arrived. The Deluder deluded you about Allah. So today no ransom will be accepted from you or from those who were kafir. Your refuge is the Fire. It is your master. What an evil destination!' Al-Hadid 12-14

88. On the Day Allah raises up all of them together, He will inform them of what they did. Allah has recorded it while they have forgotten it. Allah is a Witness of all things. Al-Mujadila 6

89. Neither their wealth nor their children will help them at all

against Allah. Such people are the Companions of the Fire, remaining in it timelessly, for ever. On the Day Allah raises up all of them together they will swear to Him just as they have sworn to you and imagine they have something to stand upon. No indeed! It is they who are the liars. Al-Mujadila 17-18

90. So when the Trumpet is blown with a single blast, and the earth and the mountains are lifted and crushed with a single blow, On that Day, the Occurrence will occur and Heaven will be split apart, for that Day it will be very frail. The angels will be gathered round its edge. On that Day, eight will bear the Throne of their Lord above their heads. On that Day you will be exposed – no concealed act you did will stay concealed. Al-Haqqa 12-17

93. As for him who is given his Book in his right hand, he will say, 'Here, come and read my Book! I counted on meeting my Reckoning.' He will have a very pleasant life in an elevated Garden, its ripe fruit hanging close to hand. 'Eat and drink with relish for what you did before in days gone by!' But as for him who is given his Book in his left hand, he will say, 'If only I had not been given my Book and had not known about my Reckoning! If only death had really been the end! My wealth has been of no use to me. My power has vanished.' 'Seize him and truss him up. Then roast him in the Blazing Fire. Then bind him in a chain which is seventy cubits long. He used not to have iman in Allah the Most Great, nor did he urge the feeding of the poor. Therefore here today he has no friend nor any food except exuding pus which no one will eat except those who were in error.' Al-Haqqa 18-37

91. On the Day the sky is like molten brass and the mountains like tufts of coloured wool, no good friend will ask about his friend even though they can see each other. An evildoer will wish he could ransom himself from the punishment of that Day, by means of his sons, or his wife or his brother or his family who sheltered him or everyone else on earth, if that only meant that he could save himself. Al-Ma'arij 8-14

92. On that Day, woe to the deniers! Proceed to that which you denied! Proceed to a shadow which forks into three but gives no shade or protection from the flames, shooting up great sparks the

size of castles, like a herd of yellow camels. Al-Mursalat 28-33
93. This is the Day they will not say a single word, nor will they be allowed to offer any excuses. On that Day, woe to the deniers! 'This is the Day of Decision. We have gathered you and the earlier peoples. So if you have a ploy, use it against Me now!' Al-Mursalat 35-39
94. On the Day they see it, it will be as if they had only lingered for the evening or the morning of a single day. An-Nazi'at 45
95. On the Day We gather them all together, We will say to those who associated others with Allah 'Where are the partner-gods, for whom you made such claims?' Then they will have no recourse except to say, 'By Allah, our Lord, We were not mushrikun.' See how they lie against themselves and how what they invented has forsaken them! Al-An'am 22-25
96. 'My son, even if something weighs as little as a mustard-seed and is inside a rock or anywhere else in the heavens or earth, Allah will bring it out. Allah is All-Pervading, All-Aware. Luqman 15
97. So on the Day of Rising they will carry the full weight of their own burdens and some of the burdens of those they misguided without knowledge. What an evil load they bear! An-Nahl 25
98. On the Day We crowd the enemies of Allah into the Fire and they are driven in close-packed ranks, when they reach it, their hearing, sight and skin will testify against them concerning what they did. Fussilat 18-19
99. Say: 'As for those who are astray, let the All-Merciful prolong their term until they see what they were promised, whether it be the punishment or the Hour. Then they will know who is in the worse position and has the weaker troops.' Maryam 75-76
100. On the Day when legs are bared and they are called on to prostrate, they will not be able to do so. Their eyes will be downcast, darkened by debasement; for they were called on to prostrate when they were in full possession of their faculties. Al-Qalam 42-43
101. They ask you about the Hour: 'When will it come?' What are you doing mentioning it? Its coming is your Lord's affair. An-Nazi'at 41-43

Rewards for Right Action

1. We will grant increase to all good-doers. Al-Baqara 57
2. They have what they earned. You have what you have earned. You will not be questioned about what they did. Al-Baqara 133
3. 'We have our actions and you have your actions.' Al-Baqara 139
4. If anyone desires the reward of the dunya, We will give him some of it. If anyone desires the reward of the akhira, We will give him some of it. We will recompense the thankful. Al 'Imran 145
5. If you do good, you do it to yourselves. If you do evil, you do it to your detriment. Bani Isra'il 7
6. That abode of the akhira – We grant it to those who do not seek to exalt themselves in the earth or to cause corruption in it. The successful outcome is for those who have taqwa. Anyone who does a good action will get something better. As for anyone who does a bad action, those who have done bad actions will only be repaid for what they did. Al-Qasas 83-84
7. Everyone will be ranked according to what they did. We will pay them in full for their actions and they will not be wronged. Al-Ahqaf 18
8. Allah does not wrong anyone by so much as the smallest speck. And if there is a good deed Allah will multiply it and pay out an immense reward direct from Him. An-Nisa 40
9. Anyone, male or female, who does right actions and is a mumin, will enter the Garden. They will not be wronged by so much as the tiniest speck. An-Nisa 123
10. This Qur'an guides to the most upright Way and gives good news to the muminun who do right actions that they will have a large reward. Bani Isra'il 9
11. ...such people are the inheritors who will inherit Firdaws, remaining in it timelessly, for ever. Al-Muminun 10-11
12. ...such people will be repaid for their steadfastness with the Highest Paradise, where they will meet with welcome and with 'Peace'. They will remain in it timelessly, for ever. What an excellent lodging and abode! Al-Furqan 75-76
13. ...some outdo each other in good by Allah's permission. That is the great favour. Fatir 32

Iman

14. Those who lower their voices when they are with the Messenger of Allah are people whose hearts Allah has tested for taqwa. They will have forgiveness and an immense reward. Al-Hujurat 3

15. Allah will say, 'This is the Day when the sincerity of the sincere will benefit them. They will have Gardens with rivers flowing under them, remaining in them timelessly, for ever and ever. Allah is pleased with them and they are pleased with Him. That is the Great Victory.' Al-Ma'ida 121

16. Those who produce a good action will receive ten like it. But those who produce a bad action will only be repaid with its equivalent and they will not be wronged. Al-An'am 161

17. ...Those who were steadfast will be recompensed according to the best of what they did. An-Nahl 96

18. Anyone, male or female, who does right actions and is a mumin, will enter the Garden. An-Nisa 123

19. The forerunners – the first of the Muhajirun and the Ansar – and those who have followed them in doing good: Allah is pleased with them and they are pleased with Him. He has prepared Gardens for them with rivers flowing under them, remaining in them timelessly, for ever and ever. That is the great victory. At-Tawba 101

20. ...no thirst or weariness or hunger will afflict them in the Way of Allah,nor will they take a single step to infuriate the kafirun, nor secure any gain from the enemy, without a right action being written down for them because of it. Allah does not let the wage of the good-doers go to waste. At-Tawba 121

21. But as for anyone who desires the akhira, and strives for it with the striving it deserves, being a mumin, the striving of such people will be gratefully acknowledged. We sustain each one, the former and the latter, through the generous giving of your Lord; and the giving of your Lord is not restricted.. Bani Isra'il 19-20

22. In your Lord's sight, right actions which are lasting are better both in reward and end result. Maryam 77

23. Every self will be repaid in full for what it did. He knows best what they are doing. Az-Zumar 67

24. And those who have taqwa of their Lord will be driven to the Garden in companies and when they arrive there, finding its

gates open, its custodians will say to them, 'Peace be upon you! You have done well so enter it timelessly, for ever.' They will say, 'Praise be to Allah Who has fulfilled His promise to us and made us the inheritors of this land, letting us settle in the Garden wherever we want. How excellent is the wage of those who work!' Az-Zumar 70-71

25. But those who have taqwa of their Lord will have high-ceilinged Halls, and more such Halls built one above the other, and rivers flowing under them. That is Allah's promise. Allah does not break His promise. Az-Zumar 19

26. ...Those You safeguard from evil acts are truly the recipients of Your mercy on that Day. That is the Mighty Victory.' Al-Mumin 8

27. He who brings the truth and he who confirms it – those are the people who have taqwa. They will have anything they wish for with their Lord. That is the recompense of the good-doers. So that Allah may erase from them the worst of what they did and pay them their wages for the best of what they did. Az-Zumar 32-34

28. He punishes whom He pleases and has mercy on whom He pleases, and to Him you shall return. Al-'Ankabut 21

29. Allah will give security those who had taqwa in their victorious Safe Haven. No evil will touch them and they will know no sorrow. Az-Zumar 58

30. Or did you suppose that you would enter the Garden without facing the same as those who came before you? Poverty and illness afflicted them and they were shaken ... Al-Baqara 212

31. Those who do good will have the best and more! Neither dust nor debasement will darken their faces. They are the Companions of the Garden, remaining in it timelessly, for ever. Yunus 26

32. Then We will rescue Our Messengers and those who have iman as well. It is incumbent upon Us to rescue the muminun. Yunus 103

33. ...We gave him knowledge and right judgement too. That is how We reward all doers of good. Yusuf 22

34. ...We grant Our grace to anyone We will and We do not allow to go to waste the wage of any people who do good. But the wages of the akhira are the best for people who have iman and fear their Lord. Yusuf 56-57

35. ...We raise the rank of anyone We will. Over everyone with knowledge is a Knower. Yusuf 76
36. ...As for those who fear Allah and are steadfast, Allah does not allow to go to waste the wage of any people who do good.' Yusuf 90
37. The angels descend on those who say, 'Our Lord is Allah,' and then go straight: 'Do not fear and do not grieve but rejoice in the Garden you have been promised. Fussilat 29
38. If anyone does a good action, We will increase the good of it for him. Allah is Ever-Forgiving, Ever-Thankful.' Ash-Shura 21
39. That is the Garden you will inherit for what you did. Az-Zukhruf 72
40. Those who say, 'Our Lord is Allah,' and then go straight will feel no fear and will know no sorrow. Al-Ahqaf 12
41. Those are people whose best deeds will be accepted and whose wrong deeds will be overlooked. They are among the Companions of the Garden, in fulfilment of the true promise made to them. Al-Ahqaf 15
42. Everything in the heavens and everything in the earth belongs to Allah so that He can repay those who do evil for what they did and repay those who do good with the Very Best. An-Najm 30
43. Will the reward for doing good be anything other than good? Ar-Rahman 59
44. You who have iman! have taqwa of Allah and iman in His Messenger. He will give you a double portion of His mercy and grant you a Light by which to walk and forgive you. Allah is Ever-Forgiving, Most Merciful. Al-Hadid 27
45. The people with taqwa will be amid shade and fountains and have any fruits that they desire: 'Eat and drink with relish for what you did. This is the way We reward good-doers.' Al-Mursalat 41-44
46. For those who have taqwa there is triumph. An-Naba' 31
47. ...a recompense from your Lord, a commensurate gift. An-Naba' 36
48. 'O self at rest and at peace, return to your Lord, well-pleasing and well-pleased! Enter among My slaves! Enter My Garden.' Al-Fajr 30-32

49. You will not be denied the reward for any good thing you do. Allah knows those who have taqwa. Al 'Imran 115
50. But those who have taqwa of their Lord will have Gardens with rivers flowing under them, remaining in them timelessly, for ever: hospitality from Allah. What is with Allah is better for those who are truly good. Al 'Imran 198
51. Those who have iman in Allah and His Messengers and do not differentiate between any of them, We will pay them their wages. Allah is Ever-Forgiving, Most Merciful. An-Nisa 151
52. Your Lord's payment is better. He is the Best of Providers. Al-Muminun 73
53. Say: 'Is that better, or the Garden of Eternal Life which has been promised to those who have taqwa? That is their recompense and destination.' They will have in it whatever they want timelessly, for ever. It is a binding promise of your Lord. Al-Furqan 15-16
54. The Garden will be brought near to those who have taqwa. Ash-Shu'ara 90
55. Their recompense is forgiveness from their Lord, and Gardens with rivers flowing under them, remaining in them timelessly, for ever. How excellent is the reward of those who act! Al 'Imran 136
56. Allah has prepared Gardens for them with rivers flowing under them, remaining in them timelessly, for ever. That is the great victory. At-Tawba 90
57. Allah will say, 'This is the Day when the sincerity of the sincere will benefit them. They will have Gardens with rivers flowing under them, remaining in them timelessly, for ever and ever. Allah is pleased with them and they are pleased with Him. That is the Great Victory.' Al-Ma'ida 119
58. Do not covet what Allah has given to some of you in preference to others – men have a portion of what they acquire and women have a portion of what they acquire; but ask Allah for His bounty. Allah has knowledge of all things. An-Nisa 32
59. Or do they in fact envy other people for the bounty Allah has granted them? An-Nisa 53
60. Whoever does jihad does it entirely for himself. Allah is Rich

Beyond Need of any being. Al-Ankabut 6

61. As for those who hold fast to the Book and establish salat, We will not let the wage of the salihun be wasted. Al-A'raf 170

62. ...Those who did right were making the way easy for themselves; so that He can repay with His bounty those who had iman and did right actions. He certainly does not love the kafirun. Among His Signs is that He sends the winds bearing good news, to give you a taste of His mercy, Ar-Rum 43-45

63. Their greeting on the Day they meet Him will be 'Peace!' and He has prepared a generous reward for them. Al-Ahzab 44

Wrong Actions and Punishments

1. Anyone who commits an error or an evil action, and then ascribes it to someone innocent, bears the weight of slander and clear wrongdoing. An-Nisa 111

2. Those who were kafir invented lies against Allah. Most of them do not use their intellect. Al-Ma'idah 103

3. But do not be an advocate for the treacherous. An-Nisa 104

4. As for thieves, both male and female, cut off their hands in reprisal for what they have done: an object lesson from Allah. Allah is Almighty, All-Wise. Al-Ma'ida 38

5. Those who persecute men and women of the muminun, and then do not make tawba, will have the punishment of Hell, will have the punishment of the Burning. Al-Buruj 10

6. But those who are kafir and deny Our Signs are the Companions of the Fire, remaining in it timelessly, for ever. Al-Baqara 38

7. But those who make accusations against chaste women and then do not produce four witnesses: flog them with eighty lashes and never again accept them as witnesses. Such people are deviators – An-Nur 4

8. A woman and a man who commit fornication: flog both of them with one hundred lashes and do not let compassion for either of them possess you where Allah's deen is concerned, if you have iman in Allah and the Last Day. A number of muminun should witness their punishment. An-Nur 2

9. And Qarun and Pharaoh and Haman – Musa came with

the Clear Signs to them, but they were arrogant on the earth. They could not outstrip Us. We seized each one of them for their wrong actions. Against some We sent a sudden squall of stones; some of them were seized by the Great Blast; some We caused the earth to swallow up; and some We drowned. Allah did not wrong them; rather they wronged themselves. Al-'Ankabut 39-40

10. ...because you forgot the meeting of this Day, We have forgotten you. Taste the punishment of eternal timelessness for what you did.' As-Sajda 14

11. Enter the gates of Hell, remaining in it timelessly, for ever. How evil is the abode of the arrogant! Al-Mumin 75

12. We have not wronged them; it was they who were wrongdoers. Az-Zukhruf 76

13. Those who oppose Allah and His Messenger will be subdued and overcome as those before them were also subdued and overcome. We have sent down Clear Signs. The kafirun will have a humiliating punishment. Al-Mujadila 5

14. They made their oaths into a cloak and barred the Way of Allah, so they will have a humiliating punishment. Al-Mujadila 16

15. That is because they were entrenched in hostility towards Allah and His Messenger. If anyone is hostile towards Allah, Allah is Severe in Retribution. Al-Hashr 4

16. ...Allah will humiliate the kafirun. At-Tawba 2

17. This was because they were hostile to Allah and His Messenger. If anyone is hostile to Allah and His Messenger, Allah is severe in retribution. Al-Anfal 13

18. As for those who are kafir and die kuffar, the whole earth filled with gold would not be accepted from any of them if they were to offer it as a ransom. They will have a painful punishment. They will have no helpers. Al 'Imran 90

19. If only the people of the cities had had iman and taqwa, We would have opened up to them blessings from heaven and earth. But they denied the truth so We seized them for what they earned. Al-A'raf 95

20. But as for those who have earned bad actions – a bad action

will be repaid with one the like of it. Debasement will darken them. They will have no one to protect them from Allah. It is as if their faces were covered by dark patches of the night. Those are the Companions of the Fire, remaining in it timelessly, for ever. Yunus 27

21. The reprisal against those who wage war on Allah and His Messenger, and go about the earth corrupting it, is that they should be killed or crucified, or have their alternate hands and feet cut off, or be banished from the land. That will be their degradation in the dunya and in the akhira they will have a terrible punishment, except for those who make tawba before you gain power over them. Know that Allah is Ever-Forgiving, Most Merciful. Al-Ma'ida 33-34

Allah's Signs

1. Do not make a mockery of Allah's Signs. Al-Baqara 229
2. It has been sent down to you in the Book that when you hear Allah's Signs being rejected and mocked at by people, you must not sit with them till they start talking of other things. If you do you are just the same as them. An-Nisa 139
3. You who have iman! do not take as friends any of those given the Book before you or the kuffar who make a mockery and a game out of your deen. Have taqwa of Allah if you are muminun. Al-Ma'ida 57
4. Those who took their deen as a diversion and a game, and were deluded by the life of the dunya. Today We will forget them just as they forgot the encounter of this Day and denied Our Signs. Al-A'raf 51
5. No fresh reminder comes to them from their Lord without their listening to it as if it was a game. Their hearts are distracted... Al-Anbiya 2-3
6. The evil deeds they did will appear before them and the things they mocked at will engulf them. Al-Jathiya 32
7. 'That is because you made a mockery of Allah's Signs and the life of the dunya deluded you.' Therefore, today they will not get out of it. They will not be able to appease Allah. Al-Jathiya 34
8. It is He who sent down the Book to you from Him: ayats contain-

ing clear judgements – they are the core of the Book – and others which are open to interpretation. Those with deviation in their hearts follow what is open to interpretation in it, desiring conflict, seeking its inner meaning. No one knows its inner meaning but Allah. Those firmly rooted in knowledge say, 'We have iman in it. All of it is from our Lord.' But only people of intelligence pay heed. Al 'Imran 7

9. Allah has sent down the Supreme Discourse, a Book consistent in its frequent repetitions. The skins of those who fear their Lord tremble at it and then their skins and hearts yield softly to the remembrance of Allah. Az-Zumar 22

10. We have sent down Clear Signs to you and the example of those who passed away before you and an admonition for those who have taqwa. An-Nur 34

11. It does not befit Allah to address any human being except by inspiration, or from behind a veil, or He sends a messenger who then reveals by His permission whatever He wills. He is indeed Most High, All-Wise. Ash-Shura 48

12. Accordingly We have revealed to you a Ruh by Our command. You had no idea of what the Book was, nor faith. Nonetheless We have made it a Light by which We guide those of Our slaves We will. Truly you are guiding to a Straight Path. Ash-Shura 49

13. These are Allah's Signs which We recite to you with truth. You are indeed one of the Messengers. Al-Baqara 250

14. And do not sell My Signs for a paltry price. Those who do not judge by what Allah has sent down, such people are kafirun. Al-Ma'ida 44

15. If you ask them they will say, 'We were only joking and playing around.' Say: 'Would you make a mockery of Allah and of His Signs and of His Messenger? Do not try to excuse yourselves.' At-Tawba 65-66

16. The revelation of the Book is from Allah, the Almighty, the All-Wise. Al-Jathiyah 1 and al-Ahqaf 1

17. It is nothing but Revelation revealed, taught him by one immensely strong,. An-Najm 4-5

18. I swear both by what you see and what you do not see, that

this is the word of a noble Messenger. It is not the word of a poet – how little iman you have! Nor the word of a fortune-teller – how little heed you pay! It is a revelation from the Lord of all the worlds. Al-Haqqa 38-43

Qur'an

1. That is the Book, without any doubt. It contains guidance for those who have taqwa. Al-Baqara 2
2. Those to whom We have given the Book, who recite it in the way it should be recited, such people have iman in it. As for those who reject it, they are the losers. Al-Baqara 121
3. The month of Ramadan is the one in which the Qur'an was sent down as guidance for mankind, with Clear Signs containing guidance and discrimination. Surat al-Baqara 84.
4. He has sent down the Book to you with truth, confirming what was there before it. And He sent down the Torah and the Injil, previously, as guidance for mankind... Al 'Imran 2-3
5. It is He who sent down the Book to you from Him: ayats containing clear judgements – they are the core of the Book – and others which are open to interpretation. Those with deviation in their hearts follow what is open to interpretation in it, desiring conflict, seeking its inner meaning. No one knows its inner meaning but Allah. Those firmly rooted in knowledge say, 'We have iman in it. All of it is from our Lord.' But only people of intelligence pay heed. Al 'Imran 7
6. This is a clear explanation for all mankind, and guidance and admonition for those who have taqwa. Al 'Imran 138
7. Will they not ponder the Qur'an? If it had been from other than Allah, they would have found many inconsistencies in it. An-Nisa 81
8. A Light has come to you from Allah and a Clear Book. By it, Allah guides those who follow what pleases Him to the ways of Peace. He will bring them from the darkness to the light by His permission, and guide them to a straight path. Al-Ma'ida 15 & 16
9. This is the path of your Lord – straight. We have made the Signs clear for people who remember. Al-An'am 127
10. Say, 'I follow only what has been revealed to me from my Lord.'

This is clear insight from your Lord, and guidance and mercy, for people who have iman. Al-A'raf 203

11. When the Qur'an is recited listen to it and be quiet so that hopefully you will gain mercy. Al-A'raf 204

12. Mankind! admonition has come to you from your Lord and also healing for what is in the breasts and guidance and mercy for the muminun. Yunus 57

13. Say: 'It is the favour of Allah and His mercy that should be the cause of their rejoicing. That is better than anything they accumulate.' Yunus 58

14. A Book whose ayats are perfectly constructed, and then demarcated, coming directly from One who is All-Wise, All-Aware. Hud 1

15. It is only a reminder to all beings. Yusuf 104

16. It is We Who have sent down the Reminder and We Who will preserve it. Al-Hijr 9

17. We have given you the Seven Oft repeated and the Magnificent Qur'an. Al-Hijr 87

18. Whenever you recite the Qur'an, seek refuge with Allah from the accursed Shaytan. An-Nahl 98

19. If We replace one ayat with another one –and Allah knows best what He is sending down... An-Nahl 101

20. This Qur'an guides to the most upright Way and gives good news to the muminun who do right actions that they will have a large reward. But as for those who do not have iman in the akhira, We have prepared for them a painful punishment. Bani Isra'il 9-10

21. We have made things clear in this Qur'an so that they might pay heed, but it only makes them run away the more! Bani Isra'il 41

22. When you recite the Qur'an, We place an obscuring veil between you and those who do not believe in the akhira. We have placed covers on their hearts, preventing them from understanding it, and heaviness in their ears. When you mention your Lord alone in the Qur'an, they turn their backs and run away. Bani Isra'il 45-46

23. ...and also the recitation at dawn. The dawn recitation is certainly witnessed. Bani Isra'il 78

24. We have divided up the Qur'an, so you can recite it to mankind at intervals, and We have sent it down little by little. Bani Isra'il 106

25. Praise belongs to Allah Who has sent down the Book to His slave and has put no crookedness in it. Al-Kahf 1

26. Recite what has been revealed to you of your Lord's Book. No one can change His Words. You will never find any safe haven apart from Him. Al-Kahf 27

27. ...When the Signs of the All-Merciful were recited to them they fell on their faces, weeping, in prostration. Maryam 58

28. In this way We give you news of what has gone before and We have given you a reminder direct from Us. Ta Ha 97

29. In this way We have sent it down as an Arabic Qur'an and We have made various threats in it so that hopefully they will have taqwa or it will spur them into remembrance. Ta Ha 110

30. This is a blessed Reminder which We have sent down. So are you going to ignore it? Al-Anbiya 50

31. Those who are kafir say, 'Why was the Qur'an not sent down to him all in one go?' It is so that We can fortify your heart by it. We have recited it distinctly, little by little. Al-Furqan 32

32. ...and I have been ordered to be one of the Muslims and to recite the Qur'an. An-Naml 92, Recite what has been revealed to you of the Book ... Al-'Ankabu/t 45

33. Those We gave the Book before this have iman in it. When it is recited to them they say, 'We have iman in it; it is the truth from our Lord. We were already Muslims before it came.' Al-Qasas 52-53

34. Is it not enough for them that We have sent down to you the Book which is recited to them? There is certainly a mercy and reminder in that for people who have iman. Al-'Ankabut 51

35. Alif Lam Mim Those are the Signs of the Wise Book – guidance and mercy for the good-doers. Luqman 1-2

36. Those who recite the Book of Allah and establish salat and give of what We have provided for them, secretly and openly, hope for a transaction which will not prove profitless. Fatir 29

37. It is a Book We have sent down to you, full of blessing, so let people of intelligence ponder its Signs and take heed. Sad 28

38. ...an Arabic Qur'an with no distortion in it... Az-Zumar 27

39. Follow the best that has been sent down to you from your Lord before the punishment comes upon you suddenly when you are not expecting it. Az-Zumar 52

40. ...truly it is a Mighty Book; falsehood cannot reach it from before it or behind it – it is a revelation from One who is All-Wise, Praiseworthy. Fussilat 40-41

41. If We had made it a Qur'an in a foreign tongue they would have said, 'Why have its Signs not been made plain? What! A foreign language for an Arab?' Fussilat 43

42. Surely We have made it an Arabic Qur'an that you may understand. And surely it is in the original of the Book with Us, truly elevated, full of wisdom. Az-Zukhruf 3 & 4

43. This is clear insight for mankind and guidance and mercy for people with certainty. Al-Jathiya 19

44. We have made the Qur'an easy to remember. But is there any rememberer there? Al-Qamar 17, 22, 32 & 40

45. ...and recite the Qur'an distinctly. Al-Muzzammil 4

46. Recite as much of the Qur'an as is easy for you. Al-Muzzammil 18

47. We have only sent down the Book to you so that you can make clear to them the things about which they differ, and as a guidance and a mercy to people who have iman. An-Nahl 64

48. The Messenger says, 'My Lord, my people treat this Qur'an as something to be ignored.' Al-Furqan 30 ???

49. Those who are kafir say, 'Why was the Qur'an not sent down to him all in one go?' It is so that We can fortify your heart by it. We have recited it distinctly, little by little. Al-Furqan 32

50. [The slaves of the All-Merciful are]...those who, when they are reminded of the Signs of their Lord, do not turn their backs, deaf and blind to them. Al-Furqan 73

51. ...and by the reciters of the Reminder[1]: your God is One: As-Saffat 3-4

52. If We wished We could take away what We have revealed to you and then you would not find any to guard you from Us – but

---

[1] A name for the Qur'an.

for a mercy from your Lord. His favour to you is indeed immense. Say: 'If both men and jinn banded together to produce the like of this Qur'an, they could never produce anything like it, even if they backed each other up.' Bani Isra'il 86-88

53. He who has imposed the Qur'an upon you will most certainly bring you back home again. Al-Qasas 85

54. ...We have sent it down as a judgement in Arabic... Ar-Ra'd 38

55. ...this is in clear and lucid Arabic. An-Nahl 103

56. Accordingly We have revealed to you an Arabic Qur'an so that you may warn the Mother of Cities [Makkah] and those around it. Ash-Shura 5

57. A Book whose verses have been demarcated for people who know as an Arabic Qur'an, Fussilat 2

58. ... [it is] in a clear Arabic tongue. Ash-Shu'ara 195

59. We have made it [Qur'an] easy in your own tongue so that hopefully they will pay heed. Ad-Dukhan 55

60. ...And this is a corroborating Book in the Arabic tongue... Al-Ahqaf 11

61. The Faithful Ruh brought it down to your heart so you would be one of the Warners in a clear Arabic tongue. It is certainly in the scriptures of the previous peoples. Ash-Shu'ara 193-5

62. This is a communication to be transmitted to mankind so that they may be warned by it and so that they will know that He is One God and so that people of intelligence will pay heed. Ibrahim 54

63. ...This is nothing but a reminder to all human beings. Al-Muddaththir 31

64. Recite what has been revealed to you of the Book and establish salat. Salat precludes indecency and wrongdoing. And remembrance of Allah is greater still. Allah knows what you do. Al-'Ankabut 45

65. Do not move your tongue trying to hasten it. Its collection and recitation are Our affair. So when We recite it, follow its recitation. Then its explanation is Our concern. Al-Qiyama 16-18

66. Will they not then ponder the Qur'an or are there locks upon their hearts? Muhammad 25

67. And We diverted a group of jinn towards you to listen to the Qur'an. When they were in earshot of it they said, 'Be quiet and listen.' When it was over they went back to their people, warning them. They said, 'Our people, we have heard a Book which was sent down after Musa, confirming what came before it, guiding to the truth and to a straight path. Al-Ahqaf 28-29

68. We know best what they say. You are not a dictator over them. So remind, with the Qur'an, whoever fears My Threat. Qaf 45

69. ...it truly is a Noble Qur'an in a well protected Book. No one may touch it except the purified. Revelation sent down from the Lord of all the worlds. Al-Waqi'a 80-83

70. But it is nothing less than a Reminder to all the worlds. Al-Qalam 52

71. Truly it is the speech of a noble Messenger, possessing great strength, securely placed with the Lord of the Throne, obeyed there, trustworthy. At-Takwir 19-21

72. It is indeed a Glorious Qur'an preserved on a Tablet. Al-Buruj 21-22

73. Ya Sin. By the Wise Qur'an. Yasin 1

74. Follow what has been revealed to you from your Lord. Allah is aware of what you do. Al-Ahzab 2

75. Has the time not arrived for the hearts of those who have iman to yield to the remembrance of Allah and to the truth He has sent down... Al-Hadid 15

76. Accordingly We have revealed to you a Ruh by Our command. You had no idea of what the Book was, nor faith. Nonetheless We have made it a Light by which We guide those of Our slaves We will. Truly you are guiding to a Straight Path. Ash-Shura 49

77. Your refuge is the Fire and you have no helpers. That is because you made a mockery of Allah's Signs and the life of the dunya deluded you. Al-Jathiya 33-34

78. The All-Merciful taught the Qur'an. Ar-Rahman 1

79. No indeed! Truly it is a reminder, and whoever wills pays heed to it. Inscribed on Honoured Pages, exalted, purified by the hands of scribes, noble, virtuous. 'Abasa 11-16

80. If you have doubts about what We have sent down to Our slave, produce another sura equal to it, and call your witnesses, besides Allah, if you are telling the truth. Al-Baqara 22

81. That is because Allah has sent down the Book with truth and those who differ from the Book are entrenched in hostility. Al-Baqara 176

82. When you see people engrossed in mockery of Our Signs, turn from them until they start to talk of other things. And if Shaytan should ever cause you to forget, once you remember, do not stay sitting with the wrongdoers. Al-An'am 68

83. ...Say, 'I follow only what has been revealed to me from my Lord.' This is clear insight from your Lord, and guidance and mercy, for people who have iman. Al-A'raf 203

84. When you recite the Qur'an, We place an obscuring veil between you and those who do not believe in the akhira. Bani Isra'il 45

85. This truly is a reminder, so let anyone who wills take a Way towards his Lord. Al-Muzzammil 17

86. It has been sent down to you in the Book that when you hear Allah's Signs being rejected and mocked at by people, you must not sit with them till they start talking of other things. If you do you are just the same as them. An-Nisa 139

87. You who have iman! do not ask about matters which, if they were made known to you, would make things difficult for you. If you do ask about them when the Qur'an is being sent down, they will be made known to you. Al-Ma'ida 101

88. Warn by it [the Qur'an] those who fear they will be gathered to their Lord, having no protector or intercessor apart from Him, so that hopefully they will have taqwa. Al-An'am 52

89. What We have revealed to you of the Book is the truth, confirming what came before it. Allah is aware of and sees His slaves. Fatir 31

90. ...'Seize hold vigorously of what We have given you and remember what is in it, so that hopefully you will have taqwa.' Al-A'raf 171

91. This Qur'an could never have been devised by any besides

Allah. Rather it is confirmation of what came before it and an elucidation of the Book which contains no doubt from the Lord of all the worlds. Do they say, 'He has invented it'? Say: 'Then produce a sura like it and call on anyone you can besides Allah if you are telling the truth. Yunus 37-38

92. Or do they say, 'He has invented it?' Say, 'Then produce ten invented suras like this, and call on anyone you can besides Allah if you are telling the truth. Hud 13

93. If men and jinn should combine together to bring the like of this Qur'an, they could not bring the like of it, even though they help each other. Al-Hijr 87

94. And this is a Book We have sent down and blessed, so follow it and have taqwa so that hopefully you will gain mercy. So you cannot say: 'The Book was only sent down to the two groups before us and we were ignorant of their studies.' Nor can you say: 'If the Book had been sent down to us, We would have been better guided than they were.' For a Clear Sign has come to you from your Lord, and guidance and mercy. Who could do greater wrong than someone who denies Allah's Signs and turns away from them? We will repay those who turn away from Our Signs with the worst kind of punishment because they turned away. Al-An'am 156-158

95. It is a Book sent down to you – so let there be no constriction in your breast because of it – so that you can give warning by it and as a reminder to the muminun. Follow what has been sent down to you from your Lord and do not follow any protectors apart from Him. How little you remember! Al-A'raf 1-2

96. ...Be in no doubt about it (the Qur'an). It is the Truth from your Lord. But most people have no iman. Hud 17

97. We have sent it down as an Arabic Qur'an so that hopefully you will use your intellect. Yusuf 2

98. ...This is not a narration which has been invented but confirmation of all that came before, a clarification of everything, and a guidance and a mercy for people who have iman. Yusuf 111

99. Those to whom We gave the Book rejoice at what has been sent down to you but some of the parties refuse to acknowledge

part of it. Say: 'I have only been ordered to worship Allah and not to associate anything with Him. I summon to Him and to Him I will return.' Ar-Ra'd 37

100. ...This is a Book We have sent down to you so that you can bring mankind from the darkness to the light, by the permission of their Lord, to the Path of the Almighty, the Praiseworthy. Ibrahim 1-2

101. Say: 'It is the truth from your Lord; so let whoever wishes have iman and whoever wishes be kafir.' Al-Kahf 29

102. Just as We sent down punishment on the dissectors, those who divide the Qur'an into little pieces. Al-Hijr 90-91

103. We have sent down the Book to you making all things clear and as guidance and mercy and good news for the Muslims. An-Nahl 89

104. Say: 'The Purest Ruh has brought it down from your Lord with truth, to make those who have iman firm, and as guidance and good news for the Muslims.' An-Nahl 102

105. We have variegated throughout this Qur'an all kinds of examples for people, but most people spurn anything but kufr. Bani Isra'il 89

106. We have sent it down with truth and with truth it has come down. We only sent you to bring good news and to give warning. Bani Isra'il 105

107. We have variegated throughout this Qur'an all kinds of examples for people... Al-Kahf 53

108. We have made it easy on your tongue so that you can give good news to those who have taqwa and warn stubbornly hostile people by it. Maryam 98 (See also Ta Ha 113)

109. Ta Ha. We did not send down the Qur'an to you to make you miserable, but only as a reminder for those who have fear, a Revelation from Him who created the earth and the high heavens. Ta Ha 1-3

110. In this way We have sent it down as Clear Signs. Allah guides anyone He wills. Al-Hajj 16

111. 'My Signs were recited to you and you turned round on your heels, arrogant towards it, talking arrant nonsense all night long.' Do they not ponder these words? Al-Muminun 67-69

112. We have given them their Reminder, but they have turned away from it. Al-Muminun 72

113. Blessed be He who has sent down the Furqan to His slave so that he can be a warner to all beings; Al-Furqan 1

114. Those who are kafir say, 'This is nothing but a lie he has invented and other people have helped him to do it. They have brought injustice and falsehood.' Al-Furqan 4

115. Those who are kafir say, 'Why was the Qur'an not sent down to him all in one go?' It is so that We can fortify your heart by it. We have recited it distinctly, little by little. Al-Furqan 32

116. Ta Sin Mim. Those are the Signs of the Clear Book. Ash-Shu'ara 1

117. Ta Sin. Those are the Signs of the Qur'an and a Clear Book. It is guidance and good news for the muminun, those who establish salat and pay zakat and are certain about the akhira. An-Naml 1-3

118. You receive the Qur'an directly from One who is All-Wise, All-Knowing. An-Naml 6

119. Certainly it [Qur'an] is guidance and a mercy for the muminun. An-Naml 79

120. ...recite the Qur'an.' Whoever is guided is only guided to his own good; if someone is misguided just say, 'I am only a warner.' An-Naml 94

121. Accordingly We have sent down the Book to you, and those to whom We gave the Book have iman in it, and some of these people have iman in it as well. Only the kafirun deny Our Signs. Al-'Ankabu/t 47

122. The revelation of the Book, without any doubt of it, is from the Lord of the worlds. Or do they say, 'He has invented it'? No indeed! It is the truth from your Lord to warn a people to whom, before you, no warner came, so that hopefully they will be guided. As-Sajda 1-2

123. Those who have been given knowledge see that what has been sent down to you from your Lord is the truth and that it guides to the Path of the Almighty, the Praiseworthy. Saba 6

124. [It is] The revelation of the Almighty, the Most Merciful. Ya Sin 5

125. We did not teach him poetry nor would it be right for him. It is simply a reminder and a clear Qur'an so that you may warn those who are truly alive and so that the Word may be carried out against the kafirun. Yasin 68-69

126. Sad. By the Qur'an holding the Remembrance! Sad 1

127. It is simply a reminder to all the worlds. Sad 86

128. The revelation of the Book is from Allah, the Almighty, the All-Wise. We have sent down the Book to you with truth. So worship Allah, making your deen sincerely His. Az-Zumar 1-2

129. Allah has sent down the Supreme Discourse, a Book consistent in its frequent repetitions. Az-Zumar 22

130. We have given all kinds of examples to people in this Qur'an, so that hopefully they will pay heed. Az-Zumar 26

131. ...The revelation of the Book is from Allah, the Almighty, the All-Knowing. Al-Mumin 1

132. Those who argue about the Signs of Allah without any authority coming to them do something hateful in the sight of Allah and in the sight of the people who have iman. That is how Allah seals up the heart of every arrogant oppressor. Al-Mumin 35

133. Those who deny the Book and that with which We sent Our Messengers will certainly come to know. Al-Mumin 70

134. A Book whose verses have been demarcated for people who know as an Arabic Qur'an, bringing good news and giving warning; but most of them have turned away and do not hear. Fussilat 2-3

135. Those who are kafir say, 'Do not listen to this Qur'an. Drown it out so that hopefully you will gain the upper hand.' Fussilat 25

136. Those who adulterate Our Signs are not concealed from Us. Who is better – someone who will be thrown into the fire or someone who will arrive in safety on the Day of Rising? Do what you like. He sees whatever you do. Those who reject the Remembrance when it comes to them – truly it is a Mighty Book; falsehood cannot reach it from before it or behind it – it is a revelation from One who is All-Wise, Praiseworthy. Nothing has been said to you that was not said to the Messengers before you. Your Lord is the Possessor of forgiveness but also of painful retribution. If We had

made it a Qur'an in a foreign tongue they would have said, 'Why have its Signs not been made plain? What! A foreign language for an Arab?' Say: 'It is guidance and healing for people who have iman. Those who do not have iman have heaviness in their ears and for them it is blindness. Such people are being called from a very distant place.' Fussilat 39-43

137. Say: 'What do you think? If it is from Allah and you reject it, who could be more misguided than someone entrenched in hostility to it?' We will show them Our Signs on the horizon and within themselves until it is clear to them that it is the truth. Is it not enough for your Lord that He is a witness of everything? Fussilat 51-52

138. Accordingly We have revealed to you an Arabic Qur'an so that you may warn the Mother of Cities [Makka] and those around it, and give warning of the Day of Gathering about which there is no doubt: one group in the Garden, the other in the Blazing Fire. Ash-Shura 5

139. It is Allah who has sent down the Book with truth and with the Just Balance. What will make you realise? Perhaps the Hour is close. Ash-Shura 15

140. ... By the Book which makes things clear. We have made it an Arabic Qur'an so that hopefully you will use your intellect. It is in the Source Book with Us, high-exalted, full of wisdom. Shall We then deprive you of the Reminder for being a profligate people? Az-Zukhruf 1-4

141. They say, 'Why was this Qur'an not sent down to one of the great men of the two cities?' [Makkah & Ta'if]. Az-Zukhruf 30

142. It is certainly a reminder to you and to your people and you will be questioned. Az-Zukhruf 43

143. By the Book which makes things clear. We sent it down on a blessed night; We are constantly giving warning. Ad-Dukhan 1-2

144. Those are Allah's Signs We recite to you with truth. In what discourse, then, after Allah and His Signs, will they have iman? Al-Jathiyyah 5

145. This is clear insight for mankind and guidance and mercy for people with certainty. Al-Jathiyah 19

146. But before it there was the Book of Musa as a model and a

mercy. And this is a corroborating Book in the Arabic tongue so that you may warn those who do wrong, and as good news for the good-doers. Al-Ahqaf 11

147. And We diverted a group of jinn towards you to listen to the Qur'an. When they were in earshot of it they said, 'Be quiet and listen.' When it was over they went back to their people, warning them. Al-Ahqaf 28

148. If We Had sent down this Qur'an onto a mountain, you would have seen it humbled, crushed to pieces out of fear of Allah. We make such examples for people so that hopefully they will reflect. Al-Hashr 21

149. The metaphor of those who were charged with the Torah but then have not upheld it, is that of a donkey loaded with weighty tomes. How evil is the metaphor of those who deny Allah's Signs! Allah does not guide wrongdoing people. Al-Jumu'a 5

150. Nor is it the word of an accursed Shaytan. At-Takwir 25

151. It is nothing but a Reminder to all the worlds, to whoever among you wishes to go straight. But you will not will unless Allah wills, the Lord of all the Worlds. At-Takwir 27-29

152. ...it is truly a Decisive Word. It is no joke. At-Tariq 13-14

153. No indeed! It is truly a reminder to which anyone who wills may pay heed. But they will only pay heed if Allah wills. He is entitled to be feared and entitled to forgive. Al-Muddaththir 53-55

154. It is We who have sent the Qur'an down to you little by little. Ad-Dahr 23

155. Truly We sent it down on the Night of Power. And what will convey to you what the Night of Power is? The Night of Power is better than a thousand months. In it the angels and the Ruh descend by their Lord's authority with every ordinance. It is Peace – until the coming of the dawn. Al-Qadr 1-5

156. When they [believing Christians] listen to what has been sent down to the Messenger, you see their eyes overflowing with tears because of what they recognise of the truth. Al-Ma'ida 83

157. Say: 'Who, then, sent down the Book which Musa brought as a Light and Guidance for the people?' You put it down on sheets of paper to display it while concealing much. You were taught

things you did not know, neither you nor your forefathers. Say: 'Allah!' Then leave them engrossed in playing their games.

158. This is a Book We have sent down and blessed, confirming what came before it, so that you can warn the Mother of Cities [Makkah] and the people around it. Those who have iman in the akhira believe in it and safeguard their salat.

159. Who could do greater wrong than someone who invents lies against Allah or denies His Signs, or who says, 'It has been revealed to me,' when nothing has been revealed to him, or someone who says, 'I will send down the same as Allah has sent down'? Al-An'am 92-94

160. Then We gave Musa the Book, complete and perfect for him who does good, elucidating everything, and a guidance and a mercy, so that hopefully they will have iman in their encounter with their Lord. Al-An'am 155

161. It is straight, to warn of violent force direct from Him, and to give the good news to the muminun, those who do right actions, that for them there is an excellent reward, a place in where they will remain for ever, and to warn those who say 'Allah has a son.' They have no knowledge of this, neither they nor their fathers. It is a monstrous utterance which has issued from their mouths. What they say is nothing but a lie. Al-Kahf 2-5

162. A sura We have sent down and imposed. We have sent down Clear Signs in it so that hopefully you will pay heed. An-Nur 1

163. We have made all kinds of examples for people in this Qur'an. If you bring them a Sign those who are kafir will say, 'You are just purveyors of falsehood!' Ar-Rum 57

164. Or do they say, 'He has simply made it up'? No, the truth is they have no iman. Let them produce a discourse like it if they are telling the truth. At-Tur 31-32

165. But you will not will unless Allah wills. Allah is All-Knowing, All-Wise. He admits whoever He wills into His mercy. But for the wrongdoers He has prepared a painful punishment. Ad-Dahr 30-31

166. ... and He has sent down the Furqan [discrimination]. Al 'Imran 4

167. We sent down the Torah containing guidance and light. Al-Ma'ida 44
168. And We sent 'Isa son of Maryam following in their footsteps, confirming the Torah that came before him. We gave him the Injil containing guidance and light, confirming the Torah that came before it, and as guidance and admonition for those who have taqwa. Al-Ma'ida 46
169. Your people deny it and yet it is the Truth. Al-An'am 67
170. In the Tablets inscription was guidance and mercy for all of them who feared their Lord. Al-A'raf 154
171. ...and before it the Book of Musa came as a model and a mercy... Hud 17
172. It is a reminder to the people with taqwa. Al-Haqqa 48
173. And it is undeniably the Truth of Certainty. Al-Haqqa 51
174. Say: It has been revealed to me that a party of the jinn listened, and they said: Surely we heard a wonderful Qur'an. Al-Jinn 1-2

Shaytan

1. And do not follow in the footsteps of Shaytan. He truly is an outright enemy to you. He only commands you to do evil and indecent acts and to say about Allah what you do not know. Al-Baqara 167-8
2. If an evil impulse from Shaytan provokes you, seek refuge in Allah. He is All-Hearing, All-Seeing. Al-A'raf 200
3. Whenever you recite the Qur'an, seek refuge with Allah from the accursed Shaytan. He has no authority over those who have iman and put their trust in their Lord. He only has authority over those who take him as a friend and associate others with Allah. An-Nahl 98-100
4. Shall I tell you upon whom the shaytans descend? They descend on every evil liar. Ash-Shu'ara 220-1
5. Anyone who associates something with Allah has gone very far astray. What they call on apart from Him are female idols. What they call on is an arrogant shaytan whom Allah has cursed. He said, 'I will take a certain fixed proportion of Your slaves. I will

lead them astray and fill them with false hopes. I will command them and they will cut off cattle's ears. I will command them and they will change Allah's creation.' Anyone who takes Shaytan as his protector in place of Allah has clearly lost everything. An-Nisa 115-118

6. He [Shaytan] makes promises to them and fills them with false hopes. But what Shaytan promises them is nothing but delusion. An-Nisa 119

7. ...and Shaytan made what they were doing seem attractive to them. Al-An'am 44

8. Shaytan has gained mastery over them and made them forget the remembrance of Allah. Such people are the party of Shaytan. No indeed! It is the party of Shaytan who are the losers. Al-Mujadila 19

9. Then I [Shaytan] will come at them, from in front of them and behind them, from their right and from their left. You will not find most of them thankful.' Al-A'raf 17

10. Children of Adam! do not let Shaytan tempt you into trouble as He expelled your parents from the Garden, stripping them of their covering and disclosing to them their private parts. He and his tribe see you from where you do not see them. We have made the shaytans friends of those who have no iman. Al-A'raf 26

11. If a whisper from the devil reaches you, then seek refuge in Allah. Indeed He is the Hearer, the Knower. Fussilat 36

12. By Allah, We sent Messengers to communities before your time, but Shaytan made their actions seem good to them. Therefore today he is their protector. They will have a painful punishment. An-Nahl 63

13. Say to My slaves that they should only say the best. Shaytan wants to stir up trouble between them. Shaytan is an outright enemy to man. Bani Isra'il 53

14. When We said to the angels, 'Prostrate yourselves to Adam!' they prostrated, except for Iblis. He said 'What! Am I to prostrate to one You have created out of clay?' He said, 'Do you see this creature you have honoured over me? If You reprieve me till the Day of Rising, I will be the master of his descendants except for

a very few.' He said, 'Go! And as for any who follow you, your repayment is Hell, repayment in full! Stir up any of them you can with your voice and rally against them your cavalry and your infantry and share with them in their children and their wealth and make them promises! The promise of Shaytan is nothing but delusion. But as for My slaves, you will not have any authority over them.' Your Lord suffices as a guardian. Bani Isra'il 61-65

15. Say: 'My Lord, I seek refuge with You from the goadings of the shaytans, and I seek refuge with You, my Lord, from their presence.' Al-Muminun 98-99

16. The shaytans did not bring it down. It does not befit them and they are not capable of it. They are debarred from hearing it. Ash-Shu'ara 210-11

17. Shaytan is your enemy so treat him as an enemy. He summons his party so they will be among the people of the Searing Blaze. Fatir 6

18. If someone shuts his eyes to the remembrance of the All-Merciful, We assign him a shaytan who becomes his bosom friend – they debar them from the path, yet they still think they are guided Az-Zukhruf 35-36

19. Do not follow in the footsteps of Shaytan. He is an outright enemy to you. Al-Baqara 206

20. But those who are kafir have false gods as protectors. They take them from the light into the darkness. Al-Baqara 256

21. Shaytan promises you poverty and commands you to avarice. Allah promises you forgiveness from Him and abundance. Allah is All-Encompassing, All-Knowing. Al-Baqara 267

22. ...Shaytan is a clear-cut enemy to man. Yusuf 5

23. When the affair is decided Shaytan will say, 'Allah made you a promise, a promise of truth, and I made you a promise but broke my promise. I had no authority over you, except that I called you and you responded to me. Do not, therefore, blame me but blame yourselves. I cannot come to your aid nor you to mine. I reject the way you associated me with Allah before.' The wrongdoers will have a painful punishment. Ibrahim 24

24. ...Shaytan was disobedient to the All-Merciful. Maryam 44

25. You who have iman! do not follow in the footsteps of Shaytan. Anyone who follows in Shaytan's footsteps should know that he commands indecency and wrongdoing. Were it not for Allah's favour to you and His mercy, not one of you would ever have been purified. But Allah purifies whoever He wills. Allah is All-Hearing, All-Knowing. *An-Nur 21*

26. They will be bundled into it [the Blazing Fire] head first, they and the misled, and every one of Iblis's regiments. *Ash-Shu'ara 94-95*

27. ...He said, 'This is part of Shaytan's handiwork. He truly is an outright and misleading enemy.' *Al-Qasas 14*

28. Shaytan made their actions seem good to them and so debarred them from the Way, even though they were intelligent people. *Al-'Ankabut 38*

29. Did I not make a contract with you, tribe of Adam, not to worship Shaytan, who truly is an outright enemy to you, but to worship Me? That is a straight path. He has led huge numbers of you into error. Why did you not use your intellect? *Ya Sin 59-61*

30. We have adorned the lowest heaven with the beauty of the planets and guarded it against every defiant shaytan. They cannot eavesdrop on the Highest Assembly and they are stoned from every side, repelled with harshness – they will suffer eternal punishment – except for him who snatches a snippet and then is pursued by a piercing flame. *As-Saffat 6-10*

31. If someone shuts his eyes to the remembrance of the All-Merciful, We assign him a shaytan who becomes his bosom friend – they debar them from the path, yet they still think they are guided – so that, when he reaches Us, he says, 'If only there was the distance of the two Easts between you and me!' What an evil companion! It will not benefit you today, since you did wrong, that you share equally in the punishment. *Az-Zukhruf 35-38*

32. Do not let Shaytan bar your way. He truly is an outright enemy to you. *Az-Zukhruf 62*

33. Those who have turned back in their tracks after the guidance became clear to them, it was Shaytan who talked them into it and filled them with false hopes. *Muhammad 26*

34. They are like Shaytan when he says to a human being, 'Be

kafir,' and then when he becomes kafir, says, 'I wash my hands of you. Truly I fear Allah, the Lord of all the worlds.' Al-Hashr 16
35. Among people there is one who argues about Allah without knowledge, and follows every rebellious shaytan. It is written of him that if anyone takes him as a friend, he will mislead him and guide him to the punishment of the Searing Blaze. Al-Hajj 3-4
36. ...The shaytans inspire their friends to dispute with you. Al-An'am 122
37. Then the angels prostrated all together, every one of them – except Iblis. He disdained to be one of the prostrators. Al-Hijr 30-31
38. He said, 'Iblis, what is it that prevents you being among the prostrators?' He said, 'I will not prostrate to a human being whom You have created out of dried clay formed from fetid black mud.' He said, 'Get out from here, you are accursed. The curse will be on you till the Day of Reckoning.' He said, 'My Lord, grant me a reprieve until the Day they are raised again.' He said, 'You are among the reprieved until the Day whose time is known.' He said, 'My Lord, because You misled me, I will make things on the earth seem good to them and I will mislead them all, every one of them, except Your slaves among them who are sincere.' He said, 'This is a Straight Path to Me. You have no authority over any of My slaves except for the misled who follow you.' Al-Hijr 32-42

The Fire of Hell

1. And beyond him [the tyrant] is Hell where he will be given pus to drink. He gulps at it but can hardly swallow it down. Death comes at him from every side but he does not die. And beyond him is relentless punishment. Ibrahim 19-20
2. Hell, where they will roast? What an evil place to stay! Ibrahim 31
3. Hell is the promised meeting-place for all of them. It has seven gates and each gate has its allotted share. Al-Hijr 43-44
4. Their shelter will be Hell. Whenever the Blaze dies down, We will increase it for them. Bani Isra'il 97
5. We have prepared for the wrongdoers a Fire whose billowing walls of smoke will hem them in. If they call for help, they will be helped with water like seething molten brass, frying their faces.

What a noxious drink! What an evil repose! Al-Kahf 29
6. As for those who reject Our Signs, We will roast them in a Fire. Every time their skins are burned off, We will replace them with new skins so that they can taste the punishment. Allah is Almighty, All-Wise. An-Nisa 55
7. ...a most evil torment engulfed Pharaoh's people – the Fire, morning and night, to which they are exposed... Al-Mumin 45-46
8. As for those who come to their Lord as evildoers, they will have Hell where they will neither die nor stay alive. Ta Ha 73
9. Those who are kafir will have garments of fire cut out for them, and boiling water poured over their heads, which will melt the contents of their bellies as well as their skin, and they will be beaten with cudgels made of iron. Every time they want to come out of it, because of their suffering, they will be driven back into it: 'Taste the punishment of the Burning!' Al-Hajj 19-20
10. The Fire will sear their faces, making them grimace horribly in it, their lips drawn back from their teeth. Al-Muminun 105
11. But instead, they deny the Hour; and We have prepared a Searing Blaze for those who deny the Hour. When it sees them coming from a long way off, they will hear it seething and rasping. When they are flung into a narrow place in it, shackled together in chains, they will cry out there for destruction. 'Do not cry out today for just one destruction, cry out for many destructions!' Al-Furqan 11-14
12. The Blazing Fire will be displayed to the misled. Ash-Shu'ara 91
13. Whereas for those who are kafir there will be the Fire of Hell. They will not be killed off so that they die and its punishment will not be lightened for them. That is how We repay every thankless man. They will shout out in it, 'Our Lord! take us out! We will act rightly, differently from the way we used to act!' Did We not let you live long enough for anyone who was going to pay heed to pay heed? And did not the warner come to you? Taste it then! There is no helper for the wrongdoers. Fatir 36-37
14. Is that better by way of hospitality or the tree of Zaqqum which We have made to be an ordeal for the wrongdoers? It is a tree that emerges in the depths of the Blazing Fire. Its fruits are

just like the heads of shaytans. They will eat from it and fill their bellies with it. Then they will have a boiling brew to drink on top of it. Then their destination will be the Blazing Fire. They found their fathers misguided and they are following hard upon their heels. As-Saffat 61-70

15. This! Whereas for the profligate there is an evil Homecoming: Hell, where they will roast. What an evil resting-place! This! So let them taste it – boiling water and scalding pus, and other such torments. This! A crowd hurtling in with you. There is no welcome for them. They will certainly roast in the Fire. Sad 54-58

16. Those who are kafir will be driven to Hell in companies and when they arrive there and its gates are opened its custodians will say to them, 'Did Messengers from yourselves not come to you, reciting your Lord's Signs to you and warning you of the meeting on this Day of yours?' They will say, 'Indeed they did, but the decree of punishment is justly carried out against the kafirun.' Az-Zumar 68

17. When they are squabbling with one another in the Fire, the weak will say to those deemed great, 'We were your followers, so why do you not relieve us of a portion of the Fire?' Those deemed great will say, 'All of us are in it. Allah has clearly judged between His slaves.' Those in the Fire will say to the custodians of Hell, 'Call on your Lord to make the punishment less for us for just one day.' They will ask, 'Did your Messengers not bring you the Clear Signs?' They will answer, 'Yes.' They will say, 'Then you call!' But the calling of the kafirun only goes astray. Al-Mumin 47-50

18. The evildoers will remain timelessly, for ever, in the punishment of Hell. It will not be eased for them. They will be crushed there by despair. We have not wronged them; it was they who were wrongdoers. They will call out, 'Malik,[1] let your Lord put an end to us!' He will say, 'You will stay the way you are.' Az-Zukhruf 74-77

19. The Tree of az-Zaqqum is the food of the wicked, seething in the belly like molten brass, as boiling water bubbles and seethes. 'Seize him and drag him bodily into the middle of the Blazing Fire.

---

[1] The name of the angel of the Fire.

Then pour the punishment of boiling water on his head.' 'Taste that! You are the mighty one, the noble one! This is the very thing you used to doubt.' Ad-Dukhan 41-47
20. On the Day when heaven sways to and fro and the mountains shift about, woe that Day to the deniers, who play at frivolous games: the Day they are shoved roughly into the Fire of Hell: 'This is the Fire which you denied! So is this magic? Or is it that you do not see? Roast in it! And bear it patiently or do not bear it patiently. It makes no difference either way. You are simply being repaid for what you did.' At-Tur 8-14
21. This is Hell which the evildoers deny. They will go back and forth between fire and scalding water. Ar-Rahman 42-43
22. And the Companions of the Left: what of the Companions of the Left? Amid searing blasts and scalding water and the murk of thick black smoke, providing no coolness and no pleasure. Al-Waqi'a 43-47
23. Then you, you misguided, you deniers will eat from the tree of Zaqqum, filling your stomachs with it and drink scalding water on top of it, slurping like thirst-crazed camels. Al-Waqi'a 54-58
24. Those who reject their Lord will have the punishment of Hell. What an evil destination! When they are flung into it they will hear it gasping harshly as it seethes. It all but bursts with rage. Each time a group is flung into it its custodians will question them: 'Did no warner come to you?' Al-Mulk 6-8
25. But no! It is a Raging Blaze stripping away the limbs and scalp, which calls for all who drew back and turned away, and amassed and hoarded up. Al-Ma'arij 15-18
26. I will roast him in Saqar. What will convey to you what Saqar is? It does not spare and does not ease up, ceaselessly scorching the flesh. There are nineteen in charge of it. We have only appointed angels as masters of the Fire and We have only specified their number as a trial for those who are kafir; Al-Muddaththir 26-31
27. Hell lies in wait – a homecoming for the profligate remaining in it for countless aeons, not tasting any coolness there or any drink, except for scalding water and burning pus – a fitting recompense. An-Naba' 21-25
28. The dissolute will be in a Blazing Fire. They will roast in it on the

Day of Judgment and will never get away from it. Al-Infitar 14-16

29. He who has fear will be reminded; but the most miserable will shun it, those who will roast in the Greatest Fire and then neither die nor live in it. Al-A'la 12-13

30. Some faces on that Day will be downcast, labouring, toiling endlessly, roasting in a red-hot Fire, drinking from a boiling spring. They have no food but a bitter thorny bush which neither nourishes nor satisfies. Al-Ghashiya 2-7

31. No indeed, if you only knew with the Knowledge of Certainty, you will certainly see the Blazing Fire! Then you will certainly see it with the Eye of Certainty. At-Takathur 5-7

32. And what will convey to you what the Shatterer is? The kindled Fire of Allah reaching right into the heart. It is sealed in above them in towering columns. Al-Humaza 5-9

33. ...then fear the Fire whose fuel is people and stones, made ready for the kafirun. Al-Baqara 23

34. Those who deny the Book and that with which We sent Our Messengers will certainly come to know when they have shackles and chains around their necks and are dragged along the ground into the boiling water and then are thrown into the Fire! Al-Mumin 70-72

35. With Us there are shackles and a Blazing Fire and food that chokes and a painful punishment, Al-Muzzammil 11-12

Description of the Garden

1. Give the good news to those who have iman and do right actions that they will have Gardens with rivers flowing under them. When they are given fruit there as provision, they will say, 'This is what we were given before.' But they were only given a simulation of it. They will have there spouses of perfect purity and will remain there timelessly, for ever. Al-Baqara 24

2. But as for those who have iman and do right actions, We will admit them into Gardens with rivers flowing under them, remaining in them timelessly, for ever and ever. In them they will have spouses of perfect purity and We will admit them into cool, refreshing shade. An-Nisa 56

3. Allah will reward them for what they say with Gardens with rivers flowing under them, remaining in them timelessly, for ever. That is the recompense of the good-doers. Al-Ma'ida 85

4. We will strip away any rancour in their hearts. Rivers will flow under them and they will say, 'Praise be to Allah who has guided us to this! We would not have been guided, had Allah not guided us. The Messengers of our Lord came with the Truth.' It will be proclaimed to them: 'This is your Garden which you have inherited for what you did.' The Companions of the Garden will call out to the Companions of the Fire, 'We have found that what our Lord promised us is true. Have you found that what your Lord promised you is true?' They will say, 'Yes, we have!' Between them a herald will proclaim: 'May the curse of Allah be on the wrongdoers those who bar access to the Way of Allah, desiring to make it crooked, and reject the akhira.' There will be a dividing wall between them and on the ramparts there will be men who recognise everyone by their mark. They will call out to the people of the Garden: 'Peace be upon you!' They will not enter it for all their ardent desire to do so. When they turn their eyes towards the Companions of the Fire, they will say, 'Our Lord, do not place us with the people of the wrongdoers!' The Companions of the Ramparts will call out to men they recognise by their mark, saying, 'What you amassed was of no use to you, nor was your arrogance. Al-A'raf 42-47

5. The Companions of the Fire will call out to the Companions of the Garden, 'Throw down some water to us or some of what Allah has given you as provision.' They will say, 'Allah has forbidden them to the kafirun: Al-A'raf 49

6. Allah has promised the men and women of the muminun Gardens with rivers flowing under them, remaining in them timelessly, for ever, and fine dwellings in the Gardens of Eden. And Allah's good pleasure is even greater. That is the great victory. At-Tawba 73

7. The forerunners – the first of the Muhajirun and the Ansar – and those who have followed them in doing good: Allah is pleased with them and they are pleased with Him. He has prepared Gardens for

them with rivers flowing under them, remaining in them timelessly, for ever and ever. That is the great victory. At-Tawba 101

8. But as for those who have iman and do right actions, their Lord will guide them by their iman. Rivers will flow under them in Gardens of Delight. Their call there is: 'Glory be to You, O Allah!' Their greeting there is: 'Peace!' The end of their call is: 'Praise be to Allah, the Lord of all the worlds!' Yunus 9-10

9. What is the Garden promised to those who have taqwa like? It has rivers flowing under it and its foodstuffs and cool shade never fail. That is the final fate of those who have taqwa. But the final fate of the kuffar is the Fire. Ar-Ra'd 36

10. Those who have taqwa will be amid Gardens and Springs: 'Enter them in peace, in complete security!' We will strip away any rancour in their hearts – brothers, resting on couches face-to-face. They will not be affected by any tiredness there and they will never be made to leave. Al-Hijr 45-48

11. But as for those who have iman and do right actions, We will not let the wage of good-doers go to waste. They will have Gardens of Eden with rivers flowing under them. They will be adorned in them with bracelets made of gold and wear green garments made of the finest silk and rich brocade, reclining there on couches under canopies. What an excellent reward! What a wonderful repose! Al-Kahf 30-31

12. Gardens of Eden which the All-Merciful has promised to His slaves in the Unseen. His promise is always kept. They will not hear any prattling there – nothing but 'Peace'. They will receive their provision there morning and night. That is the Garden which We will bequeath to those of Our slaves who have taqwa. Maryam 61-63

13. Gardens of Eden with rivers flowing under them, remaining in them timelessly, for ever. That is the reward of those who purify themselves. Ta Ha 75

14. Gardens beneath which rivers flow; they shall be adorned with bracelets of gold and with pearls and their garments shall be of silk. They will enter Gardens of Eden where they will be adorned with gold bracelets and pearls, and where their clothing will be of

silk. They will say, 'Praise be to Allah who has removed all sadness from us. Truly our Lord is Ever-Forgiving, Ever-Thankful: He who has lodged us, out of His favour, in the Abode of Permanence where no weariness or fatigue affects us.' Fatir 33-35

15. ... Allah's chosen slaves. They will have preordained provision: sweet fruits and high honour in Gardens of Delight on couches face to face; a cup from a flowing spring passing round among them, as white as driven snow, delicious to those who drink, which has no headache in it and does not leave them stupefied. There will be dark-eyed maidens with them, with eyes reserved for them alone, just like closely guarded pearls. They will confront each other, questioning one another. One of them will say, 'I used to have a friend who would say to me, "Are you one of those who say that it is true: that when we have died and are turned to dust and bones, we will face a Reckoning?"' He will say, 'Are you looking down?' So he will look down and see him in the midst of the Blazing Fire and say, 'By Allah, you almost ruined me! If it were not for the blessing of my Lord, I would have been among those arraigned. Are we not going to die, except for our first death? Are we not going to be punished? Truly this is the Great Victory! It is for the like of this that all workers should work!' As-Saffat 40-61

16. This is a Reminder. Those who have taqwa will have a good Homecoming: Gardens of Eden, whose gates will be open to them, where they will recline, calling for plentiful fruit and drink; and there will be dark-eyed maidens with them with eyes reserved for them alone. This is what you are promised on the Day of Reckoning. This is Our provision which will never run out. Sad 48-53

17. The angels descend on those who say, 'Our Lord is Allah,' and then go straight: 'Do not fear and do not grieve but rejoice in the Garden you have been promised. We are your protectors in the life of the dunya and the akhira. You will have there all that your selves could wish for. You will have there everything you demand. Hospitality from One who is Ever-Forgiving, Most Merciful.' Fussilat 29-31

18. 'Enter the Garden, you and your wives, delighting in your joy.' Platters and cups of gold will passed around among them

and they will have there all that their hearts desire and their eyes find delight in. You will remain in it timelessly, for ever. That is the Garden you will inherit for what you did. There will be many fruits in it for you to eat. Az-Zukhruf 70-73

19. The people who have taqwa will be in a safe place amid gardens and fountains, wearing fine silk and rich brocade, face to face with one another. So it will be. We will marry them to dark-eyed maidens. They will call there for fruit of every kind, in complete security. They will not taste any death there – except for the first one. He will safeguard them from the punishment of the Blazing Fire. A favour from your Lord. That is the Great Victory. Ad-Dukhan 48-54

20. An image of the Garden which is promised to those who have taqwa: in it there are rivers of water which will never spoil and rivers of milk whose taste will never change and rivers of wine, delightful to all who drink it, and rivers of honey of undiluted purity; in it they will have fruit of every kind and forgiveness from their Lord.... Muhammad 15

21. ... so that He may admit the men and women of the muminun into Gardens with rivers flowing under them, remaining in them timelessly, for ever, and erase their bad actions from them; and in Allah's sight that is a mighty victory. Al-Fath 5

22. Enter it in peace. This is the Day of Timeless Eternity.' They will have there everything they want and with Us there is still more. Qaf 34-35

23. The people who have taqwa will be in Gardens of Delight, savouring what their Lord has given them. Their Lord will safeguard them from the punishment of the Blazing Fire: 'Eat and drink with relish for what you did.' They will recline on couches ranged in rows and We will marry them to dark-eyed maidens. And We will unite those who had iman with their offspring, who followed them in iman, and We will not undervalue their own actions in any way. Every man is in pledge for what he earned. We will supply them with any kind of fruit and meat that they desire. They will pass round there a drinking cup to one another with no foolish talk and no wrong action in it. Circulating among them there will be

youths like hidden pearls. Some of them will come up to others and they will question one another. They will say, 'Beforehand we used live in fear among our families. But Allah was gracious to us and safeguarded us from the punishment of the searing wind. Beforehand we certainly used to call on Him because He is the All-Good, the Most Merciful.' At-Tur 15-26

24. For those who fear the Station of their Lord there are two Gardens. So which of your Lord's blessings do you both then deny? Shaded by spreading branches. So which of your Lord's blessings do you both then deny? In them are two clear flowing springs. So which of your Lord's blessings do you both then deny? In them are two kinds of every fruit. So which of your Lord's blessings do you both then deny? They will be reclining on couches lined with rich brocade, the fruits of the Gardens hanging close to hand. So which of your Lord's blessings do you both then deny? In them are maidens with eyes for them alone, untouched before them by either man or jinn. So which of your Lord's blessings do you both then deny? Like precious gems of ruby and pearl. So which of your Lord's blessings do you both then deny? Will the reward for doing good be anything other than good? So which of your Lord's blessings do you both then deny? As well as those two there will be two other Gardens. So which of your Lord's blessings do you both then deny? Of deep viridian green. So which of your Lord's blessings do you both then deny? In them are two gushing springs. So which of your Lord's blessings do you both then deny? In them are fruits and date-palms and pomegranates. So which of your Lord's blessings do you both then deny? In them are sweet, lovely maidens. So which of your Lord's blessings do you both then deny? Dark-eyed, secluded in cool pavilions. So which of your Lord's blessings do you both then deny? Untouched before them by either man or jinn. So which of your Lord's blessings do you both then deny? Reclining on green quilts and exquisite rugs. Ar-Rahman 45-75

25. And the Forerunners, the Forerunners. Those are the Ones Brought Near in Gardens of Delight. A large group of the earlier people but few of the later ones. On sumptuous woven couches,

reclining on them face to face. There will circulate among them, ageless youths, carrying goblets and decanters and a cup from a flowing spring – it does not give them any headache nor does it leave them stupefied. And any fruit they specify and any bird-meat they desire. And dark-eyed maidens like hidden pearls. As recompense for what they did. They will hear no prattling in it nor any word of wrong. All that is said is, 'Peace! Peace!' Al-Waqi'a 12-28

26. And the Companions of the Right: what of the Companions of the Right? Amid thornless lote-trees and fruit-laden acacias and wide-spreading shade and outpouring water and fruits in abundance never failing, unrestricted. And on elevated couches We have brought maidens into being and made them purest virgins, devoted, passionate, of like age, for the Companions of the Right. A large group of the earlier people and a large group of the later ones. Al-Waqi'a 29-42

27. But the truth is that if he is one of Those Brought Near, there is solace and sweetness and a Garden of Delight. And if he is one of the Companions of the Right, 'Peace be upon you!' from the Companions of the Right Al-Waqi'a 91-94

28. He will forgive you your wrong actions and admit you into Gardens with rivers flowing under them, and fine dwellings in the Gardens of Eden. That is the Great Victory. As-Saff 12

29. The truly good will drink from a cup mixed with the coolness of camphor, a spring from which Allah's slaves will drink, making it gush forth at will abundantly. Ad-Dahr 5-6

30. So Allah has safeguarded them from the evil of that Day and has made them meet with radiance and pure joy, and will reward them for their steadfastness with a Garden and with silk. Reclining in it on couches, they will experience there neither burning sun nor bitter cold. Its shading branches will droop down over them, its ripe fruit hanging ready to be picked. Vessels of silver and goblets of pure crystal will be passed round among them, crystalline silver – they have measured them very exactly. They will be given there a cup to drink mixed with the warmth of ginger. In it there is a flowing spring called Salsabil. Ageless youths will circulate among them, serving them. Seeing them, you would think them scattered

pearls. Seeing them, you see delight and a great kingdom. They will wear green garments of fine silk and rich brocade. They will be adorned with silver bracelets. And their Lord will give them a pure draught to drink. 'This is your reward. Your striving is fully acknowledged.' Ad-Dahr 11-22

31. For those who have taqwa there is triumph: Gardens and grape vines, and nubile maidens of similar age, and an overflowing cup, where they will hear no prattle and no denial, a recompense from your Lord, a commensurate gift. An-Naba' 31-36

32. Some faces on that Day will be radiant, well-pleased with their efforts in an elevated Garden where no prattle is ever heard. In it is a gushing spring and raised-up couches, and set-out goblets, and lined-up cushions, and spread-out rugs. Al-Ghashiya 8-16

33. Those who have taqwa will have Gardens with their Lord, with rivers flowing under them, remaining in them timelessly, for ever, and purified wives, and the Pleasure of Allah. Allah sees His slaves. Al 'Imran 15

34. Gardens of Eden which they enter, with rivers flowing under them, where they have whatever they desire. That is how Allah repays those who have taqwa. An-Nahl 31

35. As for those who have iman and do right actions, We will lodge them in lofty chambers in the Garden, with rivers flowing under them, remaining in them timelessly, for ever. How excellent is the reward of those who act: Al-'Ankabut 58

36. For those who have iman and do right actions there are Gardens of Delight, to remain in them timelessly, for ever. Allah's promise is true. He is the Almighty, the All-Wise. Luqman 7-8

Islam

Iman and Action

1. Those who have iman in what has been sent down to you and what was sent down before you, and are certain about the akhira. They are the people guided by their Lord. Al-Baqara 3-4
2. Give the good news to those who have iman and do right actions. Al-Baqara 25
3. All who have iman in Allah and the Last Day and act rightly, will have their reward with their Lord. Al-Baqara 62
4. Those who have iman and make hijra and do jihad in the Way of Allah can expect Allah's mercy. Al-Baqara 218
5. Each one [of the muminun] has iman in Allah and His angels and His Books and His Messengers. Al-Baqara 285
6. As for those who have iman and do right actions, We will pay them their wages in full. Al 'Imran 57
7. Say, 'We have iman in Allah and what has been sent down to us and what was sent down to Ibrahim, Isma'il and Ishaq and Ya'qub and the Tribes, and what Musa and 'Isa and all the Prophets were given by their Lord. We do not differentiate between any of them. We are Muslims submitted to Him.' Al 'Imran 84
8. There is a community among the People of the Book who are upright. They recite Allah's Signs throughout the night, and they prostrate. They have iman in Allah and the Last Day, and enjoin the right and forbid the wrong, and compete in doing good. They are among the salihun. Al 'Imran 113-114
9. But as for those who have iman and do right actions, We will admit them into Gardens with rivers flowing under them, remaining in them timelessly, for ever and ever. In them they will have spouses of perfect purity and We will admit them into cool, refreshing shade. An-Nisa 57. (See also an-Nisa 122)
10. You who have iman! have iman in Allah and His Messenger and in the Book He sent down to His Messenger, and the Books He sent down before. An-Nisa 136
11. Allah does not like evil words being voiced out loud, except

in the case of someone who has been wronged. Allah is All-Hearing, All-Knowing. An-Nisa 147

12. As for those who have iman and do right actions, He will pay them their wages in full and will give them increase from His favour. An-Nisa 173

13. So compete with each other in doing good. Al-Ma'ida 48

14. Those who have iman and those who are Jews and the Sabaeans and the Christians, all who have iman in Allah and the Last Day and act rightly will feel no fear and will know no sorrow. Al-Ma'ida 69

15. Those who have iman and do right actions are not to blame for anything they have eaten provided they have taqwa and iman and do right actions, and then again have taqwa and iman, and then have taqwa and do good. Allah loves good-doers. Al-Ma'ida 93

16. As for those who have iman and do right actions – We impose on no self any more than it can bear – they are the Companions of the Garden, remaining in it timelessly, for ever. Al-A'raf 42

17. Yes, the friends of Allah will feel no fear and will know no sorrow. Yunus 62

18. Obey Allah and His Messenger if you are muminun. Al-Anfal 1

19. The men and women of the muminun are friends of one another. They command what is right and forbid what is wrong, and establish salat and pay zakat, and obey Allah and His Messenger. Al-Anfal 72

20. ...there are some who have iman in Allah and the Last Day and regard what they give as something which will bring them nearer to Allah and to the prayers of the Messenger. It does indeed bring them near. At-Tawba 99

21. He brings creation out of nothing and then regenerates it so that He can repay with justice those who had iman and did right actions.... Yunus 4

22. But as for those who have iman and do right actions, their Lord will guide them by their iman. Rivers will flow under them in Gardens of Delight. Yunus 9

23. ...those who are steadfast and do right actions. They will receive forgiveness and a large reward. Hud 11

24. As for those who have iman and do right actions and humble themselves before their Lord, they are the Companions of the Garden, remaining in it timelessly, for ever. Hud 23

25. ...My mercy extends to all things but I will prescribe it for those who have taqwa and pay zakat, and those who believe in Our Signs... Al-A'raf 156

26. Those who have iman and do right actions, happiness will be theirs and a wonderful Homecoming. Ar-Ra'd 29

27. Those who had iman and did right actions will be admitted into Gardens with rivers flowing under them, remaining in them timelessly, for ever by the permission of their Lord. Their greeting there is 'Peace!' Ibrahim 23

28. Anyone who acts rightly, male or female, being a mumin, We will give them a good life and We will recompense them according to the best of what they did. An-Nahl 97

29. But as for those who have iman and do right actions, We will not let the wage of good-doers go to waste. Al-Kahf 30

30. Those who have iman and do right actions will have the Gardens of Firdaws as hospitality, Al-Kahf 107

31. ...except for those who make tawba and have iman and act rightly. They will enter the Garden and they will not be wronged in any way. Maryam 60

32. As for those who have iman and do right actions, the All-Merciful will bestow His love on them. Maryam 96

33. But as for those who come to Him as muminun, having done right actions, they will have the highest ranks. Ta Ha 75

34. But I am Ever-Forgiving to anyone who makes tawba and has iman and acts rightly and then is guided. Ta Ha 82

35. But anyone who does right actions, being a mumin, need fear no wrong or any belittlement. Ta Ha 112

36. Allah will admit those who have iman to Gardens with rivers flowing under them... Al-Hajj 14 & Muhammad 12

37. As for anyone who does right actions and is a mumin, his

striving certainly does not go unthanked. We are writing it down on his behalf. Al-Anbiya 94
38. As for those who have iman and do right actions, they will have forgiveness and generous provision. Al-Hajj 50 (See also Saba 4)
39. This is so that He may recompense those who have iman and do right actions. They will have forgiveness and generous provision. Saba' 4
40. Those who have iman and do right actions will be in Gardens of Delight. Al-Hajj 56 (See also Luqman 8)
41. You who have iman! bow and prostrate and worship your Lord, and do good, so that hopefully you will be successful. Al-Hajj 77
42. Allah has promised those of you who have iman and do right actions that He will make them successors in the land as He made those before them successors, and will firmly establish for them their deen with which He is pleased and give them, in place of their fear, security... An-Nur 55
43. ... those who make tawba and have iman and act rightly: Allah will transform the wrong actions of such people into good – Allah is Ever-Forgiving, Most Merciful. Al-Furqan 70
44. As for those who have iman and do right actions, We will erase their bad actions from them, and recompense them for the best of what they did. Al-'Ankabut 7
45. As for those who have iman and do right actions, We will lodge them in lofty chambers in the Garden, with rivers flowing under them, remaining in them timelessly, for ever. How excellent is the reward of those who act: Al-'Ankabut 58
46. As for those who had iman and did right actions, they will be made joyful in a verdant meadow. Ar-Rum 15
47. Those who did right were making the way easy for themselves; so that He can repay with His bounty those who had iman and did right actions... Ar-Rum 44-45
48. For those who have iman and do right actions there are Gardens of Delight. Luqman 8
49. As for those who have iman and do right actions, they will have the Gardens of Safe Refuge as hospitality for what they used to do. As-Sajda 19

50. It is not your wealth or your children that will bring you near to Us – only in the case of people who have iman and act rightly; such people will have a double recompense for what they did. They will be safe from all harm in the High Halls of Paradise. Saba 37

51. ...except those who have iman and do right actions, and how few they are!'... Sad 24

52. Would We make those who have iman and do right actions the same as those who cause corruption on the earth?... Sad 28

53. But whoever acts rightly, male or female, being a mumin, such a person will enter the Garden, provided for in it without any reckoning. Al-Mumin 40

54. Nor are those who have iman and do right actions the same as evildoers... Ghafir 58 (see also al-Jathiya 21)

55. Those who have iman and do right actions will have a wage which never fails. Fussilat 8

56. ...those who have iman and do right actions will be in the lush Meadows of the Gardens. They will have whatever they wish for with their Lord. That is the great favour. Ash-Shura 22

57. It is He who accepts tawba from His slave and pardons evil acts and knows what they do. He responds to those who have iman and do right action and gives them increase from His favour. Ash-Shura 25-26

58. As for those who had iman and did right actions, their Lord will admit them into His mercy. That is the Clear Victory. Al-Jathiya 30

59. But as for those who have iman and do right actions and have iman in what has been sent down to Muhammad – and it is the truth from their Lord – He will erase their bad actions from them and better their condition. Muhammad 2

60. Allah has promised those of them who have iman and do right actions forgiveness and an immense reward. Al-Fath 29

61. As for those who have iman in Allah and act rightly, We will erase their bad actions from them and admit them into Gardens with rivers flowing under them, remaining in them timelessly, for ever and ever. That is the Great Victory! Al-Taghabun 9

62. ...a Messenger reciting Allah's Clear Signs to you to bring those who have iman and do right actions out of the darkness into the Light. Whoever has iman in Allah and acts rightly, We will admit him into Gardens with rivers flowing under them remaining in them timelessly, for ever and ever. Allah has provided for him excellently! At-Talaq 11

63. ... except those who have iman and do right actions: they will have a wage which never fails. Al-Inshiqaq 25 & At-Tin 6

64. But those who have iman and do right actions will have Gardens with rivers flowing under them. That is the Great Victory. Al-Buruj 11

65. But those who have iman and do right actions - they are the best of creatures. Al-Bayyina 7

66. Truly man is in loss – except for those who have iman and do right actions and bid each other to the truth and bid each other to steadfastness. Al-'Asr 2-4

67. They should therefore respond to Me and believe in Me so that hopefully they will be rightly guided. Al-Baqara 186

68. There is good news for them [the friends of Allah] in the life of the dunya and in the akhira. Yunus 64

69. All have ranks according to what they did. Your Lord is not unaware of what they do. Al-An'am 133

70. ...those who have iman and do right actions will receive forgiveness and an immense reward. Fatir 7

71. And We rescued those who had iman and taqwa. Fussilat 18

72. How can you reject Allah, when you were dead and then He gave you life, then He will make you die and then give you life again, then you will be returned to Him? Al-Baqara 28

73. Those with iman, those who are Jews, and the Christians and Sabaeans, all who have iman in Allah and the Last Day and act rightly, will have their reward with their Lord. They will feel no fear and will know no sorrow. Al-Baqara 61

74. Do you, then, believe in one part of the Book and reject the other? What repayment will there be for any of you who do that except disgrace in the dunya? And on the Day of Rising, they will be returned to the harshest of punishments. Al-Baqara 85

75. Not so! All who submit themselves completely to Allah and are good-doers will find their reward with their Lord. They will feel no fear and will know no sorrow. Al-Baqara 112
76. So have iman in Allah and His Messengers. If you have iman and taqwa you will have an immense reward. Al 'Imran 179
77. 'It is revealed to me that your god is One God. So let him who hopes to meet his Lord act rightly and not associate anyone in the worship of his Lord.' Al-Kahf 110
78. But Allah will admit those who have iman and do right actions into Gardens with rivers flowing under them where they will be adorned with gold bracelets and pearls, and where their clothing will be of silk. They have been guided to speak good words and guided to the praiseworthy path. Al-Hajj 23-24
79. As for those who have iman and do right actions, We will admit them among the salihun. Al-'Ankabut 9
80. That is the good news which Allah gives to His slaves who have iman and do right actions. Ash-Shura 23
81. As for those who had iman in Our Signs and became Muslims: 'Enter the Garden, you and your wives, delighting in your joy.' Az-Zukhruf 69-70
82. So have iman in Allah and His Messenger and in the Light We have sent down. Allah is aware of what you do. At-Taghabun 8
83. Anyone who has iman in his Lord need fear neither belittlement nor tyranny. Al-Jinn 13
84. Allah has promised those who have iman and do right actions forgiveness and an immense reward. Al-Ma'ida 9

Doing as One Says

1. Do you order people to devoutness and forget yourselves, when you recite the Book? Will you not use your intellect? Al-Baqara 44
2. Allah would never change a blessing He has conferred on a people until they had changed what was in themselves. Al-Anfal 53
3. 'I would clearly not want to go behind your backs and do something I have forbidden you to do...' Hud 88
4. And as for poets, it is the misled who follow them. Do you not

see how they ramble on in every style and say things which they do not do, except those who have iman and do right actions and remember Allah repeatedly and defend themselves after they have been wronged? Ash-Shu'ara 223-6
5. You who have iman! why do you say what you do not do? It is deeply abhorrent to Allah that you should say what you do not do. As-Saff 2-3

Salat and Zakat

1. Establish salat and pay zakat and bow with those who bow. Al-Baqara 43
2. And establish salat and pay zakat. Al-Baqara 83
3. Establish salat and pay zakat. Any good you send ahead for yourselves, you will find with Allah. Certainly Allah sees what you do. Al-Baqara 110
4. [Rather, those with true devoutness are those who] ... establish salat and pay zakat; those who honour their contracts when they make them, and are steadfast in poverty and illness and in battle. Al-Baqara 177
5. Safeguard the salat – especially the middle one. Stand in obedience to Allah. If you are afraid, then do salat on foot or mounted. But when you are safe, remember Allah in the way He taught you when previously you did not know. Al-Baqara 238-239
6. Those who have iman and do right actions and establish salat and pay zakat, will have their reward with their Lord. Al-Baqara 277
7. The munafiqun think they deceive Allah, but He is deceiving them. When they get up to pray, they get up lazily, showing off to people, and only remembering Allah a very little. An-Nisa 143
8. ...those who establish salat and pay zakat, and have iman in Allah and the Last Day – We will pay such people an immense wage. An-Nisa 162
9. Allah said [to Bani Isra'il], 'I am with you. If you establish salat and pay zakat, and have iman in My Messengers and respect and support them, and make a generous loan to Allah, I will erase your wrong actions from you and admit you into Gardens with

rivers flowing under them. Any of you who are kafir after that have gone astray from the right way.' Al-Ma'ida 12

10. Your friend is only Allah and His Messenger and those who have iman: those who establish salat and pay zakat, and bow. Al-Ma'ida 55

11. My mercy extends to all things but I will prescribe it for those who have taqwa and pay zakat... Al-A'raf 156

12. If they [the mushrikun] make tawba and establish salat and pay zakat, let them go on their way. Allah is Ever-Forgiving, Most Merciful. At-Tawba 5

13. But if they [the mushrikun] make tawba and establish salat and pay zakat, they are your brothers in the deen. We make the Signs clear for people who have knowledge. At-Tawba 11

14. The men and women of the muminun are friends of one another. They command what is right and forbid what is wrong, and establish salat and pay zakat, and obey Allah and His Messenger... At-Tawba 71

15. We made them leaders, guiding by Our command, and revealed to them how to do good actions and establish salat and pay zakat... Al-Anbiya 73

16. ... those who, if We establish them firmly on the earth, will establish salat and pay zakat, and command what is right and forbid what is wrong. The end result of all affairs is with Allah. Al-Hajj 41

17. Ta Sin. Those are the Signs of the Qur'an and a Clear Book. It is guidance and good news for the muminun, those who establish salat and pay zakat and are certain about the akhira. An-Naml 1-3

18. The muminun are those whose hearts tremble when Allah is mentioned, whose iman is increased when His Signs are recited to them, and who put their trust in their Lord; those who establish salat and give of what We have provided for them. They are in truth the muminun... Al-Anfal 2-3-4

19. The mosques of Allah should only be frequented by those who have iman in Allah and the Last Day and establish salat and pay zakat, and fear no one but Allah. They are the ones most likely to be guided. At-Tawba 18

20. Nothing prevents what they give from being accepted from them but the fact that they have rejected Allah and His Messenger, and that they only come to salat lethargically, and that they only give reluctantly. At-Tawba 54

21. ...those who are steadfast in seeking the face of their Lord, and establish salat and give from the provision We have given them, secretly and openly, and stave off evil with good, it is they who will have the Ultimate Abode – Gardens of Eden which they will enter... Ar-Ra'd 22

22. ...and directed me to do salat and give zakat as long as I live. Maryam 31

23. He used to command his people to do salat and give zakat and he was pleasing to his Lord. Maryam 55

24. It is the muminun who are successful: those who are humble in their salat; those who turn away from worthless talk; those who pay zakat; Al-Muminun 1-4

25. ...those who safeguard their salat: such people are the inheritors who will inherit Firdaws, remaining in it timelessly, for ever. Al-Muminun 9-11

26. So establish salat and pay zakat and hold fast to Allah. He is your Protector – the Best Protector, the Best Helper. Al-Hajj 78

27. Establish salat and pay zakat and obey the Messenger so that hopefully mercy will be shown to you. An-Nur 56

28. But anything you give as zakat, seeking the Face of Allah – all who do that will get back twice as much. Ar-Rum 39

29. Alif Lam Mim. Those are the Signs of the Wise Book – guidance and mercy for the good-doers: those who establish salat and pay zakat and are certain of the akhira. Such people are following guidance from their Lord. They are the ones who are successful. Luqman 1-4

30. [Women] establish salat and pay zakat and obey Allah and His Messenger! Al-Ahzab 33

31. And establish salat and pay zakat and lend a generous loan to Allah. Al-Muzzammil 20

32. They were only ordered to worship Allah, making their deen sincerely His as people of pure natural belief, and to establish salat and pay zakat – that is the correct deen. Al-Bayyina 5

33. ...men who proclaim His glory morning and evening, not distracted by trade or commerce from the remembrance of Allah and the establishment of salat and the payment of zakat; fearing a day when all hearts and eyes will be in turmoil. An-Nur 37
34. Woe to those who associate others with Him: those who do not pay zakat and reject the akhira. Fussilat 7

Salat – prayer

1. Establish salat at each end of the day and in the first part of the night. Good actions eradicate bad actions. This is a reminder for people who pay heed. Hud 114
2. Establish salat from the time the sun declines until the darkening of the night, and also the recitation at dawn. The dawn recitation is certainly witnessed. Bani Isra'il 78
3. ... and glorify your Lord with praise before the rising of the sun and before its setting. And glorify Him during part of the night and at both ends of the day ... Ta Ha 130
4. So glory be to Allah when you start the night and when you greet the day. Praise be to Him in the heavens and the earth, in the afternoon and when you reach midday. Ar-Rum 17-18
5. ...glorify your Lord with praise before the rising of the sun and before it sets. And glorify Him during the night and after you have prostrated. Qaf 39-40
[The preceding ayat are understood to refer to the times of the prayers.]
6. ...wear fine clothing in every mosque. Al-A'raf 31
7. You who have iman! when you get up to do salat, wash your faces and your hands and your arms to the elbows, and wipe over your heads, and wash your feet to the ankles. If you are in a state of major impurity, then purify yourselves. But if you are ill or on a journey, or have come from the lavatory, or have touched women, and cannot find any water, then do tayammum with pure earth, and wipe your faces and your hands. Allah does not want to make things difficult for you, but He does want to purify you and to perfect His blessing upon you so that hopefully you will be thankful. Al-Ma'ida 6

8. An evil generation succeeded them who neglected the salat and followed their appetites. They will plunge into the Valley of Evil. Maryam 59

9. Instruct your family to do salat, and be constant in it. We do not ask you for provision. We provide for you. And the best end result is gained by taqwa. Ta Ha 132

10. ...those who establish salat... Al-Hajj 35

11. ...and establish salat. Salat precludes indecency and wrongdoing. And remembrance of Allah is greater still. Allah knows what you do. Al-'Ankabut 45

12. ...Have taqwa of Him and establish salat. Do not be among the mushrikun. Ar-Rum 31

13. [Luquman's advised his son:] 'My son, establish salat and command what is right and forbid what is wrong and be steadfast in the face of all that happens to you. That is certainly the most resolute course to follow. Do not avert your face from people out of haughtiness and do not strut about arrogantly on the earth. Allah does not love anyone who is vain or boastful. Be moderate in your tread and lower your voice. The most hateful of voices is the donkey's bray.' Luqman 17-18-19

14. ...You can only warn those who fear their Lord in the Unseen and establish salat. Whoever is purified, is purified for himself alone. Allah is your final destination. Fatir 18

15. Those who recite the Book of Allah and establish salat and give of what We have provided for them, secretly and openly, hope for a transaction which will not prove profitless. Fatir 29

16. Whatever you have been given is only the enjoyment of the life of the dunya. What is with Allah is better and longer lasting for those who have iman and trust in their Lord: those who avoid major wrong actions and indecencies and who, when they are angered, then forgive; those who respond to their Lord and establish salat, and manage their affairs by mutual consultation and give of what We have provided for them; those who, when they are wronged, defend themselves. Ash-Shura 36-38

17. ...except for those who do salat and who are constant in it,

those in whose wealth there is a known share for beggars and the destitute. Al-Ma'arij 22-25

18. He neither affirmed the truth nor did he do salat. Al-Qiyama 31

19. He who has purified himself will have success, He who invokes the Name of his Lord and prays. Al-A'la 15-16

20. So woe to those who do salat, and are forgetful of their salat... Al-Ma'un 4-5

21. You who have iman! seek help in steadfastness and salat. Al-Baqara 153

22. ...It is only people of intelligence who pay heed: those who fulfil Allah's contract and do not break their agreement; those who join what Allah has commanded to be joined and are afraid of their Lord and fear an evil Reckoning; those who are steadfast in seeking the face of their Lord, and establish salat and give from the provision We have given them, secretly and openly, and stave off evil with good, it is they who will have the Ultimate Abode... Ar-Ra'd 20-24

23. Show us our rites of worship and turn towards us. Al-Baqara 128

24. And to establish salat and have taqwa of Him. It is He to Whom you will be gathered.' Al-An'am 72

25. Seek help in steadfastness and salat. But that is a very hard thing, except for the humble. Al-Baqara 45

26. As for those who hold fast to the Book and establish salat, We will not let the wage of the salihun be wasted. Al-A'raf 170

27. Safeguard the salat – especially the middle one. Stand in obedience to Allah. Al-Baqara 238

28. If you are afraid, then do salat on foot or mounted. But when you are safe, remember Allah in the way He taught you when previously you did not know. Al-Baqara 239

29. When you are travelling in the land, there is nothing wrong in your shortening your salat if you fear that those who are kafir may harass you. An-Nisa 101

30. When you are with them and leading them in salat, a group of them should stand with you, keeping hold of their weapons. When they prostrate, the others should guard your backs. Then the other group who have not yet prayed should come and pray

with you. They too should be careful and keep hold of their weapons. An-Nisa 102

31. When you are safe again do salat in the normal way. The salat is prescribed for the muminun at specific times. An-Nisa 103

32. Both East and West belong to Allah, so wherever you turn, the Face of Allah is there. Allah is All-Encompassing, All-Knowing. Al-Baqara 115

33. Wherever you come from, turn your face to the Masjid al-Haram. Wherever you are, turn your faces towards it. Al-Baqara 150

34. You who have iman! do not approach the prayer when you are drunk, so that you will know what you are saying, nor in a state of major impurity – unless you are travelling – until you have washed yourselves completely. If you are ill or on a journey, or any of you have come from the lavatory or touched women, and you cannot find any water, then do tayammum with pure earth, wiping your faces and your hands. Allah is Ever-Pardoning, Ever-Forgiving. An-Nisa 43

35. Do you not see those who claim to be purified? No, Allah purifies whoever He wills. They will not be wronged by so much as the smallest speck. An-Nisa 49

36. ...Stand and face Him in every mosque and call on Him, making your deen sincerely His. As He originated you, so you will return.' Al-A'raf 29

37. Everyone in heaven and earth prostrates to Allah willingly or unwillingly, as do their shadows in the morning and the evening. Ar-Ra'd 15

38. You who have iman! when you are called to salat on the Day of Jumu'a, hasten to the remembrance of Allah and abandon trade. That is better for you if you only knew. Then when the salat is finished spread through the earth and seek Allah's bounty and remember Allah much so that hopefully you will be successful. But when they see a chance of trade or entertainment they scatter off to it and leave you standing there. Say: 'What is with Allah is better than trade or entertainment. Allah is the Best of Providers.' Al-Jumu'a 9-11

39. So pray to your Lord and sacrifice. Al-Kawthar 2

40. We revealed to Musa and his brother: 'Settle your people in houses in Egypt and make your houses places of worship and establish salat and give good news to the muminun.' Yunus 87

41. Among the people there is one who worships Allah right on the edge. If good befalls him, he is content with it, but if a trial befalls him, he reverts to his former ways, losing both the dunya and the akhira. That is indeed sheer loss. Al-Hajj 11

42. Say: 'Allah's guidance, that is true guidance. We are commanded to submit as Muslims to the Lord of all the worlds, and to establish salat and have taqwa of Him. It is He to Whom you will be gathered.' Al-An'am 71-72

43. ...Those who have iman in the akhira believe in it and safeguard their salat. Al-An'am 93

44. Tell My slaves who have iman that they should establish salat and give from what We have provided for them, secretly and openly, before a Day arrives on which there will be no trading and no friendship. Ibrahim 31

45. [Ibrahim prayed] 'Our Lord! Let them establish salat.' Ibrahim 39

46. I am Allah. There is no god but Me, so worship Me and establish salat to remember Me. Ta Ha 14

47. Say: 'Call on Allah or call on the All-Merciful, whichever you call upon, the Most Beautiful Names are His.' Do not be too loud in your salat or too quiet in it, but try to find a way between the two. Bani Isra'il 110

Zakat and Spending in the Way of Allah

Allah urges us to spend from whatever He has given us, to help those who are less privileged or who need this help & support. There are at least eighty-five places in Qur'an where we are asked to do so.

1. Ali Lam Mim. That is the Book, without any doubt. It contains guidance for those who have taqwa: those who have iman in the Unseen and establish salat and give of what We have provided for them. Al-Baqara 1-3

2. ... and be good to your parents and to relatives and orphans and the very poor. Al-Baqara 83

3. Rather, those with true devoutness are those who ... despite their love for it, give away their wealth to their relatives and to orphans and the very poor, and to travellers and beggars and to set slaves free. Al-Baqara 177

4. Spend in the Way of Allah. Al-Baqara 195

5. Say, 'Any wealth you give away should go to your parents and relatives and to orphans and the very poor and travellers.' Whatever good you do, Allah knows it. Al-Baqara 215

6. They will ask you what they should give away. Say, 'Whatever is surplus to your needs.' Al-Baqara 219

7. Is there anyone who will make Allah a generous loan so that He can multiply it for him many times over? Allah both restricts and expands. And you will be returned to Him. Al-Baqara 245

8. You who have iman! give away some of what We have provided for you before a Day arrives on which there is no trading, no close friendship and no intercession. Al-Baqara 254

9. The metaphor of those who spend their wealth in the Way of Allah is that of a grain which produces seven ears; in every ear there are a hundred grains. Allah gives such multiplied increase to whoever He wills. Allah is All-Encompassing, All-Knowing.

10. Those who spend their wealth in the Way of Allah, and then do not follow what they have spent by demands for gratitude or insulting words will have their reward with their Lord. They will feel no fear and will know no sorrow.

11. Correct and courteous words accompanied by forgiveness are better than sadaqa followed by insulting words. Allah is Rich Beyond Need, All-Forbearing.

12. You who have iman! do not nullify your sadaqa by demands for gratitude or insulting words, like him who spends his wealth, showing off to people and not having iman in Allah and the Last Day. His likeness is that of a smooth rock coated with soil, which, when heavy rain falls on it, is left stripped bare. They have no power over anything they have earned. Allah does not guide kafir people.

13. The metaphor of those who spend their wealth, desiring the pleasure of Allah and firmness for themselves, is that of a garden on

a hillside. When heavy rain falls on it, it doubles its produce; and if heavy rain does not fall, there is dew. Allah sees what you do.

14. Would any of you like to have a garden of dates and grapes, with rivers flowing underneath and containing all kinds of fruits, then to be stricken with old age and have children who are weak, and then for a fierce whirlwind containing fire to come and strike it so that it goes up in flames? In this way Allah makes His Signs clear to you, so that hopefully you will reflect.

15. You who have iman! give away some of the good things you have earned and some of what the earth produces for you. Do not have recourse to bad things when you give, things you would only take with your eyes tight shut! Know that Allah is Rich Beyond Need, Praiseworthy. Al-Baqara 261-267

16. Whatever amount you spend or vow you make, Allah knows it. The wrongdoers have no helpers.

17. If you make your sadaqa public, that is good. But if you conceal it and give it to the poor, that is better for you, and We will erase some of your bad actions from you. Allah is aware of what you do.

18. You are not responsible for their guidance, but Allah guides whoever He wills. Whatever good you give away is to your own benefit, when you give desiring only the Face of Allah. Whatever good you give away will be repaid to you in full. You will not be wronged.

19. It is for the poor who are held back in the Way of Allah, unable to travel in the land. The ignorant consider them rich because of their reticence. You will know them by their mark. They do not ask from people insistently. Whatever good you give away, Allah knows it.

20. Those who give away their wealth by night and day, secretly and openly, will have their reward with their Lord. They will feel no fear and will know no sorrow. Al-Baqara 269-73

21. If someone is in difficult circumstances, there should be a deferral [of repayment of the debt] until things are easier. But making a free gift of it would be better for you if you only knew. Al-Baqara 280

22. Spending in the way of Allah, is one of the qualities of pious people.
23. You will not attain true goodness until you give of what you love. Whatever you give away, Allah knows it. Al 'Imran 91-92
24. ...the people who have taqwa: those who give in times of both ease and hardship... Al 'Imran 133-4
25. Those who are tight-fisted with the bounty Allah has given them should not suppose that that is better for them. No indeed, it is worse for them! What they were tight-fisted with will be hung around their necks on the Day of Rising. Allah is the inheritor of the heavens and the earth and Allah is aware of what you do. Al 'Imran 180
26. The metaphor of what they [kuffar] spend in their life in the dunya is that of a wind with an icy bite to it which strikes the crops of a people who have wronged themselves and destroys them. Al 'Imran 117
27. If other relatives or orphans or poor people attend the sharing-out, provide for them out of it and speak to them correctly and courteously. An-Nisa 8
28. Worship Allah and do not associate anything with Him. Be good to your parents and relatives and to orphans and the very poor, and to neighbours who are related to you and neighbours who are not related to you, and to companions and travellers and your slaves. Allah does not love anyone vain or boastful.
29. As for those who are tight-fisted and direct others to be tight-fisted, and hide the bounty Allah has given them, We have prepared a humiliating punishment for those who are kafir, and also for those who spend their wealth to show off to people, not having iman in Allah and the Last Day.
30. Anyone who has made Shaytan his comrade, what an evil comrade he is! What harm would it have done them to have had iman in Allah and the Last Day and to have given of what Allah has provided for them? Allah knows everything about them. An-Nisa 36-39
31. Allah said [to Bani Isra'il], 'I am with you. If you establish salat and pay zakat, and have iman in My Messengers and respect and

support them, and make a generous loan to Allah, I will erase your wrong actions from you and admit you into Gardens with rivers flowing under them. Any of you who are kafir after that have gone astray from the right way.' Al-Ma'ida 12

32. ...and give of what We have provided for them. Al-Anfal 3

33. ...Anything you spend in the Way of Allah will be repaid to you in full. You will not be wronged. Al-Anfal 61

34. Say: 'Whether you give readily or reluctantly, it will not be accepted from you. You are people who are deviators.' At-Tawba 53

35. Zakat is for: the poor, the destitute, those who collect it, reconciling people's hearts, freeing slaves, those in debt, spending in the Way of Allah, and travellers. It is a legal obligation from Allah. Allah is All-Knowing, All-Wise. At-Tawba 60

36. The men and women of the munafiqun are as bad as one another. They command what is wrong and forbid what is right and keep their fists tightly closed. At-Tawba 67

37. Among them there were some who made an agreement with Allah: 'If He gives us of His bounty we will definitely give sadaqa and be among the salihun.' But when He does give them of His bounty they are tight-fisted with it and turn away. At-Tawba 75-76

38. ...those muminun who give sadaqa spontaneously, and those who can find nothing to give but their own effort... [both are rewarded equally]. At-Tawba 79

39. And among the desert arabs there are some who have iman in Allah and the Last Day and regard what they give as something which will bring them nearer to Allah and to the prayers of the Messenger. It does indeed bring them near. At-Tawba 99

40. Do they not know that Allah accepts tawba from His slaves and acknowledges their zakat, and that Allah is the Ever-Returning, the Most Merciful? At-Tawba 104

41. Nor will they give away any amount, whether large or small, nor will they cross any valley, without it being written down for them so that Allah can recompense them for the best of what they did. At-Tawba 121

42. ...If you fear impoverishment, Allah will enrich you from His bounty if He wills.... At-Tawba 28

43. ...As for those who hoard up gold and silver and do not spend it in the Way of Allah, give them the news of a painful punishment on the Day it is heated up in the fire of Hell and their foreheads, sides and backs are branded with it: 'This is what you hoarded for yourselves, so taste what you were hoarding!' At-Tawba 34-35

44. Spending by a disobedient will not be accepted.

45. Nothing prevents what they give from being accepted from them but the fact that they have rejected Allah and His Messenger, and that they only come to salat lethargically, and that they only give reluctantly. At-Tawba 53-54

46. [The brothers of Yusuf said] 'Allah always rewards a generous giver.' Yusuf 88

47. ...and give from the provision We have given them, secretly and openly... Ar-Ra'd 22

48. ...and give from what We have provided for them, secretly and openly, before a Day arrives on which there will be no trading and no friendship. Ibrahim 31

49. Allah does make a metaphor: an owned slave possessing no power over anything, and someone We have given plentiful provision who gives out from it secretly and openly. Are they the same? Praise be to Allah! They are not! But most people do not know it. An-Nahl 75

50. Allah commands justice and doing good and giving to relatives. An-Nahl 90

51. But if you do turn away from them [relatives, the very poor and travellers], seeking the mercy you hope for from your Lord, then speak to them with words that bring them ease. Bani Isra'il 28

52. Do not keep your hand chained to your neck but do not extend it either to its full extent so that you sit there blamed and destitute. Bani Isra'il 29

53. ...those who establish salat and give of what We have provided for them. Al-Hajj 33

54. Those of you possessing affluence and ample wealth should not make oaths that they will not give to their relatives and the very poor and those who have made hijra in the way of Allah... An-Nur 22

55. ...those who, when they spend, are neither extravagant nor mean, but take a stance mid way between the two; Al-Furqan 67
56. They will be given their reward twice over because they have been steadfast and because they ward off the bad with the good and give from what we have provided for them. Al-Qasas 54
57. [His people said to Qarun] 'Seek the abode of the akhira with what Allah has given you, without forgetting your portion of the dunya. And do good as Allah has been good to you.' Al-Qasas 77
58. Give relatives their due, and the poor and travellers. That is best for those who seek the pleasure of Allah. They are the ones who are successful. Ar-Rum 38
59. ...And they [the Muminun] give of what We have provided for them. As-Sajda 16
60. '...But anything you spend will be replaced by Him. He is the Best of Providers.' Saba 39
61. ...establish salat and give of what We have provided for them, secretly and openly, hope for a transaction which will not prove profitless. Fatir 29
62. ...and give of what We have provided for them; Ash-Shura 38
63. If He did ask you for it and put you under pressure, you would be tight-fisted and it would bring out your malevolence. Here you are then: people who are called upon to spend in the Way of Allah and then some of you are tight-fisted! But whoever is tight-fisted is only tight-fisted to himself. Allah is Rich and you are poor. If you turn away, He will replace you with a people other than yourselves and they will not be like you. Muhammad 37-38
64. And beggars and the destitute received a due share of their wealth. Adh-Dhariyat 19
65. Have iman in Allah and His Messenger and give of that to which He has made you successors. Those of you who have iman and give will have an immense reward. Al-Hadid 7
66. The men and women who give sadaqa and make a good loan to Allah will have it increased for them and they will have a generous reward. Al-Hadid 17
67. ...Allah does not love any vain or boastful man: those who are tight-fisted and tell others to be tight-fisted. If anyone turns away,

Allah is the Rich Beyond Need, the Praiseworthy. Al-Hadid 24

68. You who have iman! when women who have iman come to you as muhajirun, submit them to a test. Allah has best knowledge of their iman. If you know they are muminun, do not return them to the kuffar. They are not halal for the kuffar nor are the kuffar halal for them. Give the kuffar whatever dowry they paid. And there is nothing wrong in your marrying them provided you pay them their due. Al-Mumtahana 10

69. Give from what We have provided for you before death comes to one of you and he says, 'My Lord, if only you would give me a little more time so that I can give sadaqa and be one of the salihun!' Al-Munafiqun 10

70. So have taqwa of Allah, as much as you are able to, and listen and obey and spend for your own benefit. It is the people who are safe-guarded from the avarice of their own selves who are successful. If you make a generous loan to Allah He will multiply it for you and forgive you. Allah is All-Thankful, Most Forbearing. At-Taghabun 16-17

71. He who has plenty should spend out from his plenty, but he whose provision is restricted should spend from what Allah has given him. Allah does not demand from any self more than He has given it. Allah will appoint after difficulty, ease. At-Talaq 7

72. He used not to have iman in Allah the Most Great, nor did he urge the feeding of the poor. Therefore here today he has no friend nor any food except exuding pus which no one will eat except those who were in error. Al-Haqqa 33-37

73. Truly man was created headstrong – desperate when bad things happen, begrudging when good things come, except for those who do salat and who are constant in it... Al-Ma'arij 19

74. ...those in whose wealth there is a known share for beggars and the destitute. Al-Ma'arij 25

75. ...and lend a generous loan to Allah. Whatever good you send ahead for yourselves you will find it with Allah as something better and as a greater reward. Al-Muzzammil 20

76. They [the inhabitants of Saqar] will say, 'We were not among those who did salat and we did not feed the poor. We plunged

with those who plunged and denied the Day of Judgment until the Certain came to us.' Al-Muddaththir 42-46

77. They [the truly good] give food, despite their love for it, to the poor and orphans and captives: 'We feed you only out of desire for the Face of Allah. We do not want any repayment from you or any thanks.' Ad-Dahr 8-9

78. As for him who gives out and has taqwa and confirms the Good, We will pave his way to Ease. Al-Layl 5-7

79. But as for him who is stingy and self-satisfied, and denies the Good, We will pave his way to Difficulty. His wealth will not help him when he plummets to the depths. Al-Layl 8-11

80. Those with most taqwa will be far removed from it: those who give their wealth to purify themselves – not to repay someone else for a favour done – desiring only the Face of their Lord Most High. They will certainly be satisfied. Al-Layl 17-21

81. ...and as for beggars, do not berate them. Ad-Duha 10

82. Have you seen him who denies the deen? He is the one who harshly rebuffs the orphan and does not urge the feeding of the poor. Al-Ma'un 1-3

83. Have you seen him who turns away and gives little, and that grudgingly? An-Najm 33-34

84. And when they are told, 'Spend from the provision Allah has given you,' those who are kafir say to those who have iman, 'Why should we feed someone whom, if He wished, Allah would feed Himself? You are clearly in error.' Ya Sin 47

85. You who have iman! when you consult the Messenger privately precede your private consultation by giving sadaqa – that is better for you and purer. But if you cannot find the means, Allah is Ever-Forgiving, Most Merciful. Al-Mujadila 12

86. Woe to every faultfinding backbiter who has amassed wealth and hoarded it! He thinks his wealth will make him live for ever. No indeed! He will be flung into the Shatterer. Al-Humaza 1-4

Wastefulness and profligacy

1. Children of Adam! wear fine clothing in every mosque and eat and drink but do not be profligate. He does not love the profligate. Al-A'raf 31

2. Give your relatives their due, and the very poor and travellers but do not squander what you have. Squanderers are brothers to the shaytans, and Shaytan is always ungrateful to his Lord. Bani Isra'il 26 -27

3. ...Eat of their fruits when they bear fruit and pay their due on the day of their harvest, and do not be profligate. He does not love the profligate. Al-An'am 142

Fasting

1. You who have iman! fasting is prescribed for you, as it was prescribed for those before you – so that hopefully you will have taqwa – for a specified number of days. But any of you who are ill or on a journey should fast a number of other days. For those who are able to fast, their fidya is to feed the poor. And if someone does good of his own accord, it is better for him. But that you should fast is better for you, if you only knew. Al-Baqara 183-185

2. The month of Ramadan is the one in which the Qur'an was sent down as guidance for mankind, with Clear Signs containing guidance and discrimination. Al-Baqara 184

3. On the night of the fast it is lawful for you to have sexual relations with your wives. ...Eat and drink until you can clearly discern the white thread from the black thread of the dawn, then fulfil the fast until the night appears. But do not have sexual intercourse with them while you are in [i'tikaf] retreat in the mosques. Al-Baqara 186

Hajj

1. They will ask you about the crescent moons. Say, 'They are set times for mankind and for the hajj.' It is not devoutness for you to enter houses by the back. Rather devoutness is possessed by those who have taqwa. So come to houses by their doors and have taqwa of Allah, so that hopefully you will be successful. Al-Baqara 189

2. Do not fight them in the Masjid al-Haram until they fight you there. But if they do fight you, then kill them. Al-Baqara 191

Islam

3. Sacred month in return for sacred month – sacred things are subject to retaliation. Al-Baqara 194
4. Perform the hajj and 'umra for Allah. If you are forcibly prevented, make whatever sacrifice is feasible. But do not shave your heads until the sacrificial animal has reached the place of sacrifice. If any of you are ill or have a head injury, the expiation is fasting or sadaqa or sacrifice when you are safe and well again. Anyone who comes out of ihram between 'umra and hajj should make whatever sacrifice is feasible. For any one who cannot, there is three days' fast on hajj and seven on your return – that is ten in all. That is for anyone whose family does not live near the Masjid al-Haram. Have taqwa of Allah and know that Allah is fierce in retribution. Al-Baqara 194
5. The hajj takes place during certain well-known months. If anyone undertakes the obligation of hajj in them, there must be no sexual intercourse, no wrongdoing, nor any quarrelling during hajj. Whatever good you do, Allah knows it. Al-Baqara 196
6. Take provision; but the best provision is taqwa of Allah. So have taqwa of Me, people of intelligence! Al-Baqara 196
7. There is nothing wrong in seeking bounty from your Lord.
8. When you pour down from Arafat, remember Allah at the Sacred Landmark. Remember Him because He has guided you, even though before this you were astray.
9. Then press on from where the people press on and ask Allah's forgiveness. Allah is Ever-Forgiving, Most Merciful. Al-Baqara 197-8
10. When you have completed your rites, remember Allah as you used to remember your forefathers – or even more. Al-Baqara 199
11. Remember Allah on the designated days. Those who hurry on in two days have done no wrong, and those who stay another day have done no wrong – those of them who have taqwa. So have taqwa of Allah. And know that you will be gathered back to Him. Al-Baqara 203
12. You who have iman! do not profane the sacred rites of Allah or the sacred months, or the sacrificial animals, or the ritual garlands, or those heading for the Sacred House, desiring profit and good pleasure from their Lord. When you have come out of ihram, then

hunt for game. Do not let hatred for a people who debar you from the Masjid al-Haram incite you into going beyond the limits. Help each other to goodness and taqwa. Do not help each other to wrongdoing and enmity. Have taqwa of Allah. Allah is severe in retribution. Al-Ma'ida 2

13. You who have iman! Allah will test you with game animals which come within the reach of your hands and spears, so that Allah will know those who fear Him in the Unseen. Al-Ma'ida 94

14. You who have iman! do not kill game while you are in ihram. If one of you kills any deliberately, the reprisal for it is a livestock animal equivalent to what he killed, as judged by two just men among you, a sacrifice to reach the Ka'ba, or expiation by feeding the poor, or fasting commensurate with that, so that he may taste the evil consequences of what he did. Allah has pardoned all that took place in the past; but if anyone does it again Allah will take revenge on him. Allah is Almighty, Exactor of Revenge. Al-Ma'ida 95

15. Anything you catch in the sea is halal for you, and all food from it, for your enjoyment and that of travellers, but land game is haram for you while you are in ihram. So have taqwa of Allah, Him to whom you will be gathered. Al-Ma'ida 96

16. Allah has made the Ka'ba, the Sacred House, a special institution for mankind, and also the sacred months and the sacrificial animals and the ritual garlands. That is so you will know that Allah knows what is in the heavens and in the earth and that Allah has knowledge of all things. Al-Ma'ida 97

17. Announce the Hajj to mankind. They will come to you on foot and on every sort of lean animal, coming by every distant road so that they can be present at what will profit them and invoke Allah's name on specific days over livestock He has provided for them. Eat of them and feed those who are poor and in need. Then they should end their state of self-neglect and fulfil their vows and circle the Ancient House.' That is it. If someone honours Allah's sacred things, that is better for him in his Lord's sight. All livestock are permitted to you except what has already been recited to you. Have done with the defilement of idols and have done with telling lies. Al-Hajj 25-30

18. That is it. As for those who honour Allah's sacred rites, that comes from the taqwa in their hearts. You can make use of the sacrificial animals until a specified time, and then their place of sacrifice is by the Ancient House. We have appointed a rite of sacrifice for every nation so that they may invoke Allah's name over the livestock He has given them. Your God is One God so submit to Him. Give good news to the humble-hearted, whose hearts quake at the mention of Allah, and who are steadfast in the face of all that happens to them, those who establish salat and give of what We have provided for them. We have appointed the sacrificial animals for you as one of the sacred rites of Allah. There is good in them for you, so invoke Allah's name over them, as they stand in rows. And then when they collapse on their sides, eat of them and feed both those who ask and those who are too shy to ask. In this way We have subjected them to you so that hopefully you will be thankful. Their flesh and blood does not reach Allah but your taqwa does reach Him. In this way He has subjected them to you so that you might proclaim Allah's greatness for the way that He has guided you. Give good news to the good-doers. Al-Hajj 30-37

19. ...the mushrikun are unclean, so (after this year) they should not come near the Masjid al-Haram... At-Tawba 28

20. Have We not established a safe haven for them to which produce of every kind is brought, provision direct from Us? But most of them do not know it. They say, 'If we follow the guidance with you, we shall be forcibly uprooted from our land.' Have We not established a safe haven for them to which produce of every kind is brought, provision direct from Us? But most of them do not know it. Al-Qasas 57

21. Hajj to the House is a duty owed to Allah by all mankind – those who can find a way to do it. But if anyone is kafir, Allah is Rich Beyond Need of any being. Al 'Imran 97

22. And when We made the House [The Ka'ba] a place of return, a sanctuary for mankind: 'Take the Maqam of Ibrahim as a place of prayer.' We contracted with Ibrahim and Isma'il: 'Purify My House for those who circle it, and those who stay there, and those who bow and who prostrate.' Al-Baqara 125

23. Safa and Marwa are among the Landmarks of Allah, so anyone who goes on hajj to the House or does 'umra incurs no wrong in going back and forth between them. If anyone spontaneously does good, Allah is All-Thankful, All-Knowing. Al-Baqara 158

Mosques

1. The mosques of Allah should only be frequented by those who have iman in Allah and the Last Day and establish salat and pay zakat, and fear no one but Allah. They are the ones most likely to be guided. At-Tawba 18
2. ...A mosque founded on taqwa from the first day has a greater right for you to stand in it. In it there are men who love to purify themselves. Allah loves those who purify themselves. At-Tawba 108
3. Those who are kafir and bar access to the Way of Allah and to the Masjid al-Haram which We have appointed for all mankind – equally for those who live near it and those who come from far away – those who desire to profane it with wrongdoing, We will let them taste a painful punishment. And We located the position of the House for Ibrahim: 'Do not associate anything with Me and purify My House for those who circle it, and those who stand and bow and prostrate. Al-Hajj 25-26
4. ...those who were expelled from their homes without any right, merely for saying, 'Our Lord is Allah' (if Allah had not driven some people back by means of others, monasteries, churches, synagogues and mosques, where Allah's name is mentioned much, would have been pulled down and destroyed. Allah will certainly help those who help Him – Allah is All-Strong, Almighty, Al-Hajj 40
5. You who have iman! the mushrikun are unclean, so after this year they should not come near the Masjid al-Haram. If you fear impoverishment, Allah will enrich you from His bounty if He wills. Allah is All-Knowing, All-Wise. At-Tawba 28
6. Have We not established a safe haven for them... Al-Qasas 57
7. Who could do greater wrong than someone who bars access to the mosques of Allah, preventing His name from being remembered in them, and goes about destroying them? Al-Baqara 114

8. 'I have simply been ordered to worship the Lord of this land which He has declared sacred – everything belongs to Him – and I have been ordered to be one of the Muslims and to recite the Qur'an.' An-Naml 91

9. All mosques belong to Allah so do not call on anyone else besides Allah. Al-Jinn 18

10. The first House established for mankind was that at Bakka [Makka], a place of blessing and a guidance for all beings. Al 'Imran 96

11. But why should Allah not punish them now when they bar access to the Masjid al-Haram? They are not its guardians. Only people who have taqwa can be its guardians. But most of them do not know that. Their prayer at the House is nothing but whistling and clapping. So taste the punishment because you were kafir! Al-Anfal 34-35

12. Wherever you come from, turn your face to the Masjid al-Haram. This is certainly the truth from your Lord. Allah is not unaware of what you do. Al-Baqara 149

13. ...establish salat and command what is right and forbid what is wrong and be steadfast in the face of all that happens to you. That is certainly the most resolute course to follow. Luqman 17

14. [Allah said to Musa] 'Take off your sandals. You are in the holy valley of Tuwa.' Ta Ha 12

Praying At Night

1. Remember Allah at night and recite His revelations and prostrate. Al 'Imran 111

2. And stay awake for prayer during part of the night as a supererogatory action for yourself. It may well be that your Lord will raise you to a Praiseworthy Station. Bani Isra'il 79

3. ...[they] pass the night prostrating and standing before their Lord. Al-Furqan 64

4. Their sides eschew their beds as they call on their Lord in fear and ardent hope... As-Sajda 16

5. What of him who spends the night hours in prayer, prostrating and standing up, mindful of the akhira, hoping for the mercy of his Lord?... Az-Zumar 9

6. The part of the night they spent asleep was small and they would seek forgiveness before the dawn. Adh-Dhariyat 17-18
7. ...And glorify and praise your Lord when you get up. And glorify Him in the night and when the stars fade out. At-Tur 48-49
8. Recite as much of the Qur'an as is easy for you. Al-Muzzammil 18
9. Remember the Name of your Lord in the morning and the evening. Prostrate to Him during the night and glorify Him throughout the long night. Ad-Dahr 25-26
10. He who sees you when you stand up to pray and your movements with those who prostrate. Ash-Shu'ara 218-219
11. ...stay up at night, except a little, half of it, or a little less, or a little more, and recite the Qur'an distinctly. Al-Muzzammil 2-4
12. Certainly rising at night has a stronger effect and is more conducive to concentration. In the daytime much of your time is taken up by business matters. Remember the Name of your Lord, and devote yourself to Him completely. Al-Muzzammil 6-8
13. Your Lord knows that you stay up nearly two-thirds of the night – or half of it, or a third of it – and a group of those with you. Allah determines the night and day. He knows you will not keep count of it, so He has turned towards you. Recite as much of the Qur'an as is easy for you. He knows that some of you are ill and that others are travelling in the land seeking Allah's bounty, and that others are fighting in the Way of Allah. So recite as much of it as is easy for you. And establish salat and pay zakat and lend a generous loan to Allah. Whatever good you send ahead for yourselves you will find it with Allah as something better and as a greater reward. And seek forgiveness from Allah. Allah is Ever-Forgiving, Most Merciful. Al-Muzzammil 18

Hijra – Emigration for the sake of Allah

1. Those who have iman and make hijra and do jihad in the Way of Allah can expect Allah's mercy. Allah is Ever-Forgiving, Most Merciful. Al-Baqara 218
2. Those who made hijra and were driven from their homes and suffered harm in My Way and fought and were killed, I will erase

their bad actions from them and admit them into Gardens with rivers flowing under them, as a reward from Allah. The best of all rewards is with Allah. Al 'Imran 195

3. Those who make hijra in the Way of Allah will find many places of refuge on the earth and ample sustenance. If anyone leaves his home, making hijra to Allah and His Messenger, and death catches up with him, it is Allah Who will reward him. Allah is Ever-Forgiving, Most Merciful. An-Nisa 100

4. Those who have iman and have made hijra and done jihad in the Way of Allah and those who have given refuge and help, they are the true muminun. They will have forgiveness and generous provision. Al-Anfal 74

5. But to those who made hijra after they were persecuted and then did jihad and remained steadfast, to them your Lord is All-Compassionate, Most Merciful. An-Nahl 110

6. Those who make hijra in the Way of Allah and then are killed or die, Allah will provide for them handsomely. Truly Allah is the best Provider. Al-Hajj 56

7. For those who do good in the dunya there is good and Allah's earth is spacious. The steadfast will be paid their wages in full without any reckoning.' Az-Zumar 10

8. The angels ask those they take while they are wronging themselves, 'What were your circumstances?' They reply, 'We were oppressed on earth.' They say, 'Was Allah's earth not wide enough for you to have made hijra elsewhere in it?' The shelter of such people will be Hell. What an evil destination! An-Nisa 97

9. Those who have iman and have made hijra and done jihad with their wealth and themselves in the Way of Allah, and those who have given refuge and help, they are the friends and protectors of one another. But as for those who have iman but have not made hijra, you are not in any way responsible for their protection until they make hijra. But if they ask you for help in respect of the deen, it is your duty to help them, except against people you have a treaty with. Allah sees what you do. Al-Anfal 72

10. Those who have iman and make hijra later on and accompany you in doing jihad, they also are of your number. But blood rela-

tions are closer to one another in the Book of Allah. Allah has knowledge of all things. Al-Anfal 75
11. As for those who make hijra for Allah's sake after being wronged, We shall give them good lodging in the dunya, and the reward of the akhira is greater still if they only knew. An-Nahl 41

Jihad – fighting for the sake of Allah

1. They will ask you about the Sacred Month and fighting in it. Say, 'Fighting in it is a serious matter; but barring access to the Way of Allah and rejecting Him and barring access to the Masjid al-Haram and expelling its people from it are far more serious in the sight of Allah. Fitna is worse than killing.' Al-Baqara 217
2. Do not say that those who are killed in the Way of Allah are dead. Al-Baqara 154
3. Fight in the Way of Allah. Al-Baqara 244
4. You who have iman! take all necessary precautions, then go out to fight in separate groups or go out as one body. An-Nisa 71
5. What reason could you have for not fighting in the Way of Allah – for those men, women and children who are oppressed and say, 'Our Lord, take us out of this city whose inhabitants are wrongdoers! Give us a protector from You! Give us a helper from You!'? An-Nisa 75
6. It is Allah Who gives life and causes to die. [So, don't be afraid of going for Jihad]. Al 'Imran 156
7. You who have iman! have taqwa of Allah and seek the means of drawing near to Him, and do jihad in His Way, so that hopefully you will be successful. Al-Ma'ida 35
8. Those who have iman and have made hijra and done jihad in the Way of Allah and those who have given refuge and help, they are the true muminun. They will have forgiveness and generous provision. Al-Anfal 74
9. But to those who made hijra after they were persecuted and then did jihad and remained steadfast, to them your Lord is All-Compassionate, Most Merciful. An-Nahl 110
10. You who have iman! shall I direct you to a transaction which will save you from a painful punishment? It is to have iman in

Allah and His Messenger and do jihad in the Way of Allah with your wealth and your selves. That is better for you if you only knew. As-Saff 10-11

11. Allah loves those who fight in His Way in ranks like well-built walls. As-Saff 4

12. Fight in the Way of Allah against those who fight you, but do not go beyond the limits. Allah does not love those who go beyond the limits. ... Fitna is worse than killing. Al-Baqara 190-191

13. Permission to fight is given to those who are fought against because they have been wronged – truly Allah has the power to come to their support. Al-Hajj 37.

14. If you are killed in the Way of Allah or if you die, forgiveness and mercy from Allah are better than anything you can acquire. Al 'Imran 157

15. Do not suppose that those killed in the Way of Allah are dead. No indeed! They are alive and well provided for in the very presence of their Lord, delighting in the favour Allah has bestowed on them, rejoicing over those they left behind who have not yet joined them, feeling no fear and knowing no sorrow, rejoicing in blessings and favour from Allah and that Allah does not let the wage of the muminun go to waste. Al 'Imran 169-171

16. Allah has bought from the muminun their selves and their wealth in return for the Garden. They fight in the Way of Allah and they kill and are killed. It is a promise binding on Him in the Torah, the Injil and the Qur'an and who is truer to his contract than Allah? Rejoice then in the bargain you have made. That is the great victory. At-Tawba 111

17. So let those who sell the life of the dunya for the akhira fight in the Way of Allah. If someone fights in the Way of Allah, whether he is killed or is victorious, We will pay him an immense reward. An-Nisa 74

18. Those muminun who stay behind – other than those forced to by necessity – are not the same as those who do jihad in the Way of Allah, sacrificing their wealth and themselves. Allah has given those who do jihad with their wealth and themselves a higher rank than those who stay behind. Allah has promised the Best to

both, but Allah has preferred those who do jihad over those who stay behind by an immense reward. An-Nisa 95

19. They will ask you about booty. Say: 'Booty belongs to Allah and the Messenger. So have taqwa of Allah and put things right between you. Obey Allah and His Messenger if you are muminun.' An-Anfal 1

20. You who have iman! when you encounter those who are kafir advancing in massed ranks into battle, do not turn your backs on them. Anyone who turns his back on them that day, unless he is withdrawing to rejoin the fight or withdrawing to support another group, brings Allah's anger down upon himself. His refuge is Hell. What an evil destination! Al-Anfal 15-16

21. Know that when you take any booty a fifth of it belongs to Allah, and to the Messenger, and to close relatives, orphans, the very poor and travellers, if you believe in Allah... Al-Anfal 41

22. If they incline to peace, you too incline to it, and put your trust in Allah. He is the All-Hearing, the All-Knowing. If they intend to deceive you, Allah is enough for you. It is He who supported you with His help and with the muminun. Al-Anfal 61-62

23. O Prophet! Allah is enough for you, and for the muminun who follow you. O Prophet! spur on the muminun to fight. If there are twenty of you who are steadfast, they will overcome two hundred; and if there are a hundred of you, they will overcome a thousand of those who are kafir, because they are people who do not understand. Al-Anfal 64-65

24. So make full use of any booty you have taken which is halal and good; and have taqwa of Allah. Allah is Ever-Forgiving, Most Merciful. Al-Anfal 69

25. Then, when the sacred months are over, kill the mushrikun wherever you find them, and seize them and besiege them and lie in wait for them on every road. If they make tawba and establish salat and pay zakat, let them go on their way. Allah is Ever-Forgiving, Most Merciful. At-Tawba 5

26. If any of the mushrikun ask you for protection, give them protection until they have heard the words of Allah. Then convey them to a place where they are safe. That is because they are a people who do not know. At-Tawba 6

27. Fight them! Allah will punish them at your hands, and disgrace them and help you against them, and heal the hearts of those who have iman. At-Tawba 14

28. Those who have iman and make hijra and do jihad in the Way of Allah with their wealth and themselves have a higher rank with Allah. They are the ones who are victorious. Their Lord gives them the good news of His mercy and good pleasure and Gardens where they will enjoy everlasting delight, remaining in them timelessly, for ever and ever. Truly there is an immense reward with Allah. At-Tawba 20-21-22

29. ...'If your fathers or your sons or your brothers or your wives or your tribe, or any wealth you have acquired, or any business you fear may slump, or any house which pleases you, are dearer to you than Allah and His Messenger and doing jihad in His Way, then wait until Allah brings about His command. Allah does not guide people who are deviators.' At-Tawba 24

30. Fight those of the people who were given the Book who do not have iman in Allah and the Last Day and do not make haram what Allah and His Messenger have made haram and do not take as their deen the deen of Truth, until they pay the jizya with their own hands in a state of complete abasement. At-Tawba 29

31. When a sura is sent down saying: 'Have iman in Allah and do jihad together with His Messenger,' those among them with wealth will ask you to excuse them, saying, 'Let us remain with those who stay behind.' They are pleased to be with those who stay behind. Their hearts have been sealed up so they do not understand. But the Messenger and those who have iman along with him have done jihad with their wealth and with themselves. They are the people who will have the good things. They are the ones who are successful. At-Tawba 86-87-88

32. Nothing is held against the weak and sick nor against those who find nothing to spend, provided they are true to Allah and His Messenger – there is no way open against good-doers, Allah is Ever-Forgiving, Most Merciful – nor is anything held against those who, when they came to you for you to provide them with mounts and you said, 'I cannot find anything on which to mount

you,' turned away with their eyes overflowing with tears, overcome by grief at having nothing to give. At-Tawba 91-92

33. You who have iman! shall I direct you to a transaction which will save you from a painful punishment? It is to have iman in Allah and His Messenger and do jihad in the Way of Allah with your wealth and your selves. That is better for you if you only knew. As-Saff 10-11

34. And other things you love: support from Allah and imminent victory. Give good news to the muminun! As-Saff 13

35. You who have iman! be helpers of Allah as 'Isa son of Maryam said to the Disciples, 'Who will be my helpers to Allah?' The Disciples said, 'We will be the helpers of Allah.' As-Saff 14

36. ... and do jihad in His Way, so that hopefully you will be successful. Al-Ma'ida 35

37. Do jihad for Allah with the jihad due to Him. He has selected you and not placed any constraint upon you in the deen – the religion of your forefather Ibrahim. He named you Muslims before and also in this, so that the Messenger could be witness against you and you could be witnesses against all mankind. So establish salat and pay zakat and hold fast to Allah. He is your Protector – the Best Protector, the Best Helper. Al-Hajj 78

38. Yet they had previously made a contract with Allah that they would never turn their backs. Contracts made with Allah will be asked about. Al-Ahzab 15

39. Fighting is prescribed for you even if it is hateful to you. It may be that you hate something when it is good for you and it may be that you love something when it is bad for you. Allah knows and you do not know. Al-Baqara 216

40. Go out to fight, whatever your circumstances or desires, and do jihad with your wealth and yourselves in the Way of Allah. That is better for you if you only knew. At-Tawba 41

41. If it had been a case of easy gains and a short journey, they would have followed you, but the distance was too great for them. They will swear by Allah: 'Had we been able to, we would have gone out with you.' They are destroying their own selves. Allah knows that they are lying. At-Tawba 42

Ihsan

Nearness of Allah ﷻ

1. The colouring of Allah – and what colouring could be better than Allah's? It is Him we worship. Al-Baqara 138
2. If My slaves ask you about Me, I am near. I answer the call of the caller when he calls on Me. They should therefore respond to Me and believe in Me so that hopefully they will be rightly guided. Al-Baqara 186
3. Say, 'Shall I tell you of something better than that?' Those who have taqwa will have Gardens with their Lord, ... Al 'Imran 15
4. Allah selects whoever He wishes for His mercy. Allah is of infinite bounty. Al 'Imran 74
5. Allah knows best who your enemies are. Allah suffices as a Protector; Allah suffices as a Helper. An-Nisa 45
6. ...and seek the means of drawing near to Him... Al-Ma'ida 35
7. And among the desert arabs there are some who have iman in Allah and the Last Day and regard what they give as something which will bring them nearer to Allah and to the prayers of the Messenger. It does indeed bring them near. Allah will admit them into His mercy. Allah is Ever-Forgiving, Most Merciful. At-Tawba 99
8. ...And do not obey someone whose heart We have made neglectful of Our remembrance and who follows his own whims and desires and whose life has transgressed all bounds. Al-Kahf 28
9. We created man and We know what his own self whispers to him. We are nearer to him than his jugular vein. Qaf 16
10. He is with you wherever you are – Allah sees what you do. Al-Hadid 4
11. This truly is a reminder, so let anyone who wills take a Way towards his Lord. Al-Muzzammil 19
12. Call on your Lord humbly and secretly. He does not love those who overstep the limits. Al-A'raf 55
13. He Who responds to the oppressed when they call on Him and removes their distress, and has appointed you as khalifs on

the earth. Is there another god besides Allah? How little you pay heed! An-Naml 62

14. Your Lord says, 'Call on Me and I will answer you. Those who are too proud to worship Me will enter Hell abject. Al-Mumin 60

15. He responds to those who have iman and do right actions and gives them increase from His favour. Ash-Shura 26

16. Say: 'My salat and my rites, my living and my dying, are for Allah alone, the Lord of all the worlds. Al-An'am 163

17. Do not corrupt the earth after it has been put right. Call on Him fearfully and eagerly. Allah's mercy is close to the good-doers. Al-A'raf 56

18. To Allah belong the Most Beautiful Names, so call on Him by them and abandon those who desecrate His Names... Al-A'raf 180

19. You cannot win over Allah in the earth or in the sky and beside Allah there is no friend nor helper. Al-'Ankabut 22

20. Do not despair of solace from Allah. No one despairs of solace from Allah except for people who are kafirun.' Yusuf 87

21. Today you have forgiveness from Allah. He is the Most Merciful of the merciful. Yusuf 92

22. But those who have iman have greater love for Allah. Al-Baqara 165

23. So flee to Allah... Adh-Dhariyat 50

24. O Man! You are toiling laboriously towards your Lord but meet Him you will! Al-Inshiqaq 6

25. If only they had been pleased with what Allah and His Messenger had given them and had said, 'Allah is enough for us. Allah will give us of His bounty as will His Messenger. It is to Allah that we make our plea.' At-Tawba 59

Remembering Allah (Dhikr)

1. [Allah says] "Remember Me – I will remember you. Give thanks to Me and do not be ungrateful." Al-Baqara 152

2. ...and proclaim Allah's greatness for the guidance He has given you so that hopefully you will be thankful. Al-Baqara 184

3. ...those who, when they act indecently or wrong themselves,

Ihsan

remember Allah and ask forgiveness for their bad actions (and who can forgive bad actions except Allah?) and do not knowingly persist in what they were doing. Al 'Imran 135

4. In the creation of the heavens and the earth, and the alternation of night and day, there are Signs for people with intelligence: those who remember Allah, standing, sitting and lying on their sides, and reflect on the creation of the heavens and the earth: 'Our Lord, You have not created this for nothing. Glory be to You! Al 'Imran 190-1

5. When you have finished salat remember Allah standing, sitting and lying on your sides. An-Nisa 103

6. As for those who have taqwa, when they are bothered by visitors from Shaytan, they remember and immediately see clearly. Al-A'raf 201

7. Remember your Lord in yourself humbly and fearfully, without loudness of voice, morning and evening. Do not be one of the unaware. Al-A'raf 205

8. ...those who have iman and whose hearts find peace in the remembrance of Allah. Only in the remembrance of Allah can the heart find peace.' Ar-Ra'd 28

9. Recite what has been revealed to you of your Lord's Book. No one can change His Words. You will never find any safe haven apart from Him. Restrain yourself patiently with those who call on their Lord morning and evening, desiring His face. Do not turn your eyes from them, desiring the attractions of this world. And do not obey someone whose heart We have made neglectful of Our remembrance and who follows his own whims and desires and whose life has transgressed all bounds. Al-Kahf 28-27

10. There is no God except Allah. So, worship him and do Salat to remember Him. Ta Ha 14

11. ...proclaim Allah's greatness for the way that He has guided you. Give good news to the good-doers. Al-Hajj 37

12. ...monasteries, churches, synagogues and mosques, where Allah's name is mentioned much, would have been pulled down and destroyed. Allah will certainly help those who help Him – Allah is All-Strong, Almighty. Al-Hajj 40

13. In houses which Allah has permitted to be built and in which His name is remembered, there are men who proclaim His glory morning and evening, not distracted by trade or commerce from the remembrance of Allah and the establishment of salat and the payment of zakat; fearing a day when all hearts and eyes will be in turmoil... An-Nur 36

14. And as for poets, it is the misled who follow them. Do you not see how they ramble on in every style and say things which they do not do, except those who have iman and do right actions and remember Allah repeatedly and defend themselves after they have been wronged? Ash-Shu'ara 224-227

15. Do not let them debar you from Allah's Signs after they have been sent down to you. Call people to your Lord and on no account be one of the mushrikun. Al-Qasas 87

16. And remembrance of Allah is greater still. Al-'Ankabut 45

17. You have an excellent model in the Messenger of Allah, for all who put their hope in Allah and the Last Day and remember Allah much. Al-Ahzab 21

18. You who have iman! remember Allah much, and glorify Him in the morning and the evening. Al-Ahzab 41-42

19. Woe to those whose hearts are hardened against the remembrance of Allah! Such people are clearly misguided. Az-Zumar 22

20. The skins of those who fear their Lord tremble at it and then their skins and hearts yield softly to the remembrance of Allah. That is Allah's guidance by which He guides whoever He wills. Az-Zumar 23

21. ...So turn away from him who turns away from Our remembrance and desires nothing but the life of the dunya. An-Najm 29

22. Has the time not arrived for the hearts of those who have iman to yield to the remembrance of Allah and to the truth He has sent down, so they are not like those who were given the Book before for whom the time seemed over long so that their hearts became hard? Many of them are deviators. Al-Hadid 16

23. Remember Allah in the way He taught you when previously you did not know. Al-Baqara 239

24. You who have iman! when you meet a troop, stand firm and

remember Allah repeatedly so that hopefully you will be successful. Al-Anfal 45

25. We have sent it down with truth and with truth it has come down. We only sent you to bring good news and to give warning. The seven heavens and the earth and everyone in them glorify Him. There is nothing which does not glorify Him with praise but you do not understand their glorification. He is All-Forbearing, Ever-Forgiving. Bani Isra'il 44

26. Do you not see that everyone in the heavens and everyone on the earth prostrates to Allah, and the sun and moon and stars and the mountains, trees and beasts and many of mankind? But many of them inevitably merit punishment. Those Allah humiliates will have no one to honour them. Allah does whatever He wills. Al-Hajj 18

27. Then when the salat is finished spread through the earth and seek Allah's bounty and remember Allah much so that hopefully you will be successful. Al-Jumu'a 10

28. If someone shuts his eyes to the remembrance of the All-Merciful, We assign him a shaytan who becomes his bosom friend Az-Zukhruf 36

29. ...and do not slacken in remembering Me. Ta Ha 42

30. So when you have finished, work on, and make your Lord your goal! Al-Inshirah 7-8

Tawba – Turning to Allah in Repentance

1. Then Adam received some words from his Lord and He turned towards him. He is the Ever-Returning, the Most Merciful. Al-Baqara 37

2. ... except for those who make tawba and put things right and make things clear. I turn towards them. Al-Baqara 160

3. Allah loves those who turn back from wrongdoing and He loves those who purify themselves. Al-Baqara 222

4. Allah only accepts the tawba of those who do evil in ignorance and then quickly make tawba after doing it. An-Nisa 17

5. ... except for those who, after that, make tawba and put things right. Truly Allah is Ever-Forgiving, Most Merciful. Al 'Imran 88

6. Anyone who does evil or wrongs himself and then asks Allah's forgiveness will find Allah Ever-Forgiving, Most Merciful. An-Nisa 110

7. ...except those who make tawba and put things right and hold fast to Allah and dedicate their deen to Allah alone; they are with the muminun. Allah will give the muminun an immense reward. An-Nisa 146

8. But if anyone makes tawba after his wrongdoing and puts things right, Allah will turn towards him. Allah is Ever-Forgiving, Most Merciful. Al-Ma'ida 39

9. Why do they not turn to Allah and ask for His forgiveness? Allah is Ever-Forgiving, Most Merciful. Al-Ma'ida 74

10. They [Adam and Hawa] said, 'Our Lord, we have wronged ourselves. If you do not forgive us and have mercy on us, we will be among the lost.' Al-A'raf 23

11. But others have acknowledged their wrong actions and mixed a right action with another which is wrong. It may well be that Allah will turn towards them. Allah is Ever-Forgiving, Most Merciful. At-Tawba 102

12. Do they not know that Allah accepts tawba from His slaves and acknowledges their zakat, and that Allah is the Ever-Returning, the Most Merciful? At-Tawba 104

13. Ask your Lord for forgiveness and then make tawba to Him. He will let you enjoy a good life until a specified time, and will give His favour to all who merit it ... Hud 3

14. ...So ask His forgiveness and then make tawba to Him. My Lord is Close and Quick to Respond. Hud 61

15. Ask your Lord for forgiveness and then make tawba to Him. My Lord is Most Merciful, Most Loving.' Hud 90

16. But to those who do evil in ignorance and then after that make tawba and put things right, to them your Lord is Ever-Forgiving, Most Merciful. An-Nahl 119

17. ...except for those who make tawba and have iman and act rightly: Allah will transform the wrong actions of such people into good – Allah is Ever-Forgiving, Most Merciful. Al-Furqan 70

18. But as for those who make tawba and act rightly, they will hopefully be successful. Al-Qasas 67

19. [The Angels] ...ask forgiveness for those who have iman: 'Our Lord, You encompass everything in mercy and knowledge! Forgive those who turn to You and who follow Your Way and safeguard them from the punishment of the Blazing Fire. Al-Mumin 7

20. ...Ask forgiveness for your wrong action and glorify your Lord with praise in the evening and the early morning. Al-Mumin 55

21. ...And have taqwa of Allah. Allah is Ever-Returning, Most Merciful. Al-Hujurat 12

22. You who have iman! make tawba to Allah. It may be that your Lord will erase your bad actions from you and admit you into Gardens with rivers flowing under them... At-Tahrm 8

23. ...So be straight with Him and ask His forgiveness... Fussilat 6

24. It is He who accepts tawba from His slaves and pardons evil acts and knows what they do. Ash-Shura 25

25. ...ask forgiveness for your wrongdoing, and for the men and women who have iman. Allah knows both your activity and your repose. Muhammad 19

26. Allah loves the good-doers – those who, when they act indecently or wrong themselves, remember Allah and ask forgiveness for their bad actions (and who can forgive bad actions except Allah?) and do not knowingly persist in what they were doing. Al 'Imran 134-5

27. Your Lord knows best what is in your selves. If you are salihun, He is Ever-Forgiving to the remorseful. Bani Isra'il 25

28. Certainly before that they were good-doers. The part of the night they spent asleep was small and they would seek forgiveness before the dawn. Adh-Dhariyat 18

29. Those who become kafir after having iman and then increase in their kufr, their tawba will not be accepted. They are the misguided. Al 'Imran 90

30. There is no tawba for people who persist in doing evil until death comes to them and who then say, 'Now I make tawba,' nor for people who die kafir. We have prepared for them a painful punishment. An-Nisa 18

31. When they took full stock of what they had done and saw they had been misled, they said, 'If our Lord does not have

mercy on us and forgive us, we will certainly be among the lost.' Al-A'raf 149

32. But as for those who do evil actions and then subsequently make tawba and have iman, in that case your Lord is Ever-Forgiving, Most Merciful. Al-A'raf 153

33. My people! Ask forgiveness of your Lord and then make tawba to Him. He will send heaven down to you in abundant rain, and increase you with strength upon strength. Do not turn away as evildoers. Hud 52

34. Race each other to forgiveness from your Lord and to a Garden, whose breadth is like that of heaven and earth combined, made ready for those who have iman in Allah and His Messengers. That is Allah's favour which He gives to those He wills. Allah's favour is indeed immense. Al-Hadid 21

35. ...except those who make tawba and put things right and hold fast to Allah and dedicate their deen to Allah alone; they are with the muminun. Allah will give the muminun an immense reward. An-Nisa 146

Praise

1. Praise be to Allah, the Lord of all the worlds. Al-Fatiha 2

2. And say: 'Praise be to Allah Who has had no son and Who has no partner in His Kingdom and Who needs no one to protect Him from abasement.' And proclaim His Greatness repeatedly! Bani Isra'il 111

3. Praise be to Allah, the Bringer into Being of the heavens and earth, He who made the angels messengers, with wings – two, three or four. He adds to creation in any way He wills. Allah has power over all things. Fatir 1

4. All praise belongs to Allah, the Lord of the heavens and the Lord of the earth, Lord of all the worlds. All greatness belongs to Him in the heavens and earth He is the Almighty, the All-Wise. Al-Jathiya 36-37

5. They said, 'Glory be to our Lord. Truly we have been wrongdoers.' Al-Qalam 29

6. Magnify your Lord. Al-Muddaththir 3

7. Everyone in the heavens and the earth belongs to Him. Those in His presence do not consider themselves too great to worship Him and do not grow tired of it. They glorify Him by night and day, without ever flagging. Al-Anbiya 19-20

8. Everything in the heavens and everything in the earth belongs to Him. He is the Most High, the Magnificent. The heavens are all but rent asunder from above when the angels glorify their Lord with praise and ask forgiveness for those who are on the earth. Allah is the Ever-Forgiving, the Most Merciful. Ash-Shura 4-5

9. You will see the angels circling round the Throne, glorifying their Lord with praise. It will be decided between them with truth. And it will be said: 'Praise be to Allah, the Lord of all the worlds.' Az-Zumar 75

10. All praise is due to Allah, the Lord of the worlds. Al-Mumin 65

11. If they grow arrogant, those who are with your Lord glorify Him night and day and never grow tired. Fussilat 38

12. So glorify the name of your Lord, the Magnificent! Al-Waqi'a 74 & 96

13. Everything in the heavens and the earth glorifies Allah. He is the Almighty, the All-Wise. The kingdom of the heavens and the earth belongs to Him. He gives life and causes to die. He has power over all things. Al-Hadid 1-2

14. ...then glorify your Lord's praise and ask His forgiveness. He is the Ever-Returning. An-Nasr 3

15. So glory be to Allah when you start the night and when you greet the day. Praise be to Him in the heavens and the earth, in the afternoon and when you reach midday. Ar-Rum 17-18

16. Those who bear the Throne, and all those around it, glorify their Lord with praise and believe in Him and ask forgiveness for those who have iman. Al-Mumin 7

17. ...glorify your Lord with praise in the evening and the early morning. Al-Mumin 55

18. ...and glorify Him in the morning and the evening. Al-Fath 9

19. So be patient in the face of what they say and glorify your Lord with praise before the rising of the sun and before it sets.

And glorify Him during the night and after you have prostrated. Qaf 39-40

20. Everything in the heavens and everything in the earth glorifies Allah. He is the Almighty, the All-Wise. Al-Hashr 1

21. Everything in the heavens and everything on earth glorifies Allah. Sovereignty and praise belong to Him. He has power over all things. At-Taghabun 1

22. The best of them said, 'Did I not say to you, "Why do you not glorify Allah?"' They said, 'Glory be to our Lord. Truly we have been wrongdoers.' Al-Qalam 28-29

23. Do you not see that everyone in the heavens and earth glorifies Allah, as do the birds with their outspread wings? Each one knows its prayer and glorification. Allah knows what they do. An-Nur 41

24. The kingdom of the heavens and earth belongs to Allah and Allah is the final destination. An-Nur 42

25. Your Lord creates and chooses whatever He wills. The choice is not theirs. Glory be to Allah! He is exalted above anything they associate with Him! Al-Qasas 68

26. Allah is the Creator of everything and He is Guardian over everything. The keys of the heavens and earth belong to Him. It is those who reject Allah's Signs who are the losers. Az-Zumar 62-63

27. The kingdom of the heavens and the earth belongs to Him. All things return to Allah. Al-Hadid 5

28. He brings forth the living from the dead and brings forth the dead from the living and brings the earth to life after it was dead. In the same way you too will be brought forth. Ar-Rum 19

29. If you asked them, 'Who created the heavens and the earth?' they would say, 'Allah!' Say: 'Praise be to Allah!' But most of them do not know. Everything in the heavens and earth belongs to Allah. Allah is the Rich Beyond Need, the Praiseworthy. If all the trees on earth were pens and all the sea, with seven more seas besides, was ink Allah's words still would not run dry. Allah is Almighty, All-Wise. Luqman 25-27

30. The Forgiver of wrong action, the Accepter of tawba, the Se-

vere in retribution, the Possessor of abundance. There is no god but Him. He is the final destination. Al-Mumin 3
31. Blessed be He who has the Kingdom in His Hand. He has power over all things. Al-Mulk 1
32. ...Allah – He is the Truth, and what you call upon besides Him is falsehood. Allah is the All-High, the Most Great. Luqman 30
33. We gave Dawud great favour from Us: 'O mountains and birds! echo with him in his praise!' Saba' 10
34. So glorify your Lord with praise and be one of the prostrators. And worship your Lord until what is Certain comes to you. Al-Hijr 98-99
35. There was no group to come to his aid, besides Allah, and he was not given any help. In that situation the only protection is from Allah, the Real. He gives the best reward and the best outcome. Al-Kahf 43-44
36. Say: 'If all the sea was ink to write down the Words of my Lord, it would run out long before the Words of my Lord ran out,' even if We were to bring the same amount of ink again. Al-Kahf 109
37. ...glorify Allah in the morning and the evening. Maryam 11
38. He [Musa] said, 'Our Lord is He who gives each thing its created form and then guides it.' He [Pharaoh] said, 'What about the previous generations?' He said, 'Knowledge of them is with my Lord in a Book. My Lord does not misplace nor does He forget.' Ta Ha 49-51
39. Allah is better and longer lasting. Ta Ha 73
40. ...We subjected the mountains to Dawud, glorifying, and the birds as well... Al-Anbiya 79
41. Praise be to Allah, to Whom everything in the heavens and everything in the earth belongs, and praise be to Him in the akhira. He is the All-Wise, the All-Aware. Saba 1
42. Glory be to Him Who has the Dominion of all things in His Hand. To Him you will be returned. Yasin 83
43. Glory be to your Lord, the Lord of Might, beyond anything they describe. And peace be upon the Messengers. And praise be to Allah, the Lord of all the worlds! As-Saffat 180-182
44. Everything in the heavens and everything in the earth glorifies

Allah. He is the Almighty, the All-Wise. As-Saff 1
45. Glorify then the name of your Lord, the Magnificent. Al-Haqqa 52
46. ...By the Pen and what they write down! By the blessing of your Lord, you are not mad. Al-Qalam 1-2
47. [Musa said] 'Strengthen my back by him [Harun] and let him share in my task, so that we can glorify You much and remember You much, for You are watching us.' Ta Ha 30-34

Gratitude and Ingratitude

1. Give thanks to Me and do not be ungrateful. Al-Baqara 152
2. And proclaim Allah's greatness for the guidance He has given you so that hopefully you will be thankful. Al-Baqara 185
3. Remember Allah's blessing to you and the Book and Wisdom He has sent down to you to admonish you. Have taqwa of Allah and know that Allah has knowledge of all things. Al-Baqara 231
4. Allah will recompense the thankful. Al 'Imran 144
5. Why should Allah punish you if you are thankful and have iman? Allah is All-Thankful, All-Knowing. An-Nisa 147
6. If only they had been pleased with what Allah and His Messenger had given them and had said, 'Allah is enough for us. Allah will give us of His bounty as will His Messenger. It is to Allah that we make our plea.' At-Tawba 59
7. ...then a violent squall comes upon them and the waves come at them from every side and they realise there is no way of escape, they call on Allah, making their deen sincerely His: 'If You rescue us from this, we will truly be among the thankful.' But then, when He does rescue them, they become rebellious in the earth... Yunus 22 & 23
8. And when your Lord announced: "If you are grateful, I will certainly give you increase, but if you are ungrateful, My punishment is severe."' Ibrahim 7
9. Allah helped you at Badr when you were weak so have taqwa of Allah, so that hopefully you will be thankful. Al 'Imran 123
10. ...it [a city] showed ingratitude for Allah's blessings so Allah made it wear the robes of hunger and fear for what it did. An-Nahl 112

11. So eat from what Allah has provided for you, halal and good, and be thankful for the blessing of Allah if it is Him you worship. An-Nahl 114

12. We have appointed the sacrificial animals for you as one of the sacred rites of Allah. There is good in them for you, so invoke Allah's name over them, as they stand in rows. And then when they collapse on their sides, eat of them and feed both those who ask and those who are too shy to ask. In this way We have subjected them to you so that hopefully you will be thankful. Al-Hajj 36

13. It is He who has created hearing, sight and hearts for you. What little thanks you show! Al-Muminun 78

14. It is He who made night and day succeed each other for those who want to pay heed or to give thanks. Al-Furqan 62

15. We gave knowledge to Dawud and Sulayman who said, 'Praise be to Allah who has favoured us over many of His slaves who are muminun.' An-Naml 15

16. Then, when they reached the Valley of the Ants, an ant said, 'Ants! enter your dwellings so that Sulayman and his troops do not crush you unwittingly.' He smiled, laughing at its words, and said, 'My Lord, keep me thankful for the blessing You have bestowed on me and on my parents, and keep me acting rightly, pleasing You, and admit me, by Your mercy, among Your slaves who are salihun.' An-Naml 18-19

17. …And when he [Sulayman] saw it [the throne of Bilqis] standing firmly in his presence, he said, 'This is part of my Lord's favour to test me to see if I will give thanks or show ingratitude. Whoever gives thanks only does so to his own gain. Whoever is ungrateful, my Lord is Rich Beyond Need, Generous.' An-Naml 40

18. Allah shows favour to mankind but most of them are not thankful. An-Naml 73

19. Seek your provision from Allah, and serve Him and give thanks to Him. You will be brought back to Him. Al-'Ankabut 17

20. We gave Luqman wisdom: 'Give thanks to Allah. Whoever gives thanks only does so to his own good. Whoever is ungrateful, Allah is Rich Beyond Need, Praiseworthy.' Luqman 12

21. They made for him anything he wished: high arches and statues, huge dishes like cisterns, great built-in cooking vats. 'Work, family of Dawud, in thankfulness!' But very few of My slaves are thankful. Saba 13
22. If you are ungrateful, Allah is rich beyond need of any of you and He is not pleased with ingratitude in His slaves. But if you are grateful, He is pleased with you for that. Az-Zumar 7
23. No! Worship Allah and be among the thankful. Az-Zumar 66
24. Allah is He who appointed the night for you so that you might rest in it, and the day for seeing. Allah pours out His favour on mankind but most people do not show thanks. Al-Mumin 61
25. Among His Signs are the tall ships sailing like mountains through the sea. If He wills He makes the wind stop blowing and then they lie motionless on its back. There are certainly Signs in that for everyone who is steadfast and thankful. Ash-Shura 33
26. It is Allah who has made the sea subservient to you so that the ships sail on it at His command, enabling you to seek His bounty, so that hopefully you will be thankful. Al-Jathiya 12
27. In this way Allah makes His Signs clear to you, so that hopefully you will be thankful. Al-Ma'ida 89
28. Remember the kindness of Allah who created love of each other in your hearts when you were enemies among each other. You had reached up to the edge of fire when Allah saved you. Allah explains His message clearly so that you find the guidance in it. Al 'Imran 103
29. ...Man is truly ungrateful. Al-Hajj 66
30. He has given you everything you have asked Him for. If you tried to number Allah's blessings, you could never count them. Man is indeed wrongdoing, ungrateful. Ibrahim 34
31. If you tried to number Allah's blessings, you could never count them. Allah is Ever-Forgiving, Most Merciful. An-Nahl 18
32. Allah brought you out of your mothers' wombs knowing nothing at all, and gave you hearing, sight and hearts so that perhaps you would show thanks. An-Nahl 78
33. When harm touches man, he calls on Us, lying on his side or sitting down or standing up. Then when We remove the harm

from him he carries on as if he had never called on Us when the harm first touched him. In that way We make what they have done appear good to the profligate. Yunus 12

34. When harm occurs to you at sea, those you call on vanish – except for Him alone! But when He delivers you to dry land, you turn away. Man truly is ungrateful. Bani Isra'il 67

35. When We bless man, he turns away and draws aside. When evil touches him, he despairs. Bani Isra'il 83

36. If you ask them who has sent rain from the sky and revived the dead earth, they will say that, it is Allah. Then thank Him. Al-'Ankabut 63

37. That is how We repaid them for their ingratitude. Are any but the ungrateful repaid like this? Saba 17

38. Allah does not guide anyone who is an ungrateful liar. Az-Zumar 3

39. Then We pardoned you [Bani Isra'il] after that so that perhaps you would show thanks. Al-Baqara 52

40. In this way Allah makes His Signs clear to you, so that hopefully you will be thankful. Al-Ma'ida 89

41. We have established you firmly on the earth and granted you your livelihood in it. What little thanks you show! Al-A'raf 11

42. …Take what I have given you and be among the thankful.' Al-A'raf 144

43. When you were few and oppressed in the land, afraid that the people would snatch you away, He gave you refuge and supported you with His help and provided you with good things so that hopefully you would be thankful. Al-Anfal 26

44. Allah shows favour to mankind but most of them are not thankful. Yunus 60

45. …'This is part of my Lord's favour to test me to see if I will give thanks or show ingratitude… An-Naml 40

46. When the waves hang over them like canopies, they call on Allah, making their deen sincerely His. But then when He delivers them safely to the land, some of them are ambivalent. None but a treacherous, thankless man denies Our Signs. Luqman 32

47. ...'Eat of your Lord's provision and give thanks to Him: a bountiful land and a forgiving Lord.' Saba 15
48. They [the people of the Garden] will say, 'Praise be to Allah who has removed all sadness from us. Truly our Lord is Ever-Forgiving, Ever-Thankful:He who has lodged us, out of His favour,in the Abode of Permanence where no weariness or fatigue affects us.' Fatir 34
49. We guided him on the Way, whether he is thankful or unthankful. Ad-Dahr 3
50. ...'If you were to be ungrateful, you and everyone on the earth, Allah is Rich Beyond Need, Praiseworthy.' Ibrahim 8
51. They acknowledge Allah's blessing and then deny it. Most of them are kuffar. An-Nahl 83
52. Say:"Praise be to Allah who has rescued us from the people of the wrongdoers!" Al-Muminun 28
53. It was a blessing direct from Our presence. That is how We recompense those who give thanks. Al-Qamar 35
54. You who have iman! eat of the good things We have provided for you and give thanks to Allah if you worship Him alone. Al-Baqara 171
55. Do you not see that Allah has subjected to you everything in the heavens and earth and has showered His blessings upon you, both outwardly and inwardly? Yet there are people who argue about Allah without knowledge or guidance or any illuminating Book. Luqman 20

Sabr – Steadfastness

1. You who have iman! when you meet a troop, stand firm and remember Allah repeatedly so that hopefully you will be successful. Obey Allah and His Messenger and do not quarrel among yourselves lest you lose heart and your momentum disappear. And be steadfast. Allah is with the steadfast. Al-Anfal 46-47
2. ...be steadfast until Allah's judgement comes. He is the Best of Judges. Yunus 109
3. Those who are steadfast and do right actions. They will receive forgiveness and a large reward. Hud 11
4. Those who were steadfast will be recompensed according to the best of what they did. An-Nahl 96

Ihsan

5. Be patient. But your patience is only by Allah… An-Nahl 127
6. They will be given their reward twice over because they have been steadfast and because they ward off the bad with the good and give from what we have provided for them. Al-Qasas 54
7. Allah's reward is better for those who have iman and act rightly. But only the steadfast will obtain it.' Al-Qasas 80
8. So be steadfast. Allah's promise is true. Do not let those who have no certainty belittle you. Ar-Rum 60
9. …command what is right and forbid what is wrong and be steadfast in the face of all that happens to you. That is certainly the most resolute course to follow. Luqman 17
10. The steadfast will be paid their wages in full without any reckoning. Az-Zumar 11
11. So remain steadfast. Allah's promise is true. Ask forgiveness for your wrong action and glorify your Lord with praise in the evening and the early morning. Al-Mumin 55
12. So be steadfast as the Messengers with firm resolve were also steadfast. Al-Ahqaf 35
13. Be steadfast for your Lord. Al-Muddaththir 7
14. Therefore wait patiently for the judgement of your Lord. Do not obey any evildoer or thankless man among them. Ad-Dahr 24
15. And be steadfast. Allah does not let the wage of good-doers go to waste. Hud 115
16. So be steadfast. The best end result is for those who have taqwa. Hud 49
17. For truly with hardship comes ease; truly with hardship comes ease. Al-Inshirah 5-6
18. Today I have rewarded them for being steadfast. They are the ones who are victorious.' Al-Muminun 111
19. You who have iman! seek help in steadfastness and salat. Allah is with the steadfast. Al-Baqara 153
20. But if you are steadfast and have taqwa, that is the most resolute course to take. Al 'Imran 186
21. You who have iman, be steadfast; be supreme in steadfastness; be firm on the battlefield; and have taqwa of Allah; so that hopefully you will be successful. Al 'Imran 200

22. How excellent is the reward of those who act: those who are steadfast and put their trust in their Lord. Al-Ankabu/t 58-59
23. So be steadfast. Allah's promise is true. Do not let those who have no certainty belittle you. Ar-Rum 60
24. ...and who are steadfast in the face of all that happens to them... Al-Hajj 35
25. ...those who are steadfast in seeking the face of their Lord, and establish salat and give from the provision We have given them, secretly and openly, and stave off evil with good, it is they who will have the Ultimate Abode – Gardens of Eden which they will enter... Ar-Ra'd 24-25
26. Allah loves the steadfast. Al 'Imran 146
27. Do you not see that ships sail on the sea by Allah's blessing so that He can show you something of His Signs? There are certainly Signs in that for everyone who is steadfast and thankful. Luqman 31
28. If He wills He makes the wind stop blowing and then they lie motionless on its back. There are certainly Signs in that for everyone who is steadfast and thankful. Ash-Shura 33

Taqwa and Fear of Allah

1. That is the Book, without any doubt. It contains guidance for those who have taqwa. Al-Baqara 2
2. Take provision; but the best provision is taqwa of Allah. So have taqwa of Me, people of intelligence! Al-Baqara 197
3. Do not make a mockery of Allah's Signs. Remember Allah's blessing to you and the Book and Wisdom He has sent down to you to admonish you. Have taqwa of Allah and know that Allah has knowledge of all things. Al-Baqara 231
4. ...have taqwa of Allah, so that hopefully you will be thankful. Al 'Imran 123
5. Have taqwa of Allah so that hopefully you will be successful. Al 'Imran 130
6. But do not fear them – fear Me if you are muminun. Al 'Imran 175
7. But if you are steadfast and have taqwa, that is the most resolute course to take. Al 'Imran 186

8. You who have iman! have taqwa of Allah and seek the means of drawing near to Him. Al-Ma'ida 35

9. You who have iman! do not take as friends any of those given the Book before you or the kuffar who make a mockery and a game out of your deen. Have taqwa of Allah if you are muminun. Al-Ma'ida 57

10. 'We are commanded to submit as Muslims to the Lord of all the worlds, and to establish salat and have taqwa of Him.' Al-An'am 71-72

11. 'Prescribe good for us in the dunya and the akhira. We have truly turned to You.' Al-A'raf 156

12. You who have iman! have taqwa of Allah and be with the sadiqun. At-Tawba 119

13. In the alternation of night and day and what Allah has created in the heavens and the earth there are Signs for people who have taqwa. Yunus 6

14. [Intelligent are] those who join what Allah has commanded to be joined and are afraid of their Lord and fear an evil Reckoning... Ar-Ra'd 21

15. Those who were kafir said to their Messengers, 'We will drive you from our land unless you return to our religion.' Their Lord revealed to them, 'We will destroy those who do wrong. We will leave you the land to live in after them. That is the reward of those who fear My station and fear My threat.' Ibrahim 13-14

16. They fear their Lord above them and do everything they are ordered to do. Allah says, 'Do not take two gods. He is only One God. So dread Me alone.' An-Nahl 50-51

17. Give good news to the humble-hearted, whose hearts quake at the mention of Allah, Al-Hajj 34-35

18. So have taqwa of Allah and obey me. Ash-Shu'ara 131

19. ...That is the true Deen – but most people do not know – turning towards Him. Have taqwa of Him and establish salat. Ar-Rum 29-30

20. Mankind! have taqwa of your Lord and fear a day when no father will be able to atone for his son, or son for his father, in any way. Allah's promise is true. So do not let the life of the dunya

delude you and do not let the Deluder delude you concerning Allah. Luqman 33
21. O Prophet! Have taqwa of Allah and do not obey the kafirun and munafiqun. Allah is All-Knowing, All-Wise. Al-Ahzab 1
22. Say: 'Slaves of Mine who have iman! have taqwa of your Lord.' Az-Zumar 10
23. But those who have taqwa of their Lord will have high-ceilinged Halls, and more such Halls built one above the other, and rivers flowing under them. That is Allah's promise. Allah does not break His promise. Az-Zumar 20
24. And those who have taqwa of their Lord will be driven to the Garden in companies and when they arrive there, finding its gates open, its custodians will say to them, 'Peace be upon you! You have done well so enter it timelessly, for ever.' Az-Zumar 73
25. ...people whose hearts Allah has tested for taqwa. They will have forgiveness and an immense reward. Al-Hujurat 3
26. You who have iman! avoid most suspicion. Indeed some suspicion is a crime. And do not spy and do not backbite one another. Would any of you like to eat his brother's dead flesh? No, you would hate it. And have taqwa of Allah. Allah is Ever-Returning, Most Merciful. Al-Hujurat 12
27. We know best what they say. You are not a dictator over them. So remind, with the Qur'an, whoever fears My Threat. Qaf 45
28. You who have iman! have taqwa of Allah and iman in His Messenger. He will give you a double portion of His mercy and grant you a Light by which to walk and forgive you. Allah is Ever-Forgiving, Most Merciful. Al-Hadid 28
29. ...Whoever has taqwa of Allah – He will give him a way out. At-Talaq 2
30. ...have taqwa of Allah; so that hopefully you will be successful. Al 'Imran 200
31. O mankind! have taqwa of your Lord who created you from a single self. An-Nisa 1
32. Do not be afraid of people, be afraid of Me. Al-Ma'ida 44
33. You who have iman! if you have taqwa of Allah, He will give you discrimination and erase your bad actions from you and for-

give you. Allah's favour is indeed immense. Al-Anfal 29
34. Fear Allah, as He should be feared and die only as a Muslim. Al 'Imran 102
35. ...and have taqwa of Allah, Him in Whom you have iman. Al-Ma'ida 88
36. Say: 'Bad things and good things are not the same, even though the abundance of the bad things may seem attractive to you.' Have taqwa of Allah, people of intelligence, so that hopefully you will be successful. Al-Ma'ida 100
37. Warn by it those who fear they will be gathered to their Lord, having no protector or intercessor apart from Him, so that hopefully they will have taqwa. Al-An'am 51
38. The muminun are those whose hearts tremble when Allah is mentioned... Al-Anfal 2
39. If We Had sent down this Qur'an onto a mountain, you would have seen it humbled, crushed to pieces out of fear of Allah. We make such examples for people so that hopefully they will reflect. Al-Hashr 21
40. Whoever is guided is only guided for his own good. Whoever is misguided is only misguided to his detriment. I have not been set over you as a guardian.' Follow what has been revealed to you and be steadfast until Allah's judgement comes. He is the Best of Judges. Yunus 108-109
41. Hasten for the forgiveness from your Lord and for the Paradise as wide as are the heavens and the earth, prepared for those who fear Allah & ward off evil. Al 'Imran 133
42. Mankind, have taqwa of your Lord! The quaking of the Hour is a terrible thing. Al-Hajj 1
43. ...fearing a day when all hearts and eyes will be in turmoil. An-Nur 37
44. Only those of His slaves with knowledge have fear of Allah... Fatir 28
45. Those who fear their Lord in the Unseen will have forgiveness and an immense reward. Al-Mulk 12
46. Have taqwa of Allah. Al-Ma'ida 11
47. ...Allah loves those who have taqwa. At-Tawba 4

48. ...Allah has more right to your fear if you are muminun. At-Tawba 13
49. Allah is with those who fear Him. At-Tawba 26
50. Have taqwa of Him who created you and the earlier creatures. Ash-Shu'ara 184
51. That abode of the akhira – We grant it to those who do not seek to exalt themselves in the earth or to cause corruption in it... Al-Qasas 83
52. You who have iman! have taqwa of Allah and speak words which hit the mark. Al-Ahzab 70
53. They [the kuffar] will have awnings of Fire above them and awnings below them. By that Allah strikes fear into His slaves: 'So have taqwa, My slaves, of Me!' Az-Zumar 16
54. You should not fear them but rather fear Me – and so that I can complete My blessing to you so that hopefully you will be guided. Al-Baqara 150
55. What is in the heavens and in the earth belongs to Allah. We have instructed those given the Book before you and you yourselves, to have taqwa of Allah, but if you are kafir, what is in the heavens and in the earth belongs to Allah. Allah is Rich Beyond Need, Praiseworthy. An-Nisa 131
56. So have taqwa of Allah, Him to whom you will be gathered. Al-Ma'ida 96
57. He ['Isa] said, 'Have taqwa of Allah if you are muminun!' Al-Ma'ida 112
58. Say: 'I fear, were I to disobey my Lord, the punishment of a dreadful Day.' Al-An'am 16
59. Children of Adam! if Messengers come to you from among yourselves, recounting My Signs to you, those who have taqwa and put things right, will feel no fear and will know no sorrow. Al-A'raf 35
60. The successful outcome is for those who have taqwa. Al-A'raf 128
61. The akhira is better for those who have taqwa. An-Nisa 76.
62. You can only warn those who act on the Reminder and fear the All-Merciful in the Unseen. Give them the good news of for-

giveness and a generous reward. Ya Sin 10

63. The people with taqwa will be among Gardens and Fountains. Adh-Dhariyat 10

64. You who have iman! have taqwa of Allah and let each self look to what it has sent forward for Tomorrow. Have taqwa of Allah. Allah is aware of what you do. Do not be like those who forgot Allah so He made them forget themselves. Such people are the deviators. Al-Hashr 18-19

65. He said, 'My people, I am a clear warner to you. Worship Allah, have taqwa of Him and obey me.' Nuh 3

66. What is the matter with you that you do not hope for honour from Allah, Nuh 13

67. But as for him who feared the Station of his Lord and forbade the lower self its appetites, the Garden will be his refuge. An-Nazi'at 39-40

68. Remember Allah's blessing to you and the covenant He made with you when you said, 'We hear and we obey.' Have taqwa of Allah. Allah knows what the heart contains. Al-Ma'ida 7

69. If only the people of the cities had had iman and taqwa, We would have opened up to them blessings from heaven and earth. But they denied the truth so We seized them for what they earned. Do the people of the cities feel secure against Our violent force coming down on them in the night while they are asleep? Or do the people of the cities feel secure against Our violent force coming down on them in the day while they are playing games? Do they feel secure against Allah's devising? No one feels secure against Allah's devising except for those who are lost. Is it not clear to those who have inherited the earth after these people that, if We wanted to, We could strike them for their wrong actions, sealing up their hearts so that they cannot hear? Al-A'raf 96-100

70. ...The abode of the akhira is better for those who have taqwa... Yusuf 109

71. ...you were fearing people when Allah has more right to your fear... Al-Ahzab 37

Tawakkul – Trust In Allah ﷻ and Reliance upon Him

1. Then when you have reached a firm decision, put your trust in Allah. Al 'Imran 159 (A similar meaning is in al-Ma'ida 11)
Allah loves those who put their trust in Him. Al 'Imran 160
2. [The muminun are those] ... who put their trust in their Lord. Al-Anfal 2
3. ...and put your trust in Allah. He is the All-Hearing, the All-Knowing. Al-Anfal 61
4. Say: 'Nothing can happen to us except what Allah has ordained for us. He is Our Master. It is in Allah that the muminun should put their trust.' At-Tawba 51
5. 'Allah is enough for me. There is no god but Him. I have put my trust in Him. He is the Lord of the Mighty Throne.' At-Tawba 129
6. Musa said, 'My people! if you have iman in Allah, then put your trust in Him, if you are Muslims.' Yunus 84
7. ...I have put my trust in Him and I turn to Him. Hud 88
8. The Unseen of the heavens and the earth belongs to Allah and the whole affair will be returned to Him. So worship Him and put your trust in Him. Your Lord is not unaware of what you do. Hud 123
9. 'In Him I put my trust, and let all those who put their trust, put it in Him alone.' Yusuf 67
10. Say: 'He is my Lord; there is no god but Him. I put my trust in Him and I turn to Him. Ar-Ra'd 30
11. Believers should put their trust in Allah.
12. 'So let the muminun put their trust in Allah. And why indeed should we not put our trust in Allah when He has guided us to our ways? We will be steadfast however much you harm us. Those who trust put their trust in Allah.' Ibrahim 11-12
13. ...the accursed Shaytan. He has no authority over those who have iman and put their trust in their Lord. An-Nahl 98-99
14. ...who persevere and put their trust in their Lord. Al-'Ankabut 59
15. So let the muminun put their trust in Allah. Al-Mujadila 10
16. Allah – there is no god but Him. So let the muminun put their trust in Allah. At-Taghabun 13

17. ...Whoever has taqwa of Allah – He will give him a way out and provide for him from where he does not expect. Whoever puts his trust in Allah – He will be enough for him. Allah always achieves His aim. Allah has appointed a measure for all things. At-Talaq 2-3
18. Say: 'He is the All-Merciful. We have iman in Him and trust in Him. You will soon know who is clearly misguided.' Al-Mulk 29
19. 'Allah is enough for us and the Best of Guardians.' Al 'Imran 173
20. ...know that Allah is your Master, the Best of Masters, and the Best of Helpers! Al-Anfal 40
21. Let the muminun put their trust in Allah. Al 'Imran 122
22. And put your trust in Allah. Allah suffices as a Guardian. An-Nisa 81. (See also Al-Ahzab 3)
23. The muminun are those ... who put their trust in their Lord. Al-Anfal 2
24. ...My success is with Allah alone. I have put my trust in Him and I turn to Him. Hud 88
25. Put your trust in the Living who does not die and glorify Him with praise. He is well aware of the wrong actions of His slaves: Al-Furqan 58
26. Put your trust in the Almighty, the Most Merciful. Ash-Shu'ara 217
27. So put your trust in Allah. You are clearly on a path of truth. An-Naml 79
28. ...How excellent is the reward of those who act: those who are steadfast and put their trust in their Lord. Al-'Ankabut 59
29. Say: 'Allah is enough for me. All those who truly trust put their trust in Him.' Az-Zumar 38
30. The judgement concerning anything you differ about is Allah's concern. That is Allah, my Lord – I have put my trust in Him and to Him I turn Ash-Shura 10
31. What is with Allah is better and longer lasting for those who have iman and trust in their Lord Ash-Shura 36
32. Allah – there is no god but Him. So let the muminun put their trust in Allah. At-Taghabun 13
33. '...My Lord is with me and He will guide me.' Ash-Shu'ara 62
34. I have put my trust in Allah... Hud 56

35. Do not obey the kafirun and munafiqun and disregard their abuse of you. Put your trust in Allah. Allah is a sufficient Protector. Al-Ahzab 48

36. But those who put their trust in Allah will find Allah to be Almighty, All-Wise. Al-Anfal 49

37. Say: 'If your fathers or your sons or your brothers or your wives or your tribe, or any wealth you have acquired, or any business you fear may slump, or any house which pleases you, are dearer to you than Allah and His Messenger and doing jihad in His Way, then wait until Allah brings about His command. Allah does not guide people who are deviators.' At-Tawba 24

38. [The Mumin among the people of Fir'awn who concealed his iman said] 'I consign my affair completely to Allah. Truly Allah sees His slaves.' Al-Mumin 44

39. Those who have taqwa will be amid Gardens and Springs. Al-Hijr 42

40.[Hud said] 'Surely I rely on Allah, My Lord and your Lord; there is no living creature that He does not hold it by its forelock; surely my Lord is on the right path.' Hud 56

The Creation and Allah's Swearing Oaths by His Creations

1. In the creation of the heavens and earth, and the alternation of the night and day, and the ships which sail the seas to people's benefit, and the water which Allah sends down from the sky – by which He brings the earth to life when it was dead and scatters about in it creatures of every kind – and the varying direction of the winds, and the clouds subservient between heaven and earth, there are Signs for people who use their intellect. Al-Baqara 164

2. Allah is He Who splits the seed and kernel. He brings forth the living from the dead, and produces the dead out of the living. That is Allah, so how are you perverted? It is He Who splits the sky at dawn, and appoints the night as a time of stillness and the sun and moon as a means of reckoning. That is what the Almighty, the All-Knowing has ordained. It is He Who has appointed the stars for you so you might be guided by them in the darkness of the land and sea. We have made the Signs clear for people who have knowledge. It is He Who first produced you from a single self, then from a resting-place and a repository. We have made the Signs clear for people who understand. It is He Who sends down water from the sky from which We bring forth growth of every kind, and from that We bring forth the green shoots and from them We bring forth close-packed seeds, and from the spathes of the date palm date clusters hanging down, and gardens of grapes and olives and pomegranates, both similar and dissimilar. Look at their fruits as they bear fruit and ripen. There are Signs in that for people who have iman. Al-An'am 96-100

3. Lord is Allah, Who created the heavens and the earth in six days and then settled Himself firmly on the Throne. He covers the day with the night, each pursuing the other urgently; and the sun and moon and stars are subservient to His command. Both creation and command belong to Him. Blessed be Allah, the Lord of all the worlds. Al-A'raf 54

4. Allah is He who raised up the heavens without any support – you can see that – and then established Himself firmly on the

Throne. He made the sun and moon subservient, each running for a specified term. He directs the whole affair. He makes the Signs clear so that hopefully you will be certain about the meeting with your Lord. It is He who stretched out the earth and placed firmly embedded mountains and rivers in it and made two types of every kind of fruit. He covers over day with night. There are Signs in that for people who reflect. In the earth there are diverse regions side by side and gardens of grapes and cultivated fields, and palm-trees sharing one root and others with individual roots, all watered with the same water. And We make some things better to eat than others. There are Signs in that for people who use their intellect. Ar-Ra'd 2-4

5. Do you not see that Allah has created the heavens and the earth with truth? If He wished He could eliminate you and bring about a new creation. That is not difficult for Allah. Ibrahim 19-20

6. Allah is He who created the heavens and the earth and sends down water from the sky and by it brings forth fruits as provision for you. He has made the ships subservient to you to run upon the sea by His command, and He has made the rivers subservient to you, and He has made the sun and moon subservient to you holding steady to their courses, and He has made the night and day subservient to you. Ibrahim 32-33

7. Do those who are kafir not see that the heavens and the earth were sewn together and then We unstitched them and that We made from water every living thing? So will they not have iman? We placed firmly embedded mountains on the earth, so it would not move under them, and We put broad valleys as roadways in it, so that perhaps they might be guided. We made the sky a preserved and protected roof yet still they turn away from Our Signs. It is He who created night and day and the sun and moon, each one swimming in a sphere. Al-Anbiya 30-33

8. ...Allah merges night into day and merges day into night... Al-Hajj 59

9. ...Allah sends down water from the sky and then in the morning the earth is covered in green? Al-Hajj 61

10. Do you not see that Allah has made everything on the earth

The Creation

subservient to you and the ships running upon the sea by His command? He holds back the heaven, preventing it from falling to the earth – except by His permission. Al-Hajj 63

11. Do you not see that Allah propels the clouds then makes them coalesce then heaps them up, and then you see the rain come pouring out of the middle of them? And He sends down mountains from the sky with hail inside them, striking with it anyone He wills and averting it from anyone He wills. The brightness of His lightning almost blinds the sight. Allah revolves night and day. There is surely a lesson in that for people with inner sight. An-Nur 43-45

12. Blessed be He who placed constellations in the sky and put a blazing lamp and shining moon among them. It is He who made night and day succeed each other for those who want to pay heed or to give thanks. Al-Furqan 61-62

13. Do you not see how your Lord stretches out shadows? If He had wished He could have made them stationary. Then We appoint the sun to be the pointer to them. Then We draw them back to Ourselves in gradual steps. It is He who made the night a cloak for you and sleep a rest, and He made the day a time for rising. It is He who sends out the winds, bringing advance news of His mercy. And We send down from heaven pure water so that by it We can bring a dead land to life and give drink to many of the animals and people We created. Al-Furqan 45-49

14. It is He who has unloosed both seas – the one sweet and refreshing, the other salty and bitter – and put a dividing line between them, an uncrossable barrier. And it is He who created human beings from water and then gave them relations by blood and marriage. Your Lord is All-Powerful. Al-Furqan 53-54

15. How many creatures do not carry their provision with them! Allah provides for them and He will for you. He is the All-Hearing, the All-Knowing. If you ask them, 'Who created the heavens and the earth and made the sun and moon subservient?' they will say, 'Allah.' So how have they been perverted? Al-'Ankabut 60-61

16. If you ask them, 'Who sends down water from the sky, bringing the earth back to life again after it was dead?' they will say,

'Allah.' Say: 'Praise be to Allah.' But most of them do not use their intellect. Al-'Ankabut 63

17. Allah is He who appointed the night for you so that you might rest in it, and the day for seeing. Allah pours out His favour on mankind but most people do not show thanks. Al-Mumin 61

18. It is Allah who made the earth a stable home for you and the sky a dome, and formed you, giving you the best of forms, and provided you with good and wholesome things. That is Allah, your Lord. Blessed be Allah, the Lord of all the worlds. Al-Mumin 64

19. He who created death and life to test which of you is best in action. He is the Almighty, the Ever-Forgiving. He who created the seven heavens in layers. You will not find any flaw in the creation of the All-Merciful. Look again – do you see any gaps? Then look again and again. Your sight will return to you dazzled and exhausted! We have adorned the lowest heaven with lamps and made some of them stones for the shaytans for whom We have prepared the punishment of the Blaze. Al-Mulk 2-5

20. 'Our Lord, You have not created this for nothing. Glory be to You!' Al 'Imran 191

21. Your Lord is Allah, Who created the heavens and the earth in six days and then settled Himself firmly on the Throne. He covers the day with the night, each pursuing the other urgently; and the sun and moon and stars are subservient to His command... Al-A'raf 54

22. I only created jinn and man to worship Me. Adh-Dhariyat 56

23. Do they not see that We have made the night for them to rest in and the day for seeing? There are certainly Signs in that for people who have iman. An-Naml 86

24. It is Allah who sends the winds which raise the clouds which We then drive to a dead land and by them bring the earth to life after it was dead. That is how the Resurrection will be. Fatir 9

25. Say: 'Do you reject Him who created the earth in two days, and make others equal to Him? That is the Lord of all the worlds.' He placed firmly embedded mountains on it, towering over it, and blessed it and measured out its nourishment in it, laid out for those who seek it – all in four days. Then He turned to heaven

The Creation

when it was smoke and said to it and to the earth, 'Come willingly or unwillingly.' They both said, 'We come willingly.' In two days He determined them as seven heavens and revealed, in every heaven, its own mandate. We adorned the lowest heaven with lamps and guarded it. That is the decree of the Almighty, the All-Knowing. Fussilat 9-12

26. Among His Signs are the night and day and the sun and moon. Do not prostrate to the sun nor to the moon. Prostrate to Allah who created them, if you worship Him. Fussilat 37

27. The kingdom of the heavens and earth belongs to Allah. He creates whatever He wills. He gives daughters to whoever He wishes; and He gives sons to whoever He wishes; or He gives them both sons and daughters; and He makes whoever He wishes barren. Truly He is All-Knowing, All-Powerful. Ash-Shura 49-50

28. He created man and taught him clear expression. The sun and the moon both run with precision. The stars and the trees all bow down in prostration. He erected heaven and established the balance, so that you would not transgress the balance. Give just weight – do not skimp in the balance. Ar-Rahman 3-7

29. It is He who produces gardens, both cultivated and wild, and palm-trees and crops of diverse kinds, and olives and pomegranates, both similar and dissimilar. Eat of their fruits when they bear fruit and pay their due on the day of their harvest, and do not be profligate. He does not love the profligate.

And also animals for riding and for haulage and animals for slaughtering and for wool. Eat what Allah has provided for you and do not follow in the footsteps of Shaytan. He is an outright enemy to you.

There are eight in pairs: A pair of sheep and a pair of goats – Say: 'Is it the two males He has made haram, or the two females, or what the wombs of the two females contain? Tell me with knowledge if you are being truthful.'

And a pair of camels and a pair of cattle – Say: 'Is it the two males He has made haram, or the two females, or what the wombs of the two females contain? Were you then witnesses when Allah gave you this instruction?' Who could do greater wrong than someone who invents lies against Allah thus leading people astray without any knowledge? Allah does not guide the people of the wrongdoers. Al-An'am 142-145

30. We have placed constellations in heaven and made them beautiful for those who look. We have guarded them from every cursed Shaytan – except for the one who listens stealthily, and he is followed by an open flame. As for the earth, We stretched it out and cast firmly embedded mountains in it and made everything grow in due proportion on it. And We put livelihoods in it both for you and for those you do not provide for. There is nothing that does not have its stores with Us and We only send it down in a known measure. We send forth the pollinating winds and send down water from the sky and give it to you to drink. And it is not you who keep its stores. It is We who give life and cause to die and We are the Inheritor. Al-Hijr 16-23

31. He created the heavens and the earth with truth… An-Nahl 3

32. It is He who sends down water from the sky. From it you drink and from it come the shrubs among which you graze your herds. And by it He makes crops grow for you and olives and dates and grapes and fruit of every kind. There is certainly a Sign in that for people who reflect. He has made night and day subservient to you, and the sun and moon and stars, all subject to His command. There are certainly Signs in that for people who use their intellect. And also the things of varying colours He has created for you in the earth. There is certainly a Sign in that for people who pay heed. It is He who made the sea subservient to you so that you can eat fresh flesh from it and bring out from it ornaments to wear. And you see the ships cleaving through it so that you can seek His bounty, and so that hopefully you will show thanks. He cast firmly embedded mountains on the earth so it would not move under you, and rivers and pathways so that hopefully you would be guided, and landmarks. And they are guided by the stars. An-Nahl 10-16

33. Do they not see the birds suspended in mid-air up in the sky? Nothing holds them there except Allah. There are certainly Signs in that for people who have iman. Allah has made your houses

The Creation

places of rest for you and made houses for you out of cattle hides which are light for you to carry both when you are travelling and when you are staying in one place. And from their wool and fur and hair you obtain clothing and carpets and household utensils for a time. Allah has made shaded places for you in what He has created and He has made shelters for you in the mountains and He has made shirts for you to protect you from the heat and shirts to protect you from each other's violence. In that way He perfects His blessing on you so that hopefully you will become Muslims. An-Nahl 79-81

34. It is He who made the earth a cradle for you and threaded pathways for you through it and sent down water from the sky by which We have brought forth various different types of plants. Eat and pasture your cattle. Certainly there are Signs in that for people of sound intellect. Ta Ha 53-54

35. It is He who appointed the night for you, so that you could rest in it, and the day for seeing. There are certainly Signs in that for people who listen. Yunus 67

36. Say: 'What do you think? If Allah made it permanent day for you till the Day of Rising, what god is there other than Allah to bring you night to rest in? Do you not then see?' But part of His mercy is that He has made both night and day for you so that you can have your rest and seek His bounty, and so that hopefully you will be thankful. Al-Qasas 72-73

37. He created the heavens and the earth with truth. He wraps the night around the day and wraps the day around the night, and has made the sun and moon subservient, each one running for a specified term. Is He not indeed the Almighty, the Endlessly Forgiving? Az-Zumar 5

38. We created above you seven levels and We were not unaware of the creation. We sent down a measured amount of water from heaven and lodged it firmly in the earth; and We are well able to remove it. By means of it We produce gardens of dates and grapes for you, in which there are many fruits for you and from which you eat, and a tree springing forth from Mount Sinai yielding oil and a seasoning to those who eat. And there is certainly a lesson

for you in your livestock. We give you to drink from what is in their bellies and there are many ways in which you benefit from them, and some of them you eat; and you are conveyed on them and on ships as well. Al-Muminun 17-22

39. It is He Who shows you the lightning, striking fear and bringing hope; it is He Who heaps up the heavy clouds. The thunder glorifies His praise, as do the angels, out of fear of Him. He discharges the thunderbolts, striking with them anyone He wills. Yet still they argue about Allah when He is inexorable in His power! Ar-Ra'd 12-13

40. From it We created you, to it We will return you, and from it We will bring you forth a second time. Ta Ha 55

41. He created the heavens without pillars as you see them, and put mountains upon the earth but it might turn over with you, and He spread in it animals of every kind; and it is Him who sent down water from the cloud, then caused to grow vegetation of every noble kind.

42. And of the fruits of the palms and the grapes- you obtain from them the liquor and goodly provision; most surely there is a sign in this for a people who ponder.

43. And your Lord revealed to the bee to make hives in the mountains and in the trees and in what they build.

44. So, eat of all the fruits and walk in the ways of your Lord submissively. Comes out from its belly beverage of many colours (honey) in which there is healing for men. Most surely there is sign in this for people who reflect. And from the fruit of the date-palm and the grape-vine you derive both intoxicants and wholesome provision. There is certainly a Sign in that for people who use their intellect. Your Lord revealed to the bees: 'Build dwellings in the mountains and the trees, and also in the structures which men erect. Then eat from every kind of fruit and travel the paths of your Lord, which have been made easy for you to follow.' From inside them comes a drink of varying colours, containing healing for mankind. There is certainly a Sign in that for people who reflect. An-Nahl 65-69

45. And if you should ask them, Who created the heavens and

The Creation

the earth they would most certainly say: The Mighty, the Knowing one has created them.

46. He Who made the earth a resting place for you and made in it ways for you that you may go right.

47. And he Who sends down water from the cloud according to a measure, then We raise to life a dead country, in the same way you will be brought out of earth after being dead.

48. And He Who created pairs of all things, and made for you ships and the cattle what you ride on.

49. That you may firmly sit on their backs, then remember the favour of your Lord and say: Glory be to Him Who made this subservient to us and we were not able to do it.

50. Indeed we are returning to our Lord! Az-Zukhruf 14

51. Have they not looked at the sky above them: how We structured it and made it beautiful and how there are no fissures in it? And the earth: how We stretched it out and cast firmly embedded mountains onto it and caused luxuriant plants of every kind to grow in it, an instruction and a reminder for every penitent human being. And We sent down blessed water from the sky and made gardens grow by it and grain for harvesting and soaring date-palms with layered spathes, as provision for Our slaves; by it We brought a dead land to life. That is how the Emergence will take place. Qaf 6-11

52. We did not create heaven and earth and everything in between them as a game. Al-Anbiya 16

53. It is Allah who sends the winds which stir up clouds which He spreads about the sky however He wills. He forms them into dark clumps and you see the rain come pouring out from the middle of them. When He makes it fall on those of His slaves He wills, they rejoice, even though before He sent it down on them they were in despair. So look at the effect of the mercy of Allah, how He brings the dead earth back to life. Truly He is the One Who brings the dead to life. He has power over all things. But if We send a wind, and they see it turning yellow, still they persist after that in being kafir. Ar-Rum 48-51

54. It is He who sends down abundant rain, after they have lost all

hope, and unfolds His mercy. He is the Protector, the Praiseworthy. Among His Signs is the creation of the heavens and earth and all the creatures He has spread about in them. And He has the power to gather them together whenever He wills. Ash-Shura 28-29

55. By those sent forth in succession, by the violently gusting blasts, by the scatterers scattering, by the winnowers winnowing, by those hurling a reminder, excusing or warning, what you are promised will certainly happen. Al-Mursalat 1-7

56. We created them and made their joints strong, and if We wish We can replace them with others like them. Ad-Dahr 28

57. Allah is He who created the heavens and the earth and everything between them in six days and then established Himself firmly upon the Throne. You have no protector or intercessor apart from Him. So will you not pay heed? He directs the whole affair from heaven to earth. Then it will again ascend to Him on a Day whose length is a thousand years by the way you measure. That is the Knower of the Unseen and the Visible, the Almighty, the Most Merciful: He who has created all things in the best possible way. He commenced the creation of man from clay; As-Sajda 4-7

58. It is He Who created the heavens and the earth in six days, then established Himself firmly on the Throne. He knows what goes into the earth and what comes out of it, what comes down from heaven and what goes up into it. He is with you wherever you are – Allah sees what you do. Al-Hadid 4

59. He makes night merge into day and day merge into night. He knows what the heart contains. Al-Hadid 6

60. Consider how Allah originates the creation, then reproduces it again and again surely that is easy to Allah. Travel in the earth and see how He makes the first creation then Allah creates the latter creation; surely Allah has power over all things. Al-'Ankabut 19-20

61. Among His Signs is that He shows you lightning, a source of fear and eager hope, and sends down water from the sky, bringing the dead earth back to life by it. There are certainly Signs in that for people who use their intellect. Among His Signs is that heaven and earth hold firm by His command. Then, when He calls you forth from the earth, you will emerge at once. Ar-Rum 23-25

The Creation

62. It is He who originated creation and then regenerates it. That is very easy for Him. His is the most exalted designation in the heavens and the earth. He is the Almighty, the All-Wise. Ar-Rum 27

63. He has let loose the two seas, converging together, with a barrier between them they do not break through. Ar-Rahman 19-22

64. From out of them come glistening pearls and coral. Ar-Rahman 20

65. And We have decreed set phases for the moon, until it ends up looking like an old palm spathe. Ya Sin 39

66. He Who produces fire for you from green trees so that you use them to light your fires.' Ya Sin 80

67. The Bringer into Being of the heavens and the earth: He has given you mates from among yourselves, and given mates to the livestock, in that way multiplying you. Nothing is like Him. He is the All-Hearing, the All-Seeing. Ash-Shura 11

68. We did not create the heavens and the earth and everything between them as a game. We did not create them except with truth but most of them do not know it. Ad-Dukhan 38-39

69. It is He who made the earth a couch for you, and the sky a dome. He sends down water from the sky and by it brings forth fruits for your provision. Al-Baqara 22

70. The kingdom of the heavens and earth belongs to Allah. Allah has power over all things. Al 'Imran 189

71. Praise belongs to Allah who created the heavens and the earth and appointed darkness and light. Then those who are kafir make others equal to their Lord! Al-An'am 1-2

72. It is He Who created the heavens and the earth with truth. The day He says 'Be!' it is. Al-An'am 73

73. I have turned my face to Him Who brought the heavens and earth into being, a pure natural believer. I am not one of the mushrikun.' Al-An'am 80

74. It He is who sends out the winds, bringing advance news of His mercy, so that when they have lifted up the heavy clouds, We dispatch them to a dead land and send down water to it, by means of which We bring forth all kinds of fruit. In the same way We will bring forth the dead, so that hopefully you will pay heed.

Good land yields up its plants by its Lord's permission, but that which is bad only yields up scantily. In this way We vary the Signs for people who are thankful. Al-A'raf 57-58

75. Your Lord is Allah, Who created the heavens and the earth in seven days and then established Himself firmly on the Throne. He directs the whole affair. No one can intercede except with His permission. That is Allah your Lord, so worship Him. Will you not pay heed? Each and every one of you will return to Him. Allah's promise is true. He brings creation out of nothing and then regenerates it so that he can repay with justice those who had iman and did right actions. Those who were kafir will have a drink of scalding water and a painful punishment because of their kufr. It is He who appointed the sun to give radiance, and the moon to give light, assigning it phases so you would know the number of years and the reckoning of time. Allah did not create these things except with truth. We make the Signs clear for people who know. In the alternation of night and day and what Allah has created in the heavens and the earth there are Signs for people who have taqwa. Yunus 3-6

76. It is He who created the heavens and the earth in six days when His Throne was on the water, in order to test which of you has the best actions. Hud 7

77. We created the jinn before out of the fire of a searing wind. Al-Hijr 27

78. We made the night and day two Signs. We blotted out the Sign of the night and made the Sign of the day a time for seeing so that you can seek favour from your Lord and will know the number of years and the reckoning of time. We have made all things very clear. Bani Isra'il 12

79. ...And you see the earth dead and barren; then when We send down water onto it it quivers and swells and sprouts with luxuriant plants of every kind. Al-Hajj 5

80. Have they not looked at the earth and seen how We have madeevery sort of beneficial species grow in it? Ash-Shu'ara 6

81. Have they not reflected within themselves? Allah did not create the heavens and the earth and everything between them except

with truth and for a fixed term. Yet many people reject the meeting with their Lord. Ar-Rum 8

82. Do you not see that Allah makes night merge into day and day merge into night, and that He has made the sun and moon subservient, each one running for a specified time, and that Allah is aware of what you do? Luqman 29

83. Do they not see how We drive water to barren land and bring forth crops by it which their livestock and they themselves both eat? So will they not see? As-Sajda 27

84. Do you not see that Allah sends down water from the sky and by it We bring forth fruits of varying colours? And in the mountains there are streaks of white and red, of varying shades, and rocks of deep jet black. Fatir 27

85. Allah keeps a firm hold on the heavens and earth, preventing them from vanishing away. And if they vanished no one could then keep hold of them. Certainly He is Most Forbearing, Ever-Forgiving. Fatir 41

86. A Sign for them is the dead land which We bring to life and from which We bring forth grain of which they eat. We place in it gardens of dates and grapes, and cause springs to gush out in it, so they may eat its fruits – they did not do it themselves. So will they not be thankful? Ya Sin 32-34

87. Glory be to Him who created all the pairs: from what the earth produces and from themselves and from things unknown to them. A Sign for them is the night: We peel the day away from it and there they are in darkness. And the sun runs to its resting place. That is the decree of the Almighty, the All-Knowing. And We have decreed set phases for the moon, until it ends up looking like an old palm spathe. It is not for the sun to overtake the moon nor for the night to outstrip the day; each one is swimming in a sphere. Ya Sin 35-39

88. A Sign for them is that We carried their families in the laden ship. And We have created for them the like of it in which they sail. Ya Sin 40-41

89. Have they not seen how We created for them, by Our own handiwork, livestock which are under their control? We have made

them tame for them and some they ride and some they eat. And they have other uses for them, and milk to drink. So will they not be thankful? Ya Sin 71-73

90. We have adorned the lowest heaven with the beauty of the planets. As-Saffat 6

91. We did not create heaven and earth and everything between them to no purpose. Sad 27

92. Do you not see that Allah sends down water from the sky and threads it through the earth to emerge as springs and then by it brings forth crops of varying colours, which then wither and you see them turning yellow and then He makes them into broken stubble? Az-Zumar 21

93. It is Allah who has given you livestock, some for you to ride and some to eat. You gain various benefits from them, and on them you can obtain what your hearts desire, and on them and on the ships you are transported. Al-Mumin 79-80

94. And in the alternation of night and day and the provision Allah sends down from the sky, bringing the earth to life by it after it has died, and the varying direction of the winds, there are Signs for people who use their intellect. Al-Jathiya 5

95. And He has made everything in the heavens and everything on the earth subservient to you. It is all from Him. There are certainly Signs in that for people who reflect. Al-Jathiya 13

96. We have not created the heavens and earth and everything between them except with truth and for a set term. But those who are kafir turn away from what they have been warned about. Al-Ahqaf 3

97. We created the heavens and the earth, and everything between them, in six days and We were not affected by fatigue. Qaf 38

98. By the scatterers scattering, and those bearing weighty loads, and those speeding along with ease, and those apportioning the command: Adh-Dhariyat 1-4

99. As for heaven – We built it with great power and gave it its vast expanse. And the earth – We spread it like a carpet and how well We smoothed it out! And We created all things in pairs so that hopefully you would pay heed. Adh-Dhariyat 47-49

The Creation

100. ...that He created the two sexes – male and female – out of a sperm-drop when it spurted forth. An-Najm 45-46

101. He laid out the earth for all living creatures. In it are fruits and date-palms with covered spathes, and grains on leafy stems and fragrant herbs. Ar-Rahman 10-12

102. His, too, are the ships sailing like mountain peaks on the sea. Ar-Rahman 22

103. ... and He created the jinn from a fusion of fire. Ar-Rahman 15

104. Have you thought about what you cultivate? Is it you who make it germinate or are We the Germinator? If We wished We could have made it broken stubble. You would then be left devoid of crops, distraught: Al-Waqi'a 63-65

105. Have you thought about the water that you drink? Is it you who sent it down from the clouds or are We the Sender? If We wished We could have made it bitter, so will you not give thanks? Have you thought about the fire that you light? Is it you who make the trees that fuel it grow or are We the Grower? We have made it to be a reminder and a comfort for travellers in the wild. Al-Waqi'a 68-73

106. Do you not see how He created seven heavens in layers, and placed the moon as a light in them and made the sun a blazing lamp? Nuh 15-16

107. Allah has spread the earth out as a carpet for you so that you could use its wide valleys as roadways."' Nuh 19-20

108. Did We not make the earth a receptacle for the living and the dead? Did We not place firmly embedded mountains in it, soaring high into the air, and give you sweet fresh water to drink? Al-Mursalat 25-27

109. Have We not made the earth a flat carpet and the mountains its pegs? We have created you in pairs. We made your sleep a break. We made the night a cloak. We made the day for earning a living. We built seven firm layers above you. We installed a blazing lamp. We sent down cascading water from the clouds so that by it we might bring forth grains and plants and luxuriant gardens. An-Naba' 6-16

110. Are you stronger in structure or is heaven? He built it. He raised its vault high and made it level. He darkened its night and

brought forth its morning light. After that He smoothed out the earth and brought forth from it its water and its pastureland and made the mountains firm, for you and for your livestock to enjoy. An-Nazi'at 27-33

111. Man has only to look at his food. We pour down plentiful water, then split the earth into furrows. Then We make grain grow in it, and grapes and herbs and olives and dates and luxuriant gardens and orchards and meadows, for you and your livestock to enjoy. 'Abasa 24-32

112. By Heaven with its cyclical systems and the earth with its splitting seeds. At-Tariq 11-12

113. Glorify the Name of your Lord, the Most High: He who created and moulded; He who determined and guided; He who brings forth green pasture, then makes it blackened stubble. Al-A'la 1-5

114. Have they not looked at the camel – how it was created? and at the sky – how it was raised up? and at the mountains – how they were embedded? and at the earth – how it was smoothed out? Al-Ghashiya 17-20

115. No! I swear by the planets with their retrograde motion, swiftly moving, self-concealing, and by the night when it draws in, and by the dawn when it exhales, At-Takwir 15-18

116. By Heaven with its Houses of the Zodiac. Al-Buruj 1

117. By the sun and its morning brightness, and the moon when it follows it, and the day when it displays it, and the night when it conceals it and the sky and what erected it and the earth and what extended it. Ash-Shams 1-6

118. By the night when it conceals and the day when it reveals Al-Layl 1-2

119. By the brightness of the morning and the night when it is still, your Lord has not abandoned you nor does He hate you. Ad-Duha 1-3

120. By the fig and the olive. At-Tin 1

121. By the charging horses panting hard, striking sparks from their flashing hooves, raiding at full gallop in the early dawn, leaving a trailing dust-cloud in their wake, cleaving through the

The Creation

middle of the foe, truly man is ungrateful to his Lord and indeed he bears witness to that. Truly he is fierce in his love of wealth. Al-'Adiyat 1-8

122. No, I swear by the evening glow, and the night and all it shrouds, and the moon when it is full, you will mount up stage by stage! Al-Inshiqaq 16-19

123. By the dawn and ten nights, and the even and odd, and the night when it departs, is there not in that an oath for the intelligent? Al-Fajr 1-5

124. In the creation of the heavens and the earth, and the alternation of night and day, there are Signs for people with intelligence. Al 'Imran 190

125. He created mortal with the essence of black mud, fashioned in shape. When complete, breathed into him His spirit. Al-Hijr 28-29

126. Among His Signs is that you see the earth laid bare and then when We send down water on it it quivers and swells. He who gives it life is He who gives life to the dead. Certainly He has power over all things. Fussilat 39

Creation of the Human Being

1. O mankind! have taqwa of your Lord who created you from a single self and created its mate from it and then disseminated many men and women from the two of them. Have taqwa of Allah in whose name you make demands on one another and also in respect of your families. Allah watches over you continually. An-Nisa 1

2. We created mankind out of dried clay formed from fetid black mud. Al-Hijr 26

3. We created man from the purest kind of clay; then made him a drop in a secure receptacle; then formed the drop into a clot and formed the clot into a lump and formed the lump into bones and clothed the bones in flesh; and then brought him into being as another creature. Blessed be Allah, the Best of Creators! Then subsequently you will certainly die. Then on the Day of Rising you will be raised again. Al-Muminun 12-16

4. It is Allah who created you from a weak beginning then after weakness gave you strength then after strength ordained weakness

and grey hair. He creates whatever He wills. He is All-Knowing, All-Powerful. Ar-Rum 54

5. He who has created all things in the best possible way. He commenced the creation of man from clay; then produced his seed from an extract of base fluid; then formed him and breathed His Ruh into him and gave you hearing, sight and hearts. What little thanks you show! As-Sajda 7-9

6. He created you from a single self, then produced its mate from it, and sent down livestock to you – eight kinds in pairs. He creates you stage by stage in your mothers' wombs in a threefold darkness. That is Allah, your Lord. Sovereignty is His. There is no god but Him. So what has made you deviate? Az-Zumar 6

7. Allah created you from dust and then from a drop of sperm and then made you into pairs. No female becomes pregnant or gives birth except with His knowledge. And no living thing lives long or has its life cut short without that being in a Book. That is easy for Allah. The two seas are not the same: the one is sweet, refreshing, delicious to drink, the other salty, bitter to the taste. Yet from both of them you eat fresh flesh and extract ornaments for yourselves to wear; and you see ships on them, cleaving through the waves so that you can seek His bounty and so that hopefully you will be thankful. He makes night merge into day and day merge into night, and He has made the sun and moon subservient, each one running until a specified time. That is Allah, your Lord. The Kingdom is His. Those you call on besides Him have no power over even the smallest speck. Fatir 11-13

8. It is Allah who made the earth a stable home for you and the sky a dome, and formed you, giving you the best of forms, and provided you with good and wholesome things. That is Allah, your Lord. Blessed be Allah, the Lord of all the worlds. Al-Mumin 64

9. Have you thought about the sperm that you ejaculate? Is it you who create it or are We the Creator? Al-Waqi'a 58-59

10. He created man from a drop of sperm... An-Nahl 4

11. Allah knows what every female bears and every shrinking of the womb and every swelling. Everything has its measure with Him,... Ar-Ra'd 8

The Creation

12. Allah created you and then will take you back again. And some of you revert to the lowest form of life so that after having knowledge, you know nothing at all. Allah is All-Knowing, All-Powerful. An-Nahl 70

13. It is He who created you from earth, then from a drop of sperm, then from a clot of blood, then He brings you out as infants, then so you may achieve full strength, then so you may become old men – though some of you may die before that time – so that you may reach a predetermined age and so that hopefully you will use your intellect. Al-Mumin 67

14. ...'Do you then disbelieve in Him who created you from dust, then from a drop of sperm, and then formed you as a man? Al-Kahf 37

15. Truly Allah has knowledge of the Hour ...and knows what is in the womb... Luqman 34

16. It is He who created you from a single self and made from him his spouse so that he might find repose in her. Then when he covered her she bore a light load and carried it around. Then when it became heavy they called on Allah, their Lord, 'If You grant us a healthy child, we will be among the thankful!' Al-A'raf 189

17. Mankind! if you are in any doubt about the Rising, know that We created you from dust then from a drop of sperm then from a clot of blood then from a lump of flesh, formed yet unformed, so We may make things clear to you. We make whatever We want stay in the womb until a specified time and then We bring you out as children so that you can reach your full maturity. Some of you die and some of you revert to the lowest form of life so that, after having knowledge, they then know nothing at all... Al-Hajj 5

18. Among His Signs is that He created you from dust and here you are now, widespread human beings! Ar-Rum 20

19. When We grant long life to people, We return them to their primal state. So will you not use your intellect? Ya Sin 68

20. Does not man see that We created him from a drop yet there he is, an open antagonist! Ya Sin 77

21. He created man from dry earth like baked clay. Ar-Rahman 14

22. It is He who created you. Yet among you are those who are

kafir and those who have iman. Allah sees what you do. He created the heavens and the earth with truth and formed you, giving you the best of forms. And He is your final destination. At-Taghabun 2-3

23. Say: He it is Who brought you into being and made for you the ears and the eyes and the hearts but you give little thanks. Say: He it is Who multiplied you in the earth and to Him you shall be gathered. Al-Mulk 22-23

24. ...He created you by successive stages... Nuh 14

25. Allah caused you to grow from the earth then will return you to it and bring you out again.? Nuh 17-18

26. Was he not a drop of ejaculated sperm, then a blood-clot which He created and shaped, making from it both sexes, male and female? Al-Qiyama 37-39

27. Has man ever known a point of time when he was not something remembered? We created man from a mingled drop to test him, and We made him hearing and seeing. Ad-Dahr 1-2

28. Did We not create you from a base fluid, then place it in a secure repository for a recognised term? It is We who determine. What an excellent Determiner! Al-Mursalat 20-23

29. From what thing did He create him? From a drop of sperm He created him and proportioned him. Then He eases the way for him. Then He causes him to die and buries him. Then, when He wills, He raises him from the dead. 'Abasa 18-22

30. He Who created you and formed you and proportioned you and assembled you in whatever way He willed. Al-Infitar 7-8

31. Man has only to look at what he was created from. He was created from a spurting fluid, emerging from between the backbone and the breast-bone. At-Tariq 5-7

32. We created man in the finest mould. At-Tin 4

33. He created man from a clot. Al-'Alaq 2

34. The likeness of 'Isa in Allah's sight is the same as Adam. He created him from earth and then He said to him, 'Be!' and he was. It is the truth from your Lord so do not be among the doubters. Al 'Imran 59-60

The Creation

Human Nature

1. Man was created weak. An-Nisa 28
2. But people are prone to selfish greed. An-Nisa 128
3. Yes indeed! Allah's curse is on the wrongdoers, those who bar access to the way of Allah desiring to make it crooked and reject the akhira. Hud 19
4. ...Man is indeed wrongdoing, ungrateful. Ibrahim 34
5. Man prays for evil just as he prays for good. Man is prone to be impetuous. Bani Isra'il 11
6. When harm occurs to you at sea, those you call on vanish – except for Him alone! But when He delivers you to dry land, you turn away. Man truly is ungrateful. Bani Isra'il 67
7. When We bless man, he turns away and draws aside. When evil touches him, he despairs. Bani Isra'il 83
8. Say: 'Even if you possessed the vast storehouses of my Lord's mercy, you would still hold back, fearing to spend out.' Truly man is niggardly! Bani Isra'il 100
9. We have variegated throughout this Qur'an all kinds of examples for people, but, more than anything else, man is argumentative! Al-Kahf 54
10. Man was created hasty... Al-Anbiya 37
11. It is He who gave you life and then will cause you to die and then will give you life again. Man is truly ungrateful. Al-Hajj 66
12. We offered the Trust to the heavens, the earth and the mountains but they refused to take it on and shrank from it. But man took it on. He is indeed wrongdoing and ignorant. Al-Ahzab 72
13. Man never tires of praying for the good and if evil touches him, he despairs and loses hope. Fussilat 49
14. When We grant blessing to a man, he turns away and draws aside but when any evil touches him, he is full of endless prayers! Fussilat 51
15. They have assigned to Him a portion of His creatures! Truly man is openly ungrateful. Az-Zukhruf 15
16. ...When We let a man taste mercy from Us he exults in it. But if something bad strikes him for what he has done he is ungrateful. Ash-Shura 48

17. Truly man was created headstrong – desperate when bad things happen, begrudging when good things come, except for those who do salat and who are constant in it, those in whose wealth there is a known share for beggars and the destitute, Al-Ma'arij 19-25

18. Yet man still wants to deny what is ahead of him, asking, 'So when is the Day of Rising?' Al-Qiyama 5-6

19. Curse man for his ingratitude! 'Abasa 17

20. As for man, when his Lord tests him by honouring him and favouring him, he says, 'My Lord has honoured me!' But then when He tests him by restricting his provision, he says, 'My Lord has humiliated me!' Al-Fajr-15-18

21. We created man in trouble. Al-Balad 4

22. Truly man is ungrateful to his Lord. Al-'Adiyat 6

23. When harm touches people they call on their Lord, making tawba to Him. But then, when He gives them a taste of mercy from Him, a group of them immediately associate others with their Lord... Ar-Rum 33

24. When harm touches man he calls upon his Lord, making tawba to Him. Then when He grants him a blessing from Him, he forgets what he was calling for before and ascribes rivals to Allah, so as to misguide others from His Way. Say: 'Enjoy your kufr for a little while. You are among the Companions of the Fire.' Az-Zumar 8

25. They [the angels] said, 'Why put on it one [the human being] who will cause corruption on it and shed blood when we glorify You with praise and proclaim Your purity?' Al-Baqara 30

26. But if We let him (man) taste blessings after hardship has afflicted him, he says, 'My troubles have gone away,' and he is overjoyed, boastful – except for those who are steadfast and do right actions. They will receive forgiveness and a large reward. Hud 10

27. We created man in trouble. Does he imagine that no one has power over him? He says, 'I have consumed vast quantities of wealth.' Does he imagine that no one has seen him? Have We not given him two eyes, and a tongue and two lips and shown him the two highways? Al-Balad 4-10

28. No indeed! Truly man is unbridled seeing himself as self-suffi-

The Creation

cient. Truly it is to your Lord that you will return. Have you seen him who prevents a slave when he goes to pray? Al-'Alaq 6-10
29. Truly he is fierce in his love of wealth. Al-'Adiyat 8
30. Fierce competition for this world distracted you until you went down to the graves. At-Takathur 1-2
31. Among the people there is someone whose words about the life of the dunya excite your admiration, and he calls Allah to witness what is in his heart, while he is in fact the most hostile of adversaries. Al-Baqara 204

Death

1. Every self will taste death. Al 'Imran 185, Al-Anbiya 35, Al-'Ankabut 57
2. Every nation has an appointed time. When their time comes, they cannot delay it a single hour or bring it forward. Al-A'raf 34
3. It is He who takes you back to Himself at night, while knowing the things you perpetrate by day, and then wakes you up again, so that a specified term may be fulfilled. Then you will return to Him. Then He will inform you about what you did. Al-An'am 60
4. He is the Absolute Master over His slaves. He sends angels to watch over you. Then when death comes to one of you, Our messengers take him, and they do not fail in their task. Al-An'am 61
5. Then they are returned to Allah, their Master, the Real. Jurisdiction belongs to Him alone and He is the Swiftest of Reckoners. Al-An'am 62
6. Those the angels take in a virtuous state. They say, 'Peace be upon you! Enter the Garden for what you did.' An-Nahl 32
7. No one has the power to die without Allah's will. He has appointed a fixed time for death for each and every one. Al 'Imran 145
8. It is Allah who gives life and who gives death. Al 'Imran 156
9. Then Allah sent a crow which scratched at the earth to show him [Qabil–Cain] how to conceal his brother's [Habil-Abel] corpse. Al-Ma'ida 31
10. Allah takes back people's selves when their death arrives and those who have not yet died, while they are asleep. He keeps hold of those whose death has been decreed and sends the oth-

ers back for a specified term. There are certainly Signs in that for people who reflect. Az-Zumar 42

11. It is We who give life and cause to die and We are the Inheritor. Al-Hijr 23

12. He (Allah) gives life and causes to die and you will be returned to Him. Yunus 56

13. Wherever you are, death will catch up with you, even if you are in impregnable fortresses. If a good thing happens to them, they say, 'This has come from Allah.' But if a bad thing happens to them, they say, 'This has come from you.' Say, 'Everything comes from Allah.' What is the matter with these people that they scarcely understand a single word? An-Nisa 78

14. You who have iman! when one of you is near to death and makes a will, two just men from among you should act as witnesses; or, if you are travelling when the misfortune of death occurs, two men who are strangers to you. You should detain them after salat and, if you are doubtful, they should swear by Allah: 'We will not sell it for any price, even to a near relative, and we will not conceal the testimony of Allah. If we did we would indeed be wrongdoers.'

15. If it then comes to light that the two of them have merited the allegation of wrongdoing, two others who have the most right to do so should take their place and swear by Allah: 'Our testimony is truer than their testimony. We have not committed perjury. If we had we would indeed be wrongdoers.'

16. That makes it more likely that they will give their evidence properly or be afraid that their oaths will be refuted by subsequent oaths. Have taqwa of Allah and listen carefully. Allah does not guide deviant people. Al-Ma'ida 106-108

17. Say: 'I possess no power to harm or help myself except as Allah wills. Every nation has an appointed time. When their appointed time comes, they cannot delay it a single hour or bring it forward.' Yunus 49

18. Say: 'The Angel of Death, who has been given charge of you, will take you back and then you will be sent back to your Lord.' As-Sajda 11

The Creation

19. The throes of death come revealing the truth. That is what you were trying to evade! Qaf 19

20. Everyone on it [the earth] will pass away. Ar-Rahman 26

21. Why then, when death reaches his throat and you are at that moment looking on – and We are nearer him than you but you cannot see – why then, if you are not subject to Our command, do you not send it back if you are telling the truth? Al-Waqi'a 86-90

22. Say: 'Death, from which you are fleeing, will certainly catch up with you. Then you will be returned to the Knower of the Unseen and the Visible and He will inform you about what you did.' Al-Jumu'a 8

23. Allah will not give anyone more time, once their time has come. Allah is aware of what you do. Al-Munafiqun 11

24. ...When Allah's time comes it cannot be deferred, if you only knew.'. Nuh 4

25. No indeed! When it reaches the gullet and he hears the words, 'Who can heal him now?' and he knows it is indeed the final parting, and one leg is entwined with the other: that Day he will be driven to your Lord. Al-Qiyama 26-30

26. ...If you could only see the wrongdoers in the throes of death when the angels are stretching out their hands, saying, 'Disgorge your own selves! Today you will be repaid with the punishment of humiliation for saying something other than the truth about Allah, and being arrogant about His Signs.' Al-An'am 94

27. Who could do greater wrong than someone who invents lies against Allah or denies His Signs? Such people's portion of the Book will catch up with them so that when Our messengers come to them to take them in death, saying, 'Where are those you called upon besides Allah?' they will say, 'They have forsaken us,' testifying against themselves that they were kuffar. Al-A'raf 37

28. No nation can advance its appointed time nor can they delay it. Al-Hijr 5

29. Have they not looked into the dominions of the heavens and the earth and what Allah has created, and seen that it may well be that their appointed time is near? In what discourse after this will they have iman? Al-A'raf 185

30. It is He who created you from clay and then decreed a fixed term, and another fixed term is specified with Him. Yet you still have doubts! Al-An'am 2

People

Friends

1. The muminun should not take kafirun as friends rather than muminun. Anyone who does that has nothing to do with Allah at all – unless it is because you are afraid of them. Allah advises you to be afraid of Him. Allah is the final destination. Al 'Imran 28
2. You who have iman! do not take any outside yourselves as intimates. They will do anything to harm you. They love what causes you distress. Hatred has appeared out of their mouths, but what their breasts hide is far worse. We have made the Signs clear to you if you use your intellect. Al 'Imran 118
3. Do those who take the kafirun as protectors, rather than the muminun, hope to find power and strength with them? Power and strength belong entirely to Allah. An-Nisa 139.
4. You who have iman! do not take the kafirun as friends rather than the muminun. Do you want to give Allah clear proof against you? An-Nisa 143. See also an-Nisa 144
5. You who have iman! do not take the Jews and Christians as your friends; they are the friends of one another. Any of you who takes them as friends is one of them. Allah does not guide wrongdoing people. Al-Ma'ida 51
6. Or did you suppose that you would be left without Allah knowing those of you who have done jihad and who have not taken anyone as their intimate friends besides Allah and His Messenger and the muminun? Allah is aware of what you do. At-Tawba 16
7. Abandon those who have turned their deen into a game and a diversion and who have been deluded by the life of the dunya. Remind by it lest a person is delivered up to destruction for what he has earned with no protector or intercessor besides Allah. Al-An'am 70
8. If they had had iman in Allah and the Prophet and what has been sent down to him, they would not have taken them [those who are kafir] as friends. But most of them are deviators. Al-Ma'ida 81
9. Your friend is only Allah and His Messenger and those who

have iman: those who establish salat and pay zakat, and bow. Al-Ma'ida 55

10. As for those who make Allah their friend, and His Messenger and those who have iman: it is the party of Allah who are victorious! Al-Ma'ida 56

11. You who have iman! do not take as friends any of those given the Book before you or the kuffar who make a mockery and a game out of your deen. Have taqwa of Allah if you are muminun. Al-Ma'ida 57

12. When you call to salat they [who are kafir] make a mockery and a game of it. That is because they are people who do not use their intellect. Al-Ma'ida 58

13. Do you not see those who have turned to people with whom Allah is angry? They belong neither to you nor to them. And they swear to falsehood and do so knowingly. Al-Mujadila 14

14. You will not find people who have iman in Allah and the Last Day having love for anyone who opposes Allah and His Messenger, though they be their fathers, their sons, their brothers or their clan. Allah has inscribed iman upon such people's hearts and will reinforce them with a Ruh from Him and admit them into Gardens with rivers flowing under them, remaining in them timelessly, for ever. Allah is pleased with them and they are pleased with Him. Such people are the party of Allah. Truly it is the party of Allah who are successful. Al-Mujadila 22

15. You who have iman! do not take My enemy and your enemy as friends, showing love for them when they have rejected... Al-Mumtahana 1

16. Allah merely forbids you from taking as friends those who have fought you in the deen and driven you from your homes and who supported your expulsion. Any who take them as friends are wrongdoers. Al-Mumtahana 9

17. You who have iman! do not make friends of people with whom Allah is angry, who have despaired of the akhira as the kafirun have despaired of the inhabitants of the graves. Al-Mumtahana 13

18. There you are, loving them when they do not love you, even

People

though you have iman in all the Books. When they meet you, they say, 'We have iman.' But when they leave they bite their fingers out of rage against you. Say, 'Die in your rage.' Allah knows what your hearts contain. Al 'Imran 119

19. Do not take any of them as friends until they have made hijra in the Way of Allah. An-Nisa 89

20. You will find that the people most hostile to those who have iman are the Jews and the mushrikun. You will find the people most affectionate to those who have iman are those who say, 'We are Christians.' That is because some of them are priests and monks and because they are not arrogant. Al-Ma'ida 82

21. You who have iman, do not befriend your fathers and brothers if they prefer kufr to iman. Those among you who do befriend them are wrongdoers. At-Tawba 23

22. Allah does not forbid you from being good to those who have not fought you in the deen or driven you from your homes, or from being just towards them. Allah loves those who are just. Al-Mumtahana 8

23. The men and women of the muminun are friends of one another. They command what is right and forbid what is wrong, and establish salat and pay zakat,... At-Tawba 71

24. Say: 'If your fathers or your sons or your brothers or your wives or your tribe, or any wealth you have acquired, or any business you fear may slump, or any house which pleases you, are dearer to you than Allah and His Messenger and doing jihad in His Way, then wait until Allah brings about His command. Allah does not guide people who are deviators.' At-Tawba 23

Mumin and Kafir

1. The likeness of the two groups [muminun and kafirun] is that of the blind and deaf and the seeing and hearing. Are they the same as one another? So will you not pay heed? Hud 24

2. The blind and seeing are not the same nor are darkness and light nor are cool shade and fierce heat. The living and dead are not the same. Allah makes anyone He wills hear but you cannot make those in the grave hear. Fatir 19-22

3. The blind and the seeing are not the same. Nor are those who have iman and do right actions the same as evildoers. What little heed they pay! Al-Mumin 57-58

4. Say: 'Who is the Lord of the heavens and the earth?' Say: 'Allah.' Say: 'So why have you taken protectors apart from Him who possess no power to help or harm themselves?' Say: 'Are the blind and seeing equal? Or are darkness and light the same? Or have they assigned partners to Allah who create as He creates, so that all creating seems the same to them?' Say: 'Allah is the Creator of everything. He is the One, the All-Conquering.' Ar-Ra'd 17-18

5. He sends down water from the sky and river-beds fill up and flow according to their size, and the floodwater carries with it an increasing layer of scum; a similar kind of scum comes from what you heat up in the fire, when you desire to make jewellery or other things. That is how Allah depicts the true and the false. As for the scum, it is quickly swept away. But as for that which is of use to people, it remains behind in the ground. That is a metaphor which Allah has made. Ar-Ra'd 19

6. Is he whose breast is opened to Islam, and who is therefore illuminated by his Lord . . . ? Woe to those whose hearts are hardened against the remembrance of Allah! Such people are clearly misguided. Az-Zumar 22

7. The metaphor of those who reject their Lord is that their actions are like ashes scattered by strong winds on a stormy day. They have no power at all over anything they have earned. That is extreme misguidance. Ibrahim 18

8. Do you do not see how Allah makes a metaphor of a good word: a good tree whose roots are firm and whose branches are in heaven? It bears fruit regularly by its Lord's permission. Allah makes metaphors for people so that hopefully they will pay heed. Ibrahim 24-25

9. The metaphor of a corrupt word is that of a rotten tree, uprooted on the surface of the earth. It has no staying-power. Ibrahim 26

10. But the actions of those who are kafir are like a mirage in the desert. A thirsty man thinks it is water but when he reaches it, he

finds it to be nothing at all, but he finds Allah there. He will pay him his account in full. Allah is swift at reckoning. An-Nur 39

11. Or they are like the darkness of a fathomless sea which is covered by waves above which are waves above which are clouds, layers of darkness, one upon the other. If he puts out his hand, he can scarcely see it. Those Allah gives no light to, they have no light. An-Nur 40

12. Allah makes those who have iman firm with the Firm Word in the life of the dunya and the akhira. But Allah misguides the wrongdoers. Allah does whatever He wills. Ibrahim 27

13. When Our Signs are recited to them – Clear Signs – you can detect denial in the faces of those who are kafir. They all but assault those who recite Our Signs to them!... Al-Hajj 72

14. No self knows the delight that is hidden away for it in recompense for what it used to do. Is someone who has iman like someone who is a deviator? They are not the same! As for those who have iman and do right actions, they will have the Gardens of Safe Refuge as hospitality for what they used to do. But as for those who are deviators, their refuge is the Fire. Every time that they want to get out, they are put straight back into it again and they are told, 'Taste the punishment of the Fire, which you denied.' As-Sajda 17-20

15. On the Day you see the men and women of the muminun, with their light streaming out in front of them, and to their right: 'Good news for you today of Gardens with rivers flowing under them, remaining in them timelessly, for ever. That is the Great Victory.' That Day the men and women of the munafiqun will say to those who have iman, 'Wait for us so that we can borrow some of your light.' They will be told, 'Go back and look for light!' And a wall will be erected between them with a gate in it, on the inside of which there will be mercy but before whose exterior lies the punishment... Al-Hadid 12-13

16. That is because Allah is the Protector of those who have iman and because those who are kafir have no protector. Muhammad 11

17. Is it not likely that, if you did turn away [from fighting jihad], you would cause corruption in the earth and sever your ties of kinship? Muhammad 22

18. It is He who sent down serenity into the hearts of the muminun thereby increasing their iman with more iman – the legions of the heavens and the earth belong to Allah. Allah is All-Knowing, All-Wise. Al-Fath 4

19. The muminun are only those who have had iman in Allah and His Messenger and then have had no doubt and have done jihad with their wealth and themselves in the Way of Allah. They are the ones who are true to their word. Al-Hujurat 15

20. Those who have iman in Allah and His Messengers – such people are the truly sincere – and the martyrs who are with their Lord will receive their wages and their light. But those who are kafir and deny Our Signs, will be Companions of the Blazing Fire. Al-Hadid 19

21. There are certainly Signs in the earth for people with certainty; and in yourselves as well. Do you not then see? Adh-Dhariyat 20-21

22. Allah is not ashamed to make an example of a gnat or of an even smaller thing. As for those who have iman, they know it is the truth from their Lord. But as for those who are kafir, they say, 'What does Allah mean by this example?' He misguides many by it and guides many by it. But He only misguides the deviators. Al-Baqara 26

23. Do not give up and do not be downhearted. You shall be uppermost if you are muminun. Al 'Imran 139

24. You who have iman! if you obey those who are kafir, they will turn you round on your heels and you will be transformed into losers. Al 'Imran 149

25. Those who sell iman for kufr do not harm Allah in any way. They will have a painful punishment. Those who are kafir should not imagine that the extra time We grant to them is good for them. We only allow them more time so they will increase in evildoing. They will have a humiliating punishment. Al 'Imran 177-178

26. Those who reject Allah and His Messengers and desire to cause division between Allah and His Messengers, saying, 'We have iman in some and reject the others,' wanting to take a pathway in between, such people are the true kuffar. We have prepared a humiliating punishment for the kuffar. An-Nisa 150-151

People

27. But those of them who are firmly rooted in knowledge, and the muminun, have iman in what has been sent down to you and what was sent down before you: those who establish salat and pay zakat, and have iman in Allah and the Last Day – We will pay such people an immense wage. An-Nisa 162

28. Mankind! the Messenger has brought you the truth from your Lord, so it is better for you to have iman. But if you are kafir, everything in the heavens and the earth belongs to Allah. Allah is All-Knowing, All-Wise. An-Nisa 170

29. As for those who have iman in Allah and hold fast to Him, He will admit them into mercy and favour from Him and will guide them to Him on a straight path. An-Nisa 175

30. Allah does not guide the people of the kafirun. Al-Ma'ida 67

31. Those who deny Our Signs are deaf and dumb in utter darkness. Allah misguides whoever He wills, and puts whoever He wills on a straight path. Al-An'am 39

32. In calamity you call upon Allah; so if He pleases He removes that calamity from you. Al-An'am 41

33. Say: 'Are the blind the same as those who can see? Al-An'am 50

34. Is someone who was dead and whom We brought to life, supplying him with a light by which to walk among people, the same as someone who is in utter darkness, unable to emerge from it? That is how what they were doing is made to seem attractive to the kafirun. Al-An'am 123

35. Those who kill their children foolishly without any knowledge and make what Allah has provided for them haram, inventing lies against Allah, such people are lost. They are misguided. They are not guided. Al-An'am 141

36. But as for those who reject Our Signs and are arrogant regarding them, they are the Companions of the Fire, remaining in it timelessly, for ever. Al-A'raf 36

37. Who could do greater wrong than someone who invents lies against Allah or denies His Signs? Al-A'raf 35

38. As for those who denied Our Signs and the encounter of the akhira, their actions will come to nothing. Will they be repaid except for what they did? Al-A'raf 147

39. They swear to you by Allah in order to please you, but it would be more fitting for them to please Allah and His Messenger if they are muminun. At-Tawba 62

40. They swear by Allah that they said nothing, but they definitely spoke the word of kufr and returned to kufr after their Islam. They planned something which they did not achieve and they were vindictive for no other cause than that Allah and His Messenger had enriched them from His bounty. If they were to make tawba, it would be better for them. But if they turn away, Allah will punish them with a painful punishment in the dunya and the akhira, and they will not find any protector or helper on the earth. At-Tawba 74

41. Those who respond to their Lord will receive the best. But as for those who do not respond to Him, even if they owned everything on the earth and the same again with it, they would offer it as a ransom. They will receive an evil Reckoning. Their shelter will be Hell. What an evil resting-place! Ar-Ra'd 18

42. The muminun are those who have iman in Allah and His Messenger and who, when they are with him on a matter of common concern, do not leave until they have asked him for permission. Those people who ask you for permission are the ones who truly have iman in Allah and His Messenger. If they ask your permission to attend to their own affairs, give permission to any of them you please; and ask Allah's forgiveness for them. Allah is Ever-Forgiving, Most Merciful. Do not make the Messenger's summoning of you the same as your summoning of one another. Allah knows those of you who sneak away. Those who oppose his command should beware of a testing trial coming to them or a painful punishment striking them. An-Nur 60-61

43. As for those who do not have iman in the akhira, We have made their actions appear good to them and they wander about blindly. Such people will receive an evil punishment and will be the greatest losers in the akhira. An-Naml 4-5

44. Allah knows those who have iman and He knows the munafiqun. Al-'Ankabut 11

45. When Allah is mentioned on His own, the hearts of those

who do not believe in the akhira shrink back shuddering, but when others apart from Him are mentioned, they jump for joy. Az-Zumar 45

46. ... He may admit the men and women of the muminun into Gardens with rivers flowing under them... Al-Fath 5

47. And so that He might punish the men and women of the munafiqun and the men and women of the mushrikun – those who think bad thoughts about Allah.... Al-Fath 6

48. Or were they created out of nothing, or are they the creators? Or did they create the heavens and the earth? No, in truth they have no certainty. Or do they possess the treasuries of your Lord or do they have control of them? Or do they have a ladder on which they listen? Then let their listener bring clear evidence. Or does He have daughters whereas they have sons? Or do you ask them for a wage so they are weighed down with debt? Or is the Unseen in their hands so they can write out what is to happen? Or do they desire to dupe you? But the duped ones are those who are kafir. Or do they have some god other than Allah? Glory be to Allah above any idol they propose! If they saw a lump of heaven falling down, they would just say, 'Banked-up clouds!' At-Tur 33-42

49. And those who do wrong will have a punishment besides that but most of them do not know it. At-Tur 45

50. Those who do not have iman in the akhira give the angels female names. An-Najm 27

51. And what is the matter with you with you that you do not have iman in Allah, when the Messenger calls you to have iman in your Lord, and He has made a covenant with you if you are muminun? Al-Hadid 8

52. The Companions of the Fire and the Companions of the Garden are not the same. It is the Companions of the Garden who are the victors. Al-Hashr 20

53. You who have iman! safeguard yourselves and your families from a Fire whose fuel is people and stones. Harsh, terrible angels are in charge of it who do not disobey Allah in respect of any order He gives them and carry out what they are ordered to do. At-Tahrim 6

54. 'You who are kafir! do not try to excuse yourselves today. You are merely being repaid for what you did.' At-Tahrim 7

55. You who have iman! make tawba to Allah. It may be that your Lord will erase your bad actions from you and admit you into Gardens with rivers flowing under them on the Day when Allah will not disgrace the Prophet and those who had iman along with him. Their light will stream out ahead of them and on their right. They will say, 'Our Lord, perfect our light for us and forgive us! You have power over all things.' At-Tahrim 8

56. Who is there who could be a force for you, to come to your support, apart from the All-Merciful? The kafirun are only living in delusion. Who is there who could provide for you if He withholds His provision? Yet still they obstinately persist in insolence and evasion. Who is better guided: he who goes grovelling on his face or he who walks upright on a Straight Path? Al-Mulk 20-22

57. Say: 'He is the All-Merciful. We have iman in Him and trust in Him. You will soon know who is clearly misguided.' Say: 'What do you think? If, one morning, your water disappears into the earth who will bring you running water?' Al-Mulk 29-30

58. Your Lord knows best who is misguided from His Way and He knows best those who are guided. Al-Qalam 7

59. But do not obey any vile swearer of oaths, any backbiter, slandermonger, impeder of good, evil aggressor, gross, coarse and furthermore, despicable, simply because he possesses wealth and sons. When Our Signs are recited to him, he says, 'Just myths of the previous peoples!' We will brand him on the snout! Al-Qalam 10-16

60. Would We make the Muslims the same as the evildoers? Al-Qalam 35

61. Those who did evil used to laugh at those who had iman. When they passed by them, they would wink at one another. When they returned to their families, they would make a joke of them. When they saw them, they would say, 'Those people are misguided.' But they were not sent as guardians over them. So today those who have iman are laughing at the kuffar, on couches,

People

gazing in wonder. Have the kuffar been rewarded for what they did? Al-Mutaffifin 29-34 and 36

62. So bear with the kafirun – bear with them for a while. At-Tariq 17

63. But as for anyone who turns away and is kafir, Allah will punish him with the Greatest Punishment. Certainly it is to Us they will return. Then their Reckoning is Our concern. Al-Ghashiya 23-26

64. Those who reject Our signs, they are the Companions of the Left. Above them is a sealed vault of Fire. Al-Balad 19-20

65. Anyone who rejects false gods and has iman in Allah has grasped the Firmest Handhold, which will never give way. Allah is All-Hearing, All-Knowing. Al-Baqara 256

66. As for those who are kafir, their wealth and children will not help them against Allah in any way. They are the Companions of the Fire, remaining in it timelessly, for ever. Al 'Imran 116

67. … Say:'Are the blind the same as those who can see? So will you not reflect?' Al-An'am 50

68. They are the ones to whom We gave the Book, Judgement and Prophethood. If these people reject it, We have already entrusted it to a people who did not. Al-An'am 92

69. 'Clear insights have come to you from your Lord. Whoever sees clearly, does so to his own benefit. Whoever is blind, it is to his own detriment. I am not here as your keeper.' Al-An'am 104

70. But as for those who deny Our Signs, We will lead them, step by step, into destruction from where they do not know. I will give them more time. My strategy is sure. Al-A'raf 182-183

71. Those who are kafir spend their wealth barring access to the Way of Allah. They will spend it; then they will regret it; then they will be overthrown. Those who are kafir will be gathered into Hell, so that Allah can sift the bad out from the good, and pile the bad on top of one another, heaping them all together, and tip them into Hell. They are the lost. Al-Anfal 36-37

72. …Their bad actions are made to seem good to them. Allah does not guide kafir people. At-Tawba 37

73. Among them there are some who listen to you. But can you make the deaf hear even though they cannot understand? Among

them there are some who look at you. But can you guide the blind, even though they cannot see? Yunus 42-43

74. Allah makes another metaphor: two men, one of them deaf and dumb, unable to do anything, a burden on his master, no matter where he directs him he brings no good, is he the same as someone who commands justice and is on a straight path? An-Nahl 76

75. There is no city We will not destroy before the Day of Rising, or punish with a terrible punishment. That is inscribed in the Book. Bani Isra'il 58

76. Those who are blind in the dunya will be blind in the akhira and even further off the Path. Bani Isra'il 72

77. But those who do not have iman in the akhira recoil from the path. Al-Muminun 73

78. He neither affirmed the truth nor did he do salat, but rather denied the truth and turned away, and then went off to his family, swaggering. Al-Qiyama 31-33

79. But those who have iman have greater love for Allah. Al-Baqara 165

80. The likeness of those who are kafir is that of someone who yells out to something which cannot hear – it is nothing but a cry and a call. Deaf – dumb – blind. They do not use their intellect. Al-Baqara 171

81. [Christians who have iman say]: 'How could we not have iman in Allah, and the truth that has come to us, when we long for our Lord to include us among the salihun?' Al-Ma'ida 84

82. The punishment will fall on those who deny Our Signs because they were deviators. Al-An'am 49

83. ...if they (the mushrikun) get the upper hand over you, they will respect neither kinship nor treaty. They please you with their mouths but their hearts belie their words. Most of them are deviators. At-Tawba 8

84. As for any of you who revert from their deen and die kafir, their actions will come to nothing in the dunya and the akhira. They are the Companions of the Fire, remaining in it timelessly, for ever. Al-Baqara 217

85. A group of the People of the Book say, '...Do not trust anyone except for those who follow your deen.' Al 'Imran 71-72

86. It is He who supported you with His help and with the muminun, and unified their hearts. Even if you had spent everything on the earth, you could not have unified their hearts. But Allah has unified them. He is Almighty, All-Wise. Al-Anfal 63-64

87. As for those who have iman and then return to kufr, and then again have iman and then return to kufr, and then increase in kufr, Allah will not forgive them or guide them on any path. An-Nisa 137

88. As for those who reject Allah's Signs, Allah is swift at reckoning. Al 'Imran 19

89. They do not measure Allah with His true measure. Allah is All-Strong, Almighty. Al-Hajj 74

The Muminun

1. The steadfast, the truthful, the obedient, the givers, and those who seek forgiveness before dawn. Al 'Imran 17

2. The muminun are those whose hearts tremble when Allah is mentioned, whose iman is increased when His Signs are recited to them, and who put their trust in their Lord. Al-Anfal 2

3. Those who establish salat and give of what We have provided for them. They are in truth the muminun. They have high ranks with their Lord and forgiveness and generous provision. Al-Anfal 3-4

4. Those who have iman in Allah and the Last Day do not ask you to excuse them from doing jihad with their wealth and themselves. Allah knows the people who have taqwa.. At-Tawba 44

5. The men and women of the muminun are friends of one another. They command what is right and forbid what is wrong, and establish salat and pay zakat, and obey Allah and His Messenger. They are the people on whom Allah will have mercy. Allah is Almighty, All-Wise. At-Tawba 71

6. (Successful are:) Those who make tawba, those who worship, those who praise, those who fast, those who bow, those who prostrate, those who command the right, those who forbid the wrong, those who preserve the limits of Allah: give good news to the muminun. At-Tawba 112

7. When the Signs of the All-Merciful were recited to them they [the prophets] fell on their faces, weeping, in prostration. Maryam 58

8. We wrote down in the Zabur, after the Reminder came: 'It is My slaves who are salihun who will inherit the earth.' Al-Anbiya 105

9. ...Give good news to the humble-hearted, whose hearts quake at the mention of Allah, and who are steadfast in the face of all that happens to them, those who establish salat and give of what We have provided for them. Al-Hajj 35

10. It is the muminun who are successful: those who are humble in their salat; those who turn away from worthless talk; those who pay zakat; those who guard their private parts. Al-Muminun 1-5

11. ...those who honour their trusts and their contracts; those who safeguard their salat. Al-Muminun 8-9

12. The reply of the muminun when they are summoned to Allah and His Messenger so that he can judge between them, is to say, 'We hear and we obey.' They are ones who are successful. An-Nur 51

13. The faithful slaves of the Beneficent are those who walk upon the earth modestly and when the foolish ignorant ones speak to them foolish talks, they only answer "Peace".

14. They spend the nights before their Lord prostrating and standing in humbleness and respectful.

15. They pray to their Lord to save them from the doom of hell.

16. When they spend, they are neither spend thrift nor miser. They choose the middle path.

17. ...those who pass the night prostrating and standing before their Lord; those who say, 'Our Lord, avert from us the punishment of Hell, its punishment is inescapable pain. It is indeed an evil lodging and abode'; those who, when they spend, are neither extravagant nor mean, but take a stance mid way between the two; those who do not call on any other god together with Allah and do not kill anyone Allah has made inviolate, except with the right to do so, and do not fornicate; anyone who does that will receive an evil punishment and on the Day of Rising

People

his punishment will be doubled and he will be humiliated in it timelessly, for ever, except for those who make tawba and have iman and act rightly: Allah will transform the wrong actions of such people into good – Allah is Ever-Forgiving, Most Merciful. Al-Furqan 64-70

18. Certainly all who make tawba and act rightly have turned sincerely towards Allah. Al-Furqan 71

19. ...those who do not bear false witness and who, when they pass by worthless talk, pass by with dignity; those who, when they are reminded of the Signs of their Lord, do not turn their backs, deaf and blind to them; those who say, 'Our Lord, give us joy in our wives and children and make us a good example for those who have taqwa'. Al-Furqan 72-74

20. Their sides eschew their beds as they call on their Lord in fear and ardent hope. And they give of what We have provided for them. As-Sajda 16

21. What of him who spends the night hours in prayer, prostrating and standing up, mindful of the akhira, hoping for the mercy of his Lord? Say: 'Are they the same – those who know and those who do not know?' It is only people of intelligence who pay heed. Az-Zumar 9

22. Those who listen well to what is said and follow the best of it, they are the ones whom Allah has guided, they are the people of intelligence. Az-Zumar 18

23. ...those who avoid major wrong actions and indecencies and who, when they are angered, then forgive; those who respond to their Lord and establish salat, and manage their affairs by mutual consultation and give of what We have provided for them; those who, when they are wronged, defend themselves. The repayment of a bad action is one equivalent to it. But if someone pardons and puts things right, his reward is with Allah. Certainly He does not love wrongdoers. Ash-Shura 36-40

24. But if someone is steadfast and forgives, that is the most resolute course to follow. Ash-Shura 40

25. The people with taqwa will be among Gardens and Fountains, receiving what their Lord has given them. Certainly before that

they were good-doers. The part of the night they spent asleep was small and they would seek forgiveness before the dawn. And beggars and the destitute received a due share of their wealth. Adh-Dhariyat 15-19

26. They fulfil their vows and fear a Day whose evil will spread far and wide. They give food, despite their love for it, to the poor and orphans and captives: 'We feed you only out of desire for the Face of Allah. We do not want any repayment from you or any thanks. Truly We fear from our Lord a glowering, calamitous Day.' So Allah has safeguarded them from the evil of that Day and has made them meet with radiance and pure joy. Ad-Dahr 7-11

27. ...those who, if We establish them firmly on the earth, will establish salat and pay zakat, and command what is right and forbid what is wrong... Al-Hajj 41

28. ...those who fulfil Allah's contract and do not break their agreement; those who join what Allah has commanded to be joined and are afraid of their Lord and fear an evil Reckoning; those who are steadfast in seeking the face of their Lord, and establish salat and give from the provision We have given them, secretly and openly, and stave off evil with good, it is they who will have the Ultimate Abode – Gardens of Eden which they will enter, and all of their parents, wives and children who were salihun... Ar-Ra'd 22-25

29. Those who are filled with the fear of their Lord, those who have iman in the Signs of their Lord, those who do not associate anything with their Lord, those who give what they have given, their hearts fearful of their return to their Lord, such people are truly racing towards good things, and they are the first to reach them. Al-Muminun 58-62

30. Men and women who are Muslims, men and women who are muminun, men and women who are obedient, men and women who are truthful, men and women who are steadfast, men and women who are humble, men and women who give sadaqa, men and women who fast, men and women who guard their private parts, men and women who remember Allah much: Allah has prepared forgiveness for them and an immense reward. Al-Ahzab 35

31. And who speaks better than he who calls to Allah while he himself does good and say: I am surely of those who submit. Ha Mim 33
32. You who have iman! if any of you renounce your deen, Allah will bring forward a people whom He loves and who love Him, humble to the muminun, fierce to the kafirun, who do jihad in the Way of Allah and do not fear the blame of any censurer. That is the unbounded favour of Allah which He gives to whoever He wills. Allah is Boundless, All-Knowing. Al-Ma'ida 54
33. When those who have taqwa of Allah are asked, 'What has your Lord sent down?' their reply is, 'Good!' There is good in the dunya for those who do good, and the abode of the akhira is even better. How wonderful is the abode of those who have taqwa An-Nahl 30
34. ...They outdid each other in good actions, calling out to Us in yearning and in awe, and humbling themselves to Us. Al-Anbiya 90
35. ...You see them bowing and prostrating, seeking Allah's good favour and His pleasure. Their mark is on their faces, the traces of prostration. That is their likeness in the Torah. And their likeness in the Injil... Al-Fath 29
36. Truly man was created headstrong – desperate when bad things happen, begrudging when good things come, except for those who do salat and who are constant in it, those in whose wealth there is a known share for beggars and the destitute, those who affirm the Day of Judgement, those who are fearful of the punishment of their Lord (no one is safe from the punishment of his Lord) those who guard their private parts except from their wives and any slaves they own, in which case they incur no blame, but if anyone desires any more than that, they have overstepped the limits, those who honour their trusts and contracts, those who stand by their testimony, those who safeguard their salat. Such people will be in Gardens, highly honoured. Al-Ma'arij 19-35
37. No indeed! The book of the truly good is in 'Illiyun. And what will convey to you what 'Illiyun is? A clearly written book. Those brought near will witness it. The truly good will be in perfect Bliss on couches gazing in wonder. You will recognise in their faces the radiance of delight. Al-Mutaffifin 18-24

38. ...Their father was one of the salihun and your Lord wanted them to come of age and then to unearth their treasure as a mercy from Him... Al-Kahf 82
39. Among the people of Musa there is a group who guide by the truth and act justly in accordance with it. Al-A'raf 159
40. Allah loves the good-doers. Al-Baqara 195 & Al 'Imran 134

The People of the Book

1. They are not all the same. There is a community among the People of the Book who are upright. They recite Allah's Signs throughout the night, and they prostrate. Al 'Imran 113
2. Among the people of the Book there are some who have iman in Allah and in what has been sent down to you and what was sent down to them, and who are humble before Allah. Al 'Imran 199-200
3. When Allah said, "Isa, I will take you back and raise you up to Me and purify you of those who are kafir. And I will place the people who follow you above those who are kafir until the Day of Rising. Then you will all return to Me, and I will judge between you regarding the things about which you differed. Al 'Imran 54
4. ... and their saying, 'We killed the Messiah, 'Isa son of Maryam, Messenger of Allah.' They did not kill him and they did not crucify him but it was made to seem so to them. Those who argue about him are in doubt about it. They have no real knowledge of it, just conjecture. But they certainly did not kill him. Allah raised him up to Himself. Allah is Almighty, All-Wise. An-Nisa 157-158
5. We gave Musa nine Clear Signs... Bani Isra'il 101
6. Do you really hope they [the People of the Book] will follow you in iman when a group of them heard Allah's Word and then, after grasping it, knowingly distorted it? Al-Baqara 75
7. We gave Musa the Book – be in no doubt about the meeting with him – and made it a guidance for the tribe of Israel. As-Sajda 23
8. We wrote about everything for him [Musa] on the Tablets as an admonition and making all things clear. 'Seize hold of it vigorously and command your people to adopt the best in it.' Al-A'raf 145

9. This is a communication to be transmitted to mankind so that they may be warned by it and so that they will know that He is One God and so that people of intelligence will pay heed. Ibrahim 52

Parents

1. Be good to your parents and relatives ... An-Nisa 36
2. Your Lord has decreed that you should worship none but Him, and that you should show kindness to your parents. Whether one or both of them reach old age with you, do not say 'Ugh!' to them out of irritation and do not be harsh with them but speak to them with gentleness and generosity. Take them under your wing, out of mercy, with due humility and say: 'Lord, show mercy to them as they did in looking after me when I was small.' Bani Isra'il 23-24
3. We have instructed man to honour his parents, but if they endeavour to make you associate with Me something about which you have no knowledge, do not obey them. Al-'Ankabu/t 8
4. We have instructed man concerning his parents. Bearing him caused his mother great debility and the period of his weaning was two years: 'Give thanks to Me and to your parents. I am your final destination. But if they try to make you associate something with Me about which you have no knowledge, do not obey them. Keep company with them correctly and courteously in this world but follow the Way of him who turns to Me...' Luqman 14-15
5. We have instructed man to be good to his parents. His mother bore him with difficulty and with difficulty gave birth to him; and his bearing and weaning take thirty months. Then when he achieves his full strength and reaches forty, he says, 'My Lord, keep me thankful for the blessing You bestowed on me and on my parents, and keep me acting rightly, pleasing You. And make my descendants salihun. I have made tawba to You and I am truly one of the Muslims.' Al-Ahqaf 15
6. ...that you are good to your parents... Al-An'am 152
7. ... and be good to your parents and to relatives and orphans and the very poor. Al-Baqara 83

8. It is prescribed for you, when death approaches one of you and if he has some goods to leave, to make a will in favour of his parents and relatives. Al-Baqara 180 (Abrogated by more detailed ayat on inheritance in Surat an-Nisa' – Ed.)
9. Say, 'Any wealth you give away should go to your parents and relatives ...' Al-Baqara 215
10. ...and [We gave Yahya] devotion to his parents – he was not insolent or disobedient. Maryam 14
11. ...and [He directed me] to show devotion to my mother. He has not made me insolent or arrogant. Maryam 32

Relatives

1. Those who break Allah's contract after it has been agreed, and sever what Allah has commanded to be joined1, and cause corruption on the earth, it is they who are the lost. Al-Baqara 27
2. ...those who join what Allah has commanded to be joined... Ar-Ra'd 21
3. Allah commands justice and doing good and giving to relatives... An-Nahl 90
4. Give your relatives their due... Bani Isra'il 26
5. There is no objection to the blind, no objection to the lame, no objection to the sick nor to yourselves if you eat in your own houses or your fathers' houses or your mothers' houses or your brothers' houses or your sisters' houses or the houses of your paternal uncles or paternal aunts or the houses of your maternal uncles or maternal aunts or places to which you own the keys or those of your friends. There is nothing wrong in your eating together or eating separately... An-Nur 61
6. The Prophet has closer ties to the muminun than their own selves, and his wives are their mothers. But blood-relations have closer ties to one another in the Book of Allah than the muminun and Muhajirun. All the same you should act correctly by your friends; that is inscribed in the Book. Al-Ahzab 6
7. Be good to your parents and relatives... An-Nisa 36

Orphans

1. They will ask you about the property of orphans. Say, 'Managing it in their best interests is best.' If you mix your property with theirs, they are your brothers. Allah knows a squanderer from a good manager. If Allah had wanted, He could have been hard on you. Allah is Almighty, All-Wise. Al-Baqara 220
2. Give orphans their property, and do not substitute bad things for good. Do not assimilate their property into your own. Doing that is a serious crime. An-Nisa 2
3. If you are afraid of not behaving justly towards orphans, then marry other permissible women, two, three or four. An-Nisa 3
4. Keep a close check on orphans until they reach a marriageable age, then if you perceive that they have sound judgement hand over their property to them. Do not consume it extravagantly and precipitately before they come of age. Those who are wealthy should abstain from it altogether. Those who are poor should use it sensibly and correctly. When you hand over their property to them ensure that there are witnesses on their behalf. Allah suffices as a Reckoner. An-Nisa 6
5. If other relatives or orphans or poor people attend the sharing-out, provide for them out of it and speak to them correctly and courteously. An-Nisa 8
6. People who consume the property of orphans wrongfully consume nothing in their bellies except fire. They will roast in a Searing Blaze. An-Nisa 10
7. ...and that you do not go near the property of orphans before they reach maturity – except in a good way. Al-An'am 152
8. Do not go near the property of orphans before they reach maturity, except in a good way. Fulfil your contracts. Contracts will be asked about. Bani Isra'il 32
9. No indeed! You do not honour orphans nor do you urge the feeding of the poor; Al-Fajr 19-20
10. They will ask you for a fatwa about women. Say, 'Allah gives you a fatwa about them; and also what is recited to you in the Book about orphan girls to whom you do not give the inheritance they are owed, while at the same time desiring to marry them;

and also about young children who are denied their rights: that you should act justly with respect to orphans.' Whatever good you do, Allah knows it. An-Nisa 127
11. So as for orphans, do not oppress them. Ad-Duha 9

Differences and Disagreements

1. Those given the Book only differed after knowledge had come to them, envying one another. Al 'Imran 19
2. Why do you argue about something of which you have no knowledge? Allah knows; you do not know. Al 'Imran 66
3. Hold fast to the rope of Allah all together, and do not separate. Remember Allah's blessing to you when you were enemies and He joined your hearts together so that you became brothers by His blessing. Al 'Imran 103
4. Don't be like those who dispersed and argued with each other After the clear proof had come. Al 'Imran 105
5. Say: 'He possesses the power to send you punishment from above your heads or from beneath your feet, or to confuse you in sects and make you taste one another's violence.' Look how We vary the Signs so that hopefully they will understand. Al-An'am 65
6. As for those who divide up their deen and form into sects, you have nothing whatsoever to do with them. Their affair will go back to Allah and then He will inform them about what they did. Al-An'am 160
7. Obey Allah and His Messenger and do not quarrel among yourselves lest you lose heart and your momentum disappear. And be steadfast. Allah is with the steadfast. Al-Anfal 46
8. But they disagreed and split into different sects. Each one will return to Us. Al-Anbiya 93
9. ...Do not be among the mushrikun: those who split up their deen, and form into sects, each faction exulting in what they have. Ar-Rum 30-31
10. 'Establish the deen and do not make divisions in it.' What you call the mushrikun to follow is very hard for them. Allah chooses for Himself anyone He wills and guides to Himself those who

People

turn to Him. They only split up after knowledge came to them, tyrannising one another... Ash-Shura 13-14

11. You who have iman! obey Allah and obey the Messenger and those in command among you. If you have a dispute about something, refer it back to Allah and the Messenger... An-Nisa 59

12. No, by your Lord, they are not muminun until they make you their judge in the disputes that break out between them, and then find no resistance within themselves to what you decide and submit themselves completely. An-Nisa 65

13. Say: 'O Allah, Originator of the heavens and the earth, Knower of the Unseen and the Visible, You will judge between Your slaves regarding what they differed about.' Az-Zumar 46

14. We settled the tribe of Israel in a noble place and gave them good things as provision. They did not differ until knowledge came to them. Your Lord will decide between them on the Day of Rising regarding the things about which they differed. Yunus 93

15. Those who doubt the Hour are greatly misguided. Ash-Shura 18

16. This faith of yours is a single faith and I am your Lord, so have taqwa of Me. But they disagreed and split up, dividing into sects, each party exulting in what it had. Al-Muminun 53-54

17. Among His Signs is the creation of the heavens and the earth and the variety of your languages and colours. There are certainly Signs in that for every being. Ar-Rum 22

18. Mankind! We created you from a male and female, and made you into peoples and tribes so that you might come to know each other. The noblest among you in Allah's sight is the one with the most taqwa. Allah is All-Knowing, All-Aware. Al-Hujurat 13

19. Mankind was a single community. Then Allah sent out Prophets bringing good news and giving warning, and with them He sent down the Book with truth to decide between people regarding their differences. Only those who were given it differed about it, after the Clear Signs had come to them, envying one another. Then, by His permission, Allah guided those who had iman to the truth of that about which they had differed. Allah guides whoever He wills to a straight path. Al-Baqara 213

20. Those who were given the Book did not divide into sects until after the Clear Sign came to them. Al-Bayyina 4

21. We made the Commandments very clear to them and they only differed after knowledge came to them, tyrannising one other. Your Lord will decide between them on the Day of Rising regarding the things they differed about. Al-Jathiya 17

22. ...they will swear, 'We only desired the best.' But Allah bears witness that they are truly liars. At-Tawba 107

Good and Bad Behaviour

One's Own Deeds

1. You are only answerable for yourself. An-Nisa 84
2. … 'I have my actions and you have your actions. You are not responsible for what I do and I am not responsible for what you do.' Yunus 41
3. If you do good, you do it to yourselves. If you do evil, you do it to your detriment… Bani Isra'il 7
4. No burden-bearer can bear another's burden. If someone weighed down calls for help to bear his load, none of it will be borne for him, even by his next of kin. You can only warn those who fear their Lord in the Unseen and establish salat. Whoever is purified, is purified for himself alone. Allah is your final destination. Al-Fatir 18
5. Whoever does an evil act will only be repaid with its equivalent. But whoever acts rightly, male or female, being a mumin, such a person will enter the Garden, provided for in it without any reckoning. Al-Mumin 40
6. Those who join forces for good will receive a reward for it. Those who join forces for evil will be answerable for it. Allah gives all things what they deserve. An-Nisa 85
7. …Allah will certainly help those who help Him – Allah is All-Strong, Almighty, Al-Hajj 40
8. Those who were kafir will find that their kufr was against themselves. Those who did right were making the way easy for themselves; so that He can repay with His bounty those who had iman and did right actions. He certainly does not love the kafirun. Ar-Rum 44-45
9. If anyone commits an evil action the responsibility for it is his alone. Allah is All-Knowing, All-Wise. An-Nisa 111
10. Anyone who does evil will be repaid for it. He will not find any protector or helper besides Allah. An-Nisa 123
11. Whoever is guided is only guided to his own good. Whoever is misguided is only misguided to his detriment. No burden-bearer

can bear another's burden. We never punish until We have sent a Messenger. Bani Isra'il 15

12. Say: 'You will not be asked about any evil we committed and we will not be asked about what you did.' Saba' 25

13. Whoever acts rightly, it is to his own good. Whoever does evil, it is to his detriment. Your Lord does not wrong His slaves. Fussilat 46

14. Whoever acts rightly, it is to his own good. Whoever does evil, it is to his detriment. Then you will be returned to your Lord. Al-Jathiya 15

15. Allah created the heavens and earth with truth so that every self might be repaid for what it earned and they will not be wronged. Al-Jathiya 22

16. And We will unite those who had iman with their offspring, who followed them in iman, and We will not undervalue their own actions in any way. Every man is in pledge for what he earned. At-Tur 21

17. ... no burden-bearer can bear another's burden. An-Najm 37

18. ... man will have nothing but what he strives for; that his striving will most certainly be seen; that he will then receive repayment of the fullest kind; that the ultimate end is with your Lord. An-Najm 38-41

19. ...Allah is our Lord and your Lord. We have our actions and you have your actions... Ash-Shura 15

20. Say: 'Am I to desire other than Allah as Lord when He is the Lord of all things?' What each self earns is for itself alone. No burden-bearer can bear another's burden. Then you will return to your Lord, and He will inform you regarding the things about which you differed. Al-An'am 165

21. Those who are kafir say to those who have iman, 'Follow our way and we will bear the weight of your mistakes.' They will not bear the weight of a single one of their mistakes. Truly they are liars. They will bear their own burdens and other burdens together with their own. On the Day of Rising they will be questioned about what they invented. Al-Ankabut 12-13

Obedience

1. They should therefore respond to Me and believe in Me so that hopefully they will be rightly guided. Al-Baqara 185
2. If they argue with you, say, 'I have submitted myself completely to Allah, and so have all who follow me.' Al 'Imran 20
3. Say, 'If you love Allah, then follow me and Allah will love you and forgive you for your wrong actions. Allah is Ever-Forgiving, Most Merciful.' Al 'Imran 31
4. Obey Allah and the Messenger so that hopefully you will gain mercy. Al 'Imran 132
5. Whoever obeys Allah and the Messenger will be with those whom Allah has blessed: the Prophets and the siddiqun, the martyrs and the salihun. An-Nisa 69
6. We sent no Messenger except to be obeyed by Allah's permission. An-Nisa 64
7. Whoever obeys the Messenger has obeyed Allah. An-Nisa 80
8. Obey Allah and obey the Messenger and beware! Al-Ma'ida 92
9. Follow what has been revealed to you from your Lord –there is no god but Him –and turn away from the mushrikun. Al-An'am 107
10. ...So have iman in Allah and His Messenger, the Unlettered Prophet, who has iman in Allah and His words, and follow him so that hopefully you will be guided. Al-A'raf 158
11. Follow what has been revealed to you... Yunus 109
12. They fear their Lord above them and do everything they are ordered to do. An-Nahl 50
13. Your God is One God so submit to Him. Al-Hajj 34
14. When it is recited to them they say, 'We have iman in it; it is the truth from our Lord. We were already Muslims before it came.' Al-Qasas 53
15. Those who submit themselves completely to Allah and do good have grasped the Firmest Handhold. The end result of all affairs is with Allah. Luqman 22
16. Follow what has been revealed to you from your Lord. Allah is aware of what you do. Al-Ahzab 2
17. You who have iman! obey Allah and obey the Messenger. Do not make your actions of no worth. Muhammad 33

18. If you obey Allah and His Messenger, He will not undervalue your actions in any way. Allah is Ever-Forgiving, Most Merciful.' Al-Hujurat 14
19. ...obey Allah and His Messenger. Allah desires to remove all impurity from you... Al-Ahzab 33
20. You who have iman! enter Islam totally. Do not follow in the footsteps of Shaytan. He is an outright enemy to you. Al-Baqara 206
21. Or did you suppose that you would enter the Garden without facing the same as those who came before you? Poverty and illness afflicted them ... Al-Baqara 212
22. The men and women of the muminun are friends of one another. They command what is right and forbid what is wrong, and establish salat and pay zakat, and obey Allah and His Messenger. They are the people on whom Allah will have mercy. Allah is Almighty, All-Wise. At-Tawba 71
23. ...More fitting for them would be obedience and honourable words.... Muhammad 21-22
24. Say, 'Obey Allah and the Messenger.' Then if they turn away, Allah does not love the kafirun. Al 'Imran 32
25. Then your hearts became hardened after that, so they were like stones or even harder still. There are some stones from which rivers gush out, and others which split open and water pours out, and others which crash down from fear of Allah. Allah is not unaware of what you do. Al-Baqara 74
26. ... everything in the heavens and earth, willingly or unwillingly, submits to Him and to Him you will be returned. Al 'Imran 83
27. You who have iman! enter Islam totally. Al-Baqara 208
28. You who have iman! obey Allah and His Messenger. And do not turn away from him when you are able to hear. Do not be like those who say, 'We hear,' when they do not hear. The worst of beasts in Allah's sight are the deaf and dumb who have no intellect. Al-Anfal 20-22
29. Turn to your Lord and submit to Him before punishment comes upon you, for then you cannot be helped. Az-Zumar 54
30. Follow the best that has been sent down to you from your Lord before the punishment comes upon you suddenly when you are not expecting it. Az-Zumar 55

Behaviour

31. ...Allah does not guide people who are deviators. At-Tawba 25

32. They will say on the Day their faces are rolled over in the Fire, 'If only we had obeyed Allah and obeyed the Messenger!' Al-Ahzab 66

33. ...obey Allah and His Messenger. Allah is aware of what you do. Al-Mujadila 13

34. Obey Allah and obey the Messenger. But if you turn your backs, the Messenger is only responsible for clear transmission. At-Taghabun 12

35. You who have iman! respond to Allah and to the Messenger when He calls you to what will bring you to life! Know that Allah intervenes between a man and his heart and that you will be gathered to Him. Al-Anfal 24

36. Obey Allah and His Messenger and do not quarrel among yourselves lest you lose heart and your momentum disappear. And be steadfast. Allah is with the steadfast. Al-Anfal 47

37. Do you not see that everyone in the heavens and everyone on the earth prostrates to Allah, and the sun and moon and stars and the mountains, trees and beasts and many of mankind? But many of them inevitably merit punishment. Those Allah humiliates will have no one to honour them. Allah does whatever He wills. Al-Hajj 18

38. All who obey Allah and His Messenger and have awe of Allah and taqwa of Him, they are the ones who are victorious. An-Nur 52

39. Say: 'Obey Allah and obey the Messenger. Then if they turn away he is only responsible for what he is charged with and you are responsible for what you are charged with. If you obey him, you will be guided.' The Messenger is only responsible for clear transmission. An-Nur 54

40. All who obey Allah and His Messenger have won a mighty victory. Al-Ahzab 71

41. Everyone in the heavens and earth belongs to Him. All are submissive to Him. Ar-Rum 26

42. Say: 'I fear, were I to disobey my Lord, the punishment of a Terrible Day.' Az-Zumar 13

43. Say: 'It is Allah I worship, making my deen sincerely His.' Az-Zumar 15

44. Say: 'The real losers are those who lose themselves and their families on the Day of Rising.' Is not that clear loss? Az-Zumar 14

45. Mankind! worship your Lord, who created you and those before you, so that hopefully you will have taqwa. Al-Baqara 21

46. Then when guidance comes to you from Me, those who follow My guidance will feel no fear and will know no sorrow. Al-Baqara 38

47. As for those who obey Allah and His Messenger, We will admit them into Gardens with rivers flowing under them, remaining in them timelessly, for ever. That is the Great Victory. An-Nisa 13

48. Turn your face towards the deen in pure natural faith,and on no account be among the mushrikun. Yunus 105

49. ...As for him who disobeys Allah and His Messenger, he will have the Fire of Hell, remaining in it timelessly, for ever and ever.' Al-Jinn 23

50. Every self is held in pledge against what it earned, except for the companions of the Right. In Gardens they will ask the evildoers: 'What caused you to enter Saqar?' They will say, 'We were not among those who did salat and we did not feed the poor. We plunged with those who plunged and denied the Day of Judgment until the Certain came to us.' The intercession of the interceders will not help them. Al-Muddaththir 38-47

51. If you obeyed most of those on earth,they would misguide you from Allah's Way. They follow nothing but conjecture. They are only guessing. Al-An'am 117

52. Restrain yourself patiently with those who call on their Lord morning and evening, desiring His face. Do not turn your eyes from them, desiring the attractions of this world... Al-Kahf 28

53. You who have iman! obey Allah and obey the Messenger and those in command among you. An-Nisa 59

Shirk – association of partners with Allah

1. Allah does not forgive anything being associated with Him but He forgives whoever He wills for anything other than that. Anyone who associates something with Allah has committed a terrible crime. An-Nisa 48

Behaviour

2. Allah does not forgive anything being associated with Him but He forgives whoever He wills for anything other than that. Anyone who associates something with Allah has gone very far astray. An-Nisa 116

3. ...Do not set up another god together with Allah and so be thrown into Hell, blamed and driven out. Bani Isra'il 39

4. Be people of pure natural belief in Allah, not associating anything else with Him. As for anyone who associates others with Allah, it is as though he had fallen from the sky and the birds had seized him and carried him away or the wind had dropped him in a distant place. Al-Hajj 31

5. Do not call on any other god together with Allah... Al-Furqan 68

6. Is there another god besides Allah? Say: 'Bring your proof if you are being truthful.' An-Naml 64

7. Have taqwa of Him and establish salat. Do not be among the mushrikun: those who split up their deen, and form into sects, each faction exulting in what they have. Ar-Rum 30-31

8. But if they [parents] try to make you associate something with Me about which you have no knowledge, do not obey them. Keep company with them correctly and courteously in this world but follow the Way of him who turns to Me. Then you will return to Me and I will inform you about the things you did. Luqman 15

9. He [Shaytan] only has authority over those who take him as a friend and associate others with Allah. An-Nahl 100

10. That is Allah's guidance. He guides by it those of His slaves He wills. If they had associated others with Him, nothing they did would have been of any use. Al-An'am 89

11. If people take protectors besides Him – 'We only worship them so that they may bring us nearer to Allah' – Allah will judge between them regarding the things about which they differed. Allah does not guide anyone who is an ungrateful liar. Az-Zumar 3-4

12. Mankind! an example has been made, so listen to it carefully. Those whom you call upon besides Allah are not even able to create a single fly, even if they were to join together to do it. And if a fly steals something from them, they cannot get it back. How feeble are both the seeker and the sought! Al-Hajj 73

13. If you call on them they will not hear your call, and were they to hear, they would not respond to you. On the Day of Rising they will reject your making associates of them. No one can inform you like One who is All-aware. Mankind! you are the poor in need of Allah whereas Allah is the Rich Beyond Need, the Praiseworthy. If He wills He can dispense with you and bring about a new creation. That is not difficult for Allah. Fatir 14-17

14. The metaphor of those who take protectors besides Allah is that of a spider which builds itself a house; but no house is flimsier than a spider's house, if they only knew. Al-'Ankabut 41

15. He has made an example for you from among yourselves. Are any of the slaves you own partners with you in what We have provided for you so that you are equal in respect of it, you fearing them the same as one another? In that way We make Our Signs clear for people who use their intellect. Ar-Rum 28

16. Do not, then, knowingly make others equal to Allah. Al-Baqara 22

17. Say, 'People of the Book! come to a proposition which is the same for us and you – that we should worship none but Allah and not associate any partners with Him and not take one another as lords besides Allah.' If they turn away, say, 'Bear witness that we are Muslims.' Al 'Imran 64

18. ...But Allah is far above what they associate with Him. Do they make things into partner-gods which cannot create anything and are themselves created; which are not capable of helping them and cannot even help themselves? Al-A'raf 190-191-192

19. Those you call on besides Allah are slaves just like yourselves. Call on them and let them respond to you if you are telling the truth. Al-A'raf 194

20. Those you call on besides Him are not capable of helping you. They cannot even help themselves. If you call them to guidance, they do not hear. You see them looking at you, yet they do not see. Al-A'raf 197-198

21. Say: 'Can any of your partner-gods bring creation out of nothing and then regenerate it?' Say: 'Allah brings creation out of nothing and then regenerates it. So how have you been perverted?' Yunus 34

22. We did not wrong them; rather they wronged themselves. The gods they called upon besides Allah did not help them at all when Allah's command came upon them. They did nothing but increase their ruin. Hud 101

23. How many Signs there are in the heavens and earth! Yet they pass them by, turning away from them. Most of them do not have iman in Allah without associating others with Him. Yusuf 105-106

24. The call of truth is made to Him alone. Those they call upon apart from Him do not respond to them at all. It is like someone stretching out his cupped hands towards water to convey it to his mouth: it will never get there. The call of the kuffar only goes astray. Ar-Ra'd 15

25. What then of Him who is standing over every self seeing everything it does? Yet still they associate others with Allah! Say: 'Name them! Or would you inform Him of something in the earth He does not know, or are they words which are simply guesswork on your part?' However, the plotting of those who are kafir seems good to them and they bar the way. Anyone misguided by Allah has no guide. They will receive punishment in the life of the dunya and the punishment of the akhira is harsher still. They have no defender against Allah. Ar-Ra'd 33-34

26. They have made others equal to Allah to misguide people from His Way. Say: 'Enjoy yourselves! Your destination is the Fire!' Ibrahim 30

27. He is, however, Allah, my Lord, and I will not associate anyone with my Lord. Al-Kahf 38

28. Whoever calls on another god together with Allah, has no grounds for doing so at all and his reckoning is with his Lord. Truly the kafirun have no success. Al-Muminun 117

29. He to whom the kingdom of the heavens and the earth belongs. He does not have a son and He has no partner in the Kingdom. He created everything and determined it most exactly. But they have adopted gods apart from Him which do not create anything but are themselves created. They have no power to harm or help themselves. They have no power over death or life or resurrection. Al-Furqan 2-3

30. When they embark in ships, they call on Allah, making their deen sincerely His, but then when He delivers them safely to the land, they associate others with Him. Al-'Ankabut 65

31. Let them be ungrateful for what We have given them! Let them enjoy themselves – they will soon know! Al-'Ankabut 66

32. Say: 'Call on those you make claims for besides Allah. They have no power over even the smallest particle, either in the heavens or in the earth. They have no share in them. He has no need of their support.' Saba 22

33. Say: 'Show me those you have joined to Him as associates. No indeed! He is Allah, the Almighty, the All-Wise.' Saba 27

34. They have taken gods besides Allah so that perhaps they may be helped. They cannot help them even though they are an army mobilised in their support. Ya Sin 74-75

35. Those who shun the worship of false gods and turn towards Allah will have good news. So give good news to My slaves. Az-Zumar 17

36. Or have they adopted intercessors besides Allah? Say: 'Even though they do not control a thing and have no awareness?' Az-Zumar 43

37. It has been revealed to you and those before you: 'If you associate others with Allah, your actions will come to nothing and you will be among the losers.' Az-Zumar 65

38. Say: 'I was forbidden to worship those you call upon besides Allah when the Clear Signs came to me from my Lord and I was commanded to submit to the Lord of all the worlds.' Al-Mumin 66

39. Those you call upon apart from Him possess no power of intercession – only those who bore witness to the truth and have full knowledge. Az-Zukhruf 86

40. Say: 'Have you thought about those you call upon apart from Allah? Show me what they have created on the earth. Or do they have a partnership in the heavens? Produce a Book for me before this one or a shred of knowledge if you are telling the truth.' Who could be further astray than those who call on other things besides Allah, which will not respond to them until the Day of Rising and which are unaware of their prayers? When mankind is

Behaviour

gathered together, they will be their enemies and will reject their worship. Al-Ahqaf 4-6

41. Do not set up another god together with Allah... Adh-Dhariyat 51

42. Have you really considered al-Lat and al-'Uzza and Manat, the third, the other one? Do you have males and He females? That is a most unfair division! An-Najm 19-22

43. Say: 'I call only upon my Lord and do not associate anyone else with Him.' Al-Jinn 20

44. If anyone associates anything with Allah, Allah has forbidden him the Garden and his refuge will be the Fire. The wrongdoers will have no helpers. Al-Ma'ida 72

45. Yet they make the jinn co-partners with Allah when He created them! And they attribute sons and daughters to Him without any knowledge. Glory be to Him! He is the Originator of the heavens and the earth. How could He have a son when He has no wife? He created all things and He has knowledge of all things. Al-An'am 100-101

46. Say: 'My Lord has guided me to a straight path, a well-founded deen, the religion of Ibrahim, a man of pure natural belief. He was not one of the mushrikun.' Say: 'My salat and my rites, my living and my dying, are for Allah alone, the Lord of all the worlds, Who has no partner. I am commanded to be like that and I am the first of the Muslims.' Say: 'Am I to desire other than Allah as Lord when He is the Lord of all things?...' Al-An'am 162-166

47. ...We don't associate anything with Allah. And that is how Allah has favoured us and all mankind, but most do not give thanks. Yusuf 38

48. ... are many lords better, or Allah, the only One, the Conqueror? What you serve apart from Him are only names which you and your forefathers have made up There is no mandate for them from Allah. Allah alone is qualified to judge. His order is to worship none but Him. That is in truth the straight and upright deen, but most of mankind simply do not know. Yusuf 39-40

49. Has your Lord honoured you with sons and Himself taken the angels as daughters? It is truly something terrible that you say! Bani Isra'il 40

50. They allot a portion of the provision We have given them to things they have no knowledge of at all. By Allah, you will be asked about what you invented! They allot daughters to Allah – glory be to Him! – while they have what they want! When one of them is given the good news of a baby girl, his face darkens and he is furious. He hides away from people because of the evil of the good news he has been given. Should he keep her ignominiously or bury her in the earth? What an evil judgement they make! Those who do not have iman in the akhira have an evil likeness. Allah's is the Highest Likeness. He is the Almighty, the All-Wise. If Allah were to punish people for their wrong actions, not a single creature would be left upon the earth, but He defers them till a predetermined time. When their specified time arrives, they cannot delay it for a single hour nor can they bring it forward. They allot to Allah what they themselves dislike and their tongues frame the lie that they will receive the Best. There is no doubt at all that they will receive the Fire and that they are people who go to excess. An-Nahl 56-62

51. Say: 'Call on those you make claims for apart from Him. They possess no power to remove any harm from you or to change anything.' Those they call on are themselves seeking the means by which they might approach their Lord – even those who are the closest to Him – and are hoping for His mercy and fearing his punishment. The punishment of your Lord is truly something to be feared. Bani Isra'il 56-57

52. Or have they taken gods out of the earth who can bring the dead to life? If there had been any gods besides Allah in heaven or earth, they would both be ruined. Glory be to Allah, Lord of the Throne, beyond what they describe! Al-Anbiya 21-22

53. Some people set up equals to Allah, loving them as they should love Allah. Al-Baqara 165

54. Say: 'Allah rescues you from it, and from every plight. Then you associate others with Him.' Say: 'He possesses the power to send you punishment from above your heads or from beneath your feet, or to confuse you in sects and make you taste one another's violence.' Look how We vary the Signs so that hopefully they will understand. Al-An'am 64-65

55. When Luqman said to his son, counselling him, 'My son, do not associate anything with Allah. Associating others with Him is a terrible wrong.' Luqman 13

56. The metaphor of a corrupt word is that of a rotten tree, uprooted on the surface of the earth. It has no staying-power. Ibrahim 26

57. ...and [they] worship, instead of Allah, things that have no control over their provision from the heavens or earth in any way, and are themselves completely impotent? Do not try to make metaphors for Allah. Allah knows and you do not know. An-Nahl 73-74

58. Anyone who rejects Allah and His angels and His Books and His Messengers and the Last Day has gone very far astray. An-Nisa 136

Right action

1. It is not devoutness to turn your faces to the East or to the West. Rather, those with true devoutness are those who
    i. have iman in Allah
    ii. and the Last Day,
    ii. the Angels,
    iv. the Book
    v. and the Prophets,
    vi. and who, despite their love for it, give away their wealth to
        a. their relatives
        b. and to orphans
        c. and the very poor,
        d. and to travellers
        e. and beggars
        f. and to set slaves free,
    vii. and who establish salat
    viii. and pay zakat;
    ix. those who honour their contracts when they make them,
    x. and are steadfast in poverty and illness and in battle.

Those are the people who are true. They are the people who have taqwa. Al-Baqara 177

2. If you do good and have taqwa, Allah is aware of what you do. An-Nisa 128

3. ... they have taqwa and iman and do right actions, and then again have taqwa and iman, and then have taqwa and do good. Allah loves good-doers. Al-Ma'ida 93

4. Their flesh and blood does not reach Allah but your taqwa does reach Him... Al-Hajj 37

5. ...such people are truly racing towards good things, and they are the first to reach them. Al-Muminun 61

6. Is someone who has iman like someone who is a deviator? They are not the same! As-Sajda 18

7. For those who do good in the dunya there is good and Allah's earth is spacious. Az-Zumar 10

8. Say: 'Each man acts according to his nature, but your Lord knows best who is best guided on the Path.' Bani Isra'il 84

9. If two parties of the muminun fight, make peace between them. But if one of them attacks the other unjustly, fight the attackers until they revert to Allah's command. If they revert, make peace between them with justice, and be even-handed. Allah loves those who are even-handed. Al-Hujurat 9

10. Each person faces a particular direction so race each other to the good. Wherever you are, Allah will bring you all together. Truly Allah has power over all things. Al-Baqara 148

11. Those who did good and had taqwa among those who responded to Allah and the Messenger after the wound had been inflicted will have an immense reward. Al 'Imran 172

12. You who have iman! you are only responsible for yourselves. The misguided cannot harm you as long as you are guided. All of you will return to Allah and He will inform you about what you were doing. Al-Ma'ida 105

13. Allah commands justice and doing good and giving to relatives. And He forbids indecency and doing wrong and tyranny. He warns you so that hopefully you will pay heed. An-Nahl 90

14. Then We placed you on the right road of Our Command, so follow it. Do not follow the whims and desires of those who do not know. Al-Jathiya 18

Behaviour

15. You who have iman! when you confer together secretly, do not do so in wrongdoing and enmity and disobedience to the Messenger; rather confer together in goodness and taqwa of Allah. Have taqwa of Allah – Him to Whom you will be gathered. Al-Mujadila 9

16. You who have iman! have taqwa of Allah and let each self look to what it has sent forward for Tomorrow. Have taqwa of Allah. Allah is aware of what you do. Do not be like those who forgot Allah so He made them forget themselves. Such people are the deviators. Al-Hashr 18-19

17. He who has purified himself will have success, He who invokes the Name of his Lord and prays. Al-A'la 14-15

18. But he has not braved the steep ascent. What will convey to you what the steep ascent is? It is freeing a slave or feeding on a day of hunger an orphaned relative or a poor man in the dust; then to be one of those who have iman and bid each other to steadfastness and bid each other to compassion. Those are the Companions of the Right. Al-Balad 11-18

19. You who have iman! do not betray Allah and His Messenger, and do not knowingly betray your trusts. Al-Anfal 27

20. ...Do not be too soft-spoken in your speech lest someone with sickness in his heart becomes desirous. Speak correct and courteous words. Al-Ahzab 32

21. And remind them, for truly the muminun benefit from being reminded. Adh-Dhariyat 55

22. Wealth and sons are the embellishment of the life of the dunya. But, in your Lord's sight, right actions which are lasting bring a better reward and are a better basis for hope. Al-Kahf 46

23. Say: 'Act, for Allah will see your actions, and so will His Messenger and the muminun. You will be returned to the Knower of the Unseen and the Visible and He will inform you regarding what you did.' At-Tawba 106

24. If anyone wants power, all power belongs to Allah. All good words rise to Him and He raises up all virtuous deeds. But people who plot evil deeds will suffer a harsh punishment. The plotting of such people is profitless. Fatir 10

25. So compete with each other in doing good. Al-Ma'ida 48
26. Help each other to goodness and taqwa. Do not help each other to wrongdoing and enmity. Have taqwa of Allah. Allah is severe in retribution. Al-Ma'ida 2
27. This is My Path and it is straight, so follow it. Do not follow other ways or you will become cut off from His Way. That is what He instructs you to do, so that hopefully you will have taqwa. Al-An'am 154

Tolerance And Forgiveness

1. But you should pardon and overlook until Allah gives His command. Al-Baqara 109
2. Those who control their rage and pardon other people – Allah loves the good-doers. Al 'Imran 134
3. Allah knows what is in such people's hearts so turn away from them and warn them and speak to them with words that take effect. An-Nisa 63
4. Make allowances for people, command what is right, and turn away from the ignorant. Al-A'raf 199
5. He [Yusuf] said, 'No blame at all will fall on you. Today you have forgiveness from Allah.' Yusuf 92
6. The Hour is certainly coming, so turn away graciously. Al-Hijr 85
7. They should rather pardon and overlook. Would you not love Allah to forgive you? Allah is Ever-Forgiving, Most Merciful. An-Nur 22
8. You who have iman! some of your wives and children are an enemy to you, so be wary of them. But if you pardon and exonerate and forgive, Allah is Ever-Forgiving, Most Merciful. At-Taghabun 14
9. Yet pardon them, and overlook. Allah loves good-doers. Al-Ma'ida 13
10. ...when they [the Muminun] are angered, then forgive. Ash-Shura 37
11. The repayment of a bad action is one equivalent to it. But if someone pardons and puts things right, his reward is with Allah. Certainly He does not love wrongdoers. Ash-Shura 40

12. Those who control their rage and pardon other people – Allah loves the good-doers. Al 'Imran 134
13. Whether you reveal a good act or keep it hidden, or pardon an evil act, Allah is Ever-Pardoning, All-Powerful. An-Nisa 149
14. And as for your words, 'My Lord, these are people who have no iman!' turn from them and say, 'Peace! You will soon come to know.' Az-Zukhruf 88-89
15. Tell those who have iman that they should forgive those who feel no fear about the Days of Allah, when He will repay people according to what they earned. Al-Jathiya 14
16. Be steadfast in the face of what they say and cut yourself off from them – but courteously. Leave the deniers, who live a life of ease, to Me, and tolerate them a little longer. Al-Muzzammil 10-11
17. He said, 'Peace be upon you. I will ask my Lord to forgive you.' Maryam 47

Kindness and Good Counsel

1. It is a mercy from Allah that you were gentle with them. If you had been rough or hard of heart, they would have scattered from around you. Al 'Imran 159
2. Call to the way of your Lord with wisdom and fair admonition, and argue with them in the kindest way... An-Nahl 125
3. [Allah commanded Musa] 'Go to Pharaoh; he has overstepped the bounds. But speak to him with gentle words so that hopefully he will pay heed or show some fear.' Ta Ha 44
4. When Luqman said to his son, counselling him... 'My son, establish salat and command what is right and forbid what is wrong and be steadfast in the face of all that happens to you. That is certainly the most resolute course to follow. Do not avert your face from people out of haughtiness and do not strut about arrogantly on the earth. Allah does not love anyone who is vain or boastful. Be moderate in your tread and lower your voice. The most hateful of voices is the donkey's bray.' Luqman 12 & 16-18
5. There is no good in much of their secret talk, except in the case of those who enjoin sadaqa, or what is right, or putting things right between people. If anyone does that, seeking the pleasure of Allah,

We will give him an immense reward. An-Nisa 114

6. Only argue with the People of the Book in the kindest way – except in the case of those of them who do wrong – saying, 'We have iman in what has been sent down to us and what was sent down to you. Our God and your God are one and we submit to Him.' Al-'Ankabut 46

7. It is not necessary for the muminun to go out all together. If a party from each group of them were to go out so they could increase their knowledge of the deen they would be able to notify their people when they returned to them so that hopefully they would take warning! At-Tawba 122

8. Let there be a community among you who call to the good, and enjoin the right, and forbid the wrong. Al 'Imran 104

9. They would not restrain one another from any of the wrong things that they did. How evil were the things they used to do! Al-Ma'ida 79

10. Allah knows what is in such people's hearts so turn away from them and warn them and speak to them with words that take effect. An-Nisa 63

Pride And Arrogance

1. He [Iblis] refused and was arrogant and was one of the kafirun. Al-Baqara 34

2. ... he is seized by pride which drives him to wrongdoing. Hell will be enough for him! Al-Baqara 206

3. Do not strut arrogantly about the earth. You will certainly never split the earth apart nor will you ever rival the mountains in height. Bani Isra'il 37

4. He was a man of wealth and property and he said to his companion, debating with him, 'I have more wealth than you and more people under me.' He entered his garden and wronged himself by saying, 'I do not think that this will ever end. I do not think the Hour will ever come. But if I should be sent back to my Lord, I will definitely get something better in return.' Al-Kahf 34-36

5. They say, 'If we follow the guidance with you, we shall be forcibly uprooted from our land.' Have We not established a

safe haven for them to which produce of every kind is brought, provision direct from Us? But most of them do not know it. How many cities We have destroyed which lived in insolent ingratitude! There are their houses, never again inhabited after them, except a little. It was We who were their Heir. Al-Qasas 58

6. He said, 'I have only been given it because of knowledge I have.' Did he not know that before him Allah had destroyed generations with far greater strength than his and far more possessions? The evildoers will not be questioned about their sins. Al-Qasas 78

7. The people who truly do have iman in Our Signs are those who fall to the ground prostrating when they are reminded of them, and glorify the praise of their Lord, and are not arrogant. As-Sajda 16

8. On the Day of Rising you will see those who lied against Allah with their faces blackened. Az-Zumar 59

9. They will be told, 'Enter the gates of Hell and stay there timelessly, for ever. How evil is the abode of the arrogant!' Az-Zumar 72

10. Certainly those who argue about the Signs of Allah without any authority having come to them have nothing in their breasts except for pride which they will never be able to vindicate. Therefore seek refuge with Allah. He is the All-Hearing, the All-Seeing. Al-Mumin 55

11. Those who argue about the Signs of Allah without any authority coming to them do something hateful in the sight of Allah and in the sight of the people who have iman. That is how Allah seals up the heart of every arrogant oppressor. Al-Mumin 35

12. Allah does not love anyone vain or boastful. An-Nisa 36

13. Your Lord says, 'Call on Me and I will answer you. Those who are too proud to worship Me will enter Hell abject.' Al-Mumin 60

14. That is so that you will not be grieved about the things that pass you by or exult about the things that come to you. Allah does not love any vain or boastful man: Al-Hadid 23

15. When they are told, 'Come, and the Messenger of Allah will ask forgiveness for you,' they turn their heads and you see them turn away in haughty arrogance. In their case it makes no difference whether you ask forgiveness for them or do not ask forgiveness

for them. Allah will never forgive them. Allah does not guide deviant people. Al-Munafiqun 5-6

16. He neither affirmed the truth nor did he do salat, but rather denied the truth and turned away, and then went off to his family, swaggering. Al-Qiyama 30-32

17. Arrogance entangles one into sinful life. Al-Baqara 206

18. ...So do not claim purity for yourselves. He knows best those who have taqwa. An-Najm 32

19. Those who exult in what they have done and love to be praised for what they have not done should not suppose that they have escaped the punishment. Al 'Imran 188

20. Do not be like those who left their homes in arrogance, showing off to people... Al-Anfal 47

21. Do not avert your face from people out of haughtiness and do not strut about arrogantly on the earth. Allah does not love anyone who is vain or boastful. Be moderate in your tread and lower your voice. The most hateful of voices is the donkey's bray. Luqman 17-18

22. All of that is evil action and hateful in the sight of your Lord. Bani Isra'il 38

23. Allah does not love people who gloat. Al-Qasas 76

24. He said, 'What prevented you from prostrating when I commanded you to?' He replied, 'I am better than him. You created me from fire and You created him from clay.' He said, 'Descend from Heaven. It is not for you to be arrogant in it. So get out! You are one of the abased.' Al-A'raf 11-12

25. ...'What you amassed was of no use to you, nor was your arrogance. Al-A'raf 48

26. I will divert from My Signs all those who are arrogant in the earth without any right. If they see every Sign, they will not believe in it. If they see the way of right guidance, they will not take it as a way. But if they see the way of error, they will take that as a way. That is because they denied Our Signs and paid no attention to them. Al-A'raf 146

27. How evil is the abode of the arrogant!' An-Nahl 29

28. Everything in the heavens and every creature on the earth

Behaviour

prostrates to Allah, as do the angels. They are not puffed up with pride. An-Nahl 49

29. Among people there is one who argues about Allah without knowledge or guidance or any light-giving Book, turning away arrogantly, to misguide people from the Way of Allah. He will be disgraced in this world and on the Day of Rising We will make him taste the punishment of the Burning… Al-Hajj 8-9

30. He [Qarun] said, 'I have only been given it because of knowledge I have.' Did he not know that before him Allah had destroyed generations with far greater strength than his and far more possessions? Al-Qasas 78

31. When they were told, 'There is no god but Allah,' they were arrogant. As-Saffat 35

32. But those who are kafir are full of vainglory and entrenched in hostility. Sad 2

33. He said, 'Iblis, what prevented you prostrating to what I created with My own Hands? Were you overcome by arrogance or are you one of the exalted?' He said, 'I am better than him. You created me from fire but You created him from clay.' He said, 'Get out! you are accursed! My curse is upon you until the Day of Reckoning.' Sad 74-77

34. As for those who show disdain and grow arrogant, He will punish them with a painful punishment. They will not find any protector or helper for themselves besides Allah. An-Nisa 172

35. 'Ad were arrogant in the land, without any right, saying, 'Who has greater strength than us?' Did they not see that Allah, who created them, had greater strength than them? But they renounced Our Signs. Fussilat 15

36. When they are told, 'Come, and the Messenger of Allah will ask forgiveness for you,' they turn their heads and you see them turn away in haughty arrogance. Al-Munafiqun 5

37. Those who exult in what they have done and love to be praised for what they have not done should not suppose that they have escaped the punishment. They will have a painful punishment. Al 'Imran 188

38. Woe to every wicked liar who hears the Signs of Allah recited to him and then persists in his arrogance just as if he had

never heard them. Give him the news of a painful punishment. Al-Jathiya 7-8

39. He said, 'Iblis, what is it that prevents you being among the prostrators?' He said, 'I will not prostrate to a human being whom You have created out of dried clay formed from fetid black mud.' Al-Hijr 32-33

Humility

1. Seek help in steadfastness and salat. But that is a very hard thing, except for the humble... Al-Baqara 45
2. Be humble when receiving Allah's blessing. Al-Baqara 58
3. We sent Messengers to nations before you, and afflicted those nations with hardship and distress so that hopefully they would humble themselves. Al-An'am 43
4. As for those who have iman and do right actions and humble themselves before their Lord, they are the Companions of the Garden, remaining in it timelessly, for ever. Hud 23
5. Do they not see the things Allah has created, casting their shadows to the right and to the left, prostrating themselves before Allah in complete humility? An-Nahl 48
6. ...Your God is One God so submit to Him. Give good news to the humble-hearted... Al-Hajj 34
7. ...and so that those who have been given knowledge will know it is the truth from their Lord and have iman in it and their hearts will be humbled to Him. Allah guides those who have iman to a straight path. Al-Hajj 54
8. It is the muminun who are successful: those who are humble in their salat. Al-Muminun 1-2
9. We sent Messengers to nations before you, and afflicted those nations with hardship and distress so that hopefully they would humble themselves. Al-An'am 42
10. The slaves of the All-Merciful are those who walk lightly on the earth and, who, when the ignorant speak to them, say, 'Peace'. Al-Furqan 63
11. Be moderate in your tread and lower your voice. The most hateful of voices is the donkey's bray.' Luqman 19

12. Say: 'Have iman in it or do not have iman in it.' Certainly, when it is recited to them, those who were given knowledge before it fall on their faces in prostration, saying, 'Glory be to our Lord! The promise of our Lord is truly fulfilled!' Weeping, they fall to the ground in prostration, and it increases them in humility. Bani Isra'il 107-108

13. ...but they did not go low before their Lord; nor will they humble themselves. Al-Muminun 76

Respect

1. You who have iman! do not profane the sacred rites of Allah or the sacred months, or the sacrificial animals, or the ritual garlands, or those heading for the Sacred House, desiring profit and good pleasure from their Lord. Al-Ma'ida 2

2. ...But all might belongs to Allah and to His Messenger and the muminun. But the munafiqun do not know this. Al-Munafiqun 8

3. The noblest among you in Allah's sight is the one with the most taqwa. Al-Hujurat 13

Backbiting

1. Allah does not like evil words being voiced out loud, except in the case of someone who has been wronged. Allah is All-Hearing, All-Knowing. An-Nisa 148

2. And those who abuse men and women who are muminun, when they have not merited it, bear the weight of slander and clear wrongdoing. Al-Ahzab 58

3. Woe to every faultfinding backbiter. Al-Humaza 1

4. If two parties of the muminun fight, make peace between them. But if one of them attacks the other unjustly, fight the attackers until they revert to Allah's command. If they revert, make peace between them with justice, and be even-handed. Allah loves those who are even-handed. The muminun are brothers, so make peace between your brothers and have taqwa of Allah so that hopefully you will gain mercy. Al-Hujurat 9-10

5. You who have iman! people should not ridicule others who

may be better than themselves; nor should any women ridicule other women who may be better than themselves. And do not find fault with one another or insult each other with derogatory nicknames. How evil it is to have a name for evil conduct after coming to iman! Those people who do not turn from it are wrongdoers. Al-Hujurat 11

6. You who have iman! avoid most suspicion. Indeed some suspicion is a crime. And do not spy and do not backbite one another. Would any of you like to eat his brother's dead flesh? No, you would hate it. And have taqwa of Allah. Allah is Ever-Returning, Most Merciful. Al-Hujurat 12

Mischief Making and Corruption

1. Among the people there are some who say, 'We have iman in Allah and the Last Day,' when they are not muminun. They think they deceive Allah and those who have iman. They deceive no one but themselves but they are not aware of it. Al-Baqara 8-9
2. Eat and drink of Allah's provision and do not go about the earth corrupting it. Al-Baqara 60
3. Do not devour one another's property by false means nor offer it to the judges as a bribe, trying through crime to knowingly usurp a portion of other people's property. Al-Baqara 188
4. Fitna is worse than killing. Al-Baqara 191
5. As for any of you who revert from their deen and die kafir, their actions will come to nothing in the dunya and the akhira. They are the Companions of the Fire, remaining in it timelessly, for ever. Al-Baqara 217
6. Allah does not love corruption. Al-Baqara 205
7. Corruption has appeared in both land and sea because of what people's own hands have wrought so that they may taste something of what they have done so that hopefully they will turn back. Ar-Rum 41
8. So We decreed for the tribe of Israel that if someone kills another person – unless it is in retaliation for someone else or for causing corruption in the earth – it is as if he had murdered all mankind. And if anyone gives life to another person, it is as if he

had given life to all mankind. Our Messengers came to them with Clear Signs but even after that many of them committed outrages in the earth. Al-Ma'ida 32

9. Do not lie in wait on every pathway, threatening people, barring those who have iman from the Way of Allah, desiring to make it crooked. Remember when you were few and He increased your number: see the final fate of the corrupters! Al-A'raf 86

10. But as for those who break Allah's contract after it has been agreed and sever what Allah has commanded to be joined, and cause corruption in the earth, the curse will be upon them. They will have the Evil Abode. Ar-Ra'd 25

11. ...But then when a warner did come to them, it only increased their aversion, shown by their arrogance in the land and evil plotting. But evil plotting envelops only those who do it... Fatir 41

12. Do not argue on behalf of those who betray themselves. Allah does not love any evildoing traitors. An-Nisa 107

13. And likewise in every city We set up its greatest wrongdoers to plot in it. They plot against themselves alone, but they are not aware of it. Al-An'am 124

14. Allah does not uphold the actions of corrupters. Yunus 81

Worldly Attractions

1. To those who are kafir, the life of the dunya is painted in glowing colours and they laugh at those who have iman. But on the Day of Rising those who fear Allah will be over them. Al-Baqara 212

2. The life of the dunya is nothing but a game and a diversion. The akhira is better for those who have taqwa. So will you not use your intellect? Al-An'am 32

3. When they forgot what they had been reminded of, We opened up for them the doors to everything, until, when they were exulting in what they had been given, We suddenly seized them and at once they were in despair. Al-An'am 44

4. Say: 'Who has forbidden the fine clothing Allah has produced for His slaves and the good kinds of provision?' Say: 'On the Day of Rising such things will be exclusively for those who had iman

during their life in the dunya.' In this way We make the Signs clear for people who know. Al-A'raf 32

5. Those who took their deen as a diversion and a game, and were deluded by the life of the dunya.' Today We will forget them just as they forgot the encounter of this Day and denied Our Signs. Al-A'raf 51

6. I will give them more time. My strategy is sure. Al-A'raf 183

7. ...Are you happier with the dunya than the akhira? Yet the enjoyment of the dunya is very small compared to that of the akhira. At-Tawba 38

8. Those who have iman and show taqwa, there is good news for them in the life of the dunya and in the akhira... Yunus 63-64

9. There is the enjoyment of the dunya. Then they will return to Us. Then We will let them taste the terrible punishment because they were kafir. Yunus 70

10. As for those who desire the life of the dunya and its finery, We will give them full payment in it for their actions. They will not be deprived here of their due. But such people will have nothing in the akhira but the Fire. What they achieved here will come to nothing. What they did will prove to be null and void. Hud 15-16

11. ...desiring His face. Do not turn your eyes from them, desiring the attractions of this world. And do not obey someone whose heart We have made neglectful of Our remembrance and who follows his own whims and desires and whose life has transgressed all bounds. Al-Kahf 28

12. [They said] 'Seek the abode of the akhira with what Allah has given you, without forgetting your portion of the dunya. And do good as Allah has been good to you. And do not seek to cause corruption in the earth. Allah does not love corrupters.' Al-Qasas 77

13. So do not let the life of the dunya delude you. Luqman 33

14. If anyone desires to cultivate the akhira, We will increase him in his cultivation. If anyone desires to cultivate the dunya, We will give him some of it but he will have no share in the akhira. Ash-Shura 20

15. Whatever you have been given is only the enjoyment of the life of the dunya. What is with Allah is better and longer lasting for those who have iman and trust in their Lord: Ash-Shura 33

16. No indeed! But you love this fleeting world and you disregard the akhira. Al-Qiyama 20-21
17. Do not let their wealth and children impress you. Allah merely wants to punish them by them... At-Tawba 55
18. What is with you runs out but what is with Allah goes on for ever. Those who were steadfast will be recompensed according to the best of what they did. An-Nahl 96
19. Do not direct your eyes longingly to what We have given certain of them to enjoy, the flower of the life of this world, so that We can test them by it. Your Lord's provision is better and longer lasting. Ta Ha 131
20. The life of the dunya is nothing but a game and a diversion. The abode of the akhira – that is truly Life if they only knew. Al-'Ankabut 64
21. You who have iman! do not let your wealth or children divert you from the remembrance of Allah. Whoever does that is lost. Al-Munafiqun 9
22. As for man, when his Lord tests him by honouring him and favouring him, he says, 'My Lord has honoured me!' But then when He tests him by restricting his provision, he says, 'My Lord has humiliated me!' Al-Fajr 15-18
23. ...But then, when He gives them a taste of mercy from Him, a group of them immediately associate others with their Lord to show ingratitude for what We have given them. 'Enjoy yourselves – you will soon know.' Ar-Rum 34
24. The life of the dunya is just the enjoyment of delusion. Al 'Imran 185
25. To mankind the love of worldly appetites is painted in glowing colours: women and children, and heaped-up mounds of gold and silver, and horses with fine markings, and livestock and fertile farmland. All that is merely the enjoyment of the life of the dunya. The best homecoming is in the presence of Allah. Al 'Imran 14
26. Mankind! have taqwa of your Lord and fear a day when no father will be able to atone for his son, or son for his father, in any way. Allah's promise is true. So do not let the life of the dunya delude you and do not let the Deluder delude you concerning Allah. Luqman 33

27. Mankind! Allah's promise is true. Do not let the life of the dunya delude you and do not let the Deluder delude you about Allah. Fatir 5

28. ...His metaphor is that of a dog: if you chase it away, it lolls out its tongue and pants, and if you leave it alone, it lolls out its tongue and pants. That is the metaphor of those who deny Our Signs... Al-A'raf 176

29. If they do not respond to you then know that they are merely following their whims and desires. And who could be further astray than someone who follows his whims and desires without any guidance from Allah? Allah does not guide the people of the wrongdoers. Al-Qasas 50

30. The life of the dunya is merely a game and a diversion. If you have iman and taqwa, He will pay you your wages and not ask you for all your wealth. Muhammad 36

31. Know that the life of the dunya is merely a game and a diversion and ostentation and a cause of boasting among yourselves and trying to outdo one another in wealth and children: like the plant-growth after rain which delights the cultivators, but then it withers and you see it turning yellow, and then it becomes broken stubble. In the akhira there is terrible punishment but also forgiveness from Allah and His good pleasure. The life of the dunya is nothing but the enjoyment of delusion. Al-Hadid 20

32. Do not be deceived by the fact that those who are kafir move freely about the earth. A brief enjoyment; then their shelter will be Hell. Al 'Imran 196-197

33. So the last remnant of the people who did wrong was cut off. Praise belongs to Allah, the Lord of all the worlds! Al-An'am 44

34. Like those before you who had greater strength than you and more wealth and children. They enjoyed their portion; so enjoy your portion as those before you enjoyed theirs. You have plunged into defamation as they plunged into it. The actions of such people come to nothing in the dunya or the akhira. They are the lost. At-Tawba 69

35. Those who were left behind were glad to stay behind the Messenger of Allah. They did not want to do jihad with their wealth

and themselves in the Way of Allah. They said, 'Do not go out to fight in the heat.' Say: 'The Fire of Hell is much hotter, if they only understood.' At-Tawba 82

36. ...'People who invent lies against Allah will not be successful.' Yunus 69

37. As for anyone who desires this fleeting existence, We hasten in it whatever We will to whoever We want. Then We will consign him to Hell Bani Isra'il 18

38. No indeed! But you love this fleeting world and you disregard the akhira. Al-Qiyama 20-21

39. Make a metaphor for them of the life of the dunya. It is like water which We send down from the sky and the plants of the earth combine with it but then become dry chaff scattered by the winds. Allah has absolute power over everything. Al-Kahf 45

40. Do you build a tower on every hilltop, just to amuse yourselves, and construct great fortresses, hoping to live for ever, and when you attack, attack as tyrants do? So have taqwa of Allah and obey me. Ash-Shu'ara 128-131

41. [Do you think] ... that what they enjoyed will be of any use to them? Ash-Shu'ara 207

42. These people love this fleeting world and have put the thought of a Momentous Day behind their backs. Ad-Dahr 27

43. They know an outward aspect of the life of the dunya but are heedless of the akhira. Ar-Rum 7

44. He said, 'I will let anyone who becomes a kafir enjoy himself a little but then I will drive him to the punishment of the Fire. What an evil destination!' Al-Baqara 126

45. Those [the Jews] are the people who trade the akhira for the dunya. The punishment will not be lightened for them. They will not be helped. Al-Baqara 86

46. 'You have come to Us all alone just as We created you at first, leaving behind you everything We bestowed on you. We do not see your intercessors accompanying you. Al-An'am 95

47. Do not let their wealth and their children impress you. Allah merely wants to punish them by them in the dunya, and for them to expire while they are kafirun. At-Tawba 85

48. The metaphor of the life of the dunya is that of water which We send down from the sky, and which then mingles with the plants of the earth to provide food for both people and animals. Then, when the earth is at its loveliest and takes on its fairest guise and its people think they have it under their control, Our command comes upon it by night or day and We reduce it to dried-out stubble, as though it had not been flourishing just the day before! In this way We make Our Signs clear for people who reflect. Yunus 24

49. Those who reject Allah after having had iman – except for someone forced to do it whose heart remains at rest in its iman – but as for those whose breasts become dilated with kufr, anger from Allah will come down on them. They will have a terrible punishment. That is because they prefer the life of the dunya to the akhira and because Allah does not guide kafir people. Those are the people whose hearts, hearing and sight Allah has sealed up. They are the unaware. There is no doubt that in the akhira they will be the losers. An-Nahl 106-109

50. A brief enjoyment, then they will have a painful punishment. An-Nahl 117

51. Say: 'Shall I inform you of the greatest losers in their actions? People whose efforts in the life of the dunya are misguided while they suppose that they are doing good.' Al-Kahf 103-104

52. Do they imagine that, in the wealth and children We extend to them, We are hastening to them with good things? No indeed, but they have no awareness! Al-Muminun 56-57

53. He went out among his people in his finery. Those who desired the life of the dunya said, 'Oh! If only we had the same as Qarun has been given! What immense good fortune he possesses.' Al-Qasas 79

54. But those who had been given knowledge said, 'Woe to you! Allah's reward is better for those who have iman and act rightly... Al-Qasas 80

55. We will let them enjoy themselves a little, then drive them to a harsh punishment. Luqman 24

56. No one disputes Allah's Signs except those who are kafir.

Do not let their free movement about the earth deceive you. Al-Mumin 4

57. [The mmumin who concealed his iman said] 'My people! the life of the dunya is only fleeting enjoyment. It is the akhira which is the abode of permanence.' Al-Mumin 39

58. Were it not that mankind might all become one community, We would have given those who reject the All-Merciful silver roofs to their houses and silver stairways to ascend and silver doors to their houses and silver couches on which to recline, and gold ornaments. All that is merely the trappings of the life of the dunya. But the akhira with your Lord is for those who have taqwa. Az-Zukhruf 33-35

59. 'Eat and enjoy yourselves for a little while. You are evildoers.' Al-Mursalat 46

60. Yet still you prefer the life of the dunya when the akhira is better and longer lasting. Al-A'la 16-17

61. Say, 'The enjoyment of the dunya is very brief. The akhira is better for those who have taqwa. You will not be wronged by so much as the smallest speck.' An-Nisa 77

62. Do not direct your eyes longingly to what We have given certain of them to enjoy. Do not feel sad concerning them. And take the muminun under your wing. Al-Hijr 88

63. When Our Clear Signs are recited to them, those who are kafir say to those who have iman, 'Which of the two parties has the better position and the more illustrious gathering?' How many generations We have destroyed before them who had finer furnishings and a better outward show! Maryam 73-74

64. On the Day when those who were kafir are exposed to the Fire:'You dissipated the good things you had in your worldly life and enjoyed yourself in it. So today you are being repaid with the punishment of humiliation for being arrogant in the earth without any right and for being deviators.' Al-Ahqaf 20

65. Look how We favour some of them over others. But the akhira has higher ranks and greater favours. Bani Isra'il 21

66. Is it, then, they who allocate the mercy of your Lord? We have allocated their livelihood among them in the life of the dunya and

raised some of them above others in rank so that some of them are subservient to others. But the mercy of your Lord is better than anything they amass. Az-Zukhruf 32
67. When man tastes Allah's mercy after some hurt had touched him, he says: "This is my own fortune and I don't think the Hour will ever come; even if I am brought back to my Lord I am sure I will be better off with Him as well". But Allah will make him taste hard punishment. Fusilat 50

Sustenance and provision

1. Praise be to Allah, the Lord of all the worlds. Al-Fatiha 1
2. Allah provides for whoever He wills without any reckoning. Al-Baqara 212
3. Allah both restricts and expands. Al-Baqara 245
4. 'You provide for whoever You will without any reckoning.' Al 'Imran 27
5. Say: 'Am I to take anyone other than Allah as my protector,the Bringer into Being of the heavens and the earth,He who feeds and is not fed?' Al-An'am 14
6. There is no creature on the earth which is not dependent upon Allah for its provision. He knows where it lives and where it dies. They are all in a Clear Book. Hud 6
7. And We put livelihoods in it [the earth] both for you and for those you do not provide for. There is nothing that does not have its stores with Us and We only send it down in a known measure. We send forth the pollinating winds and send down water from the sky and give it to you to drink. And it is not you who keep its stores. Al-Hijr 20-22
8. Allah has favoured some of you over others in provision, but those who have been favoured do not give their provision to their slaves so they become the same in respect of it. So why do they renounce the blessings of Allah? An-Nahl 71
9. Your Lord expands the provision of anyone He wills and restricts it. He is aware of and sees His slaves. Bani Isra'il 30
10. [Allah said to Adam and Hawa] 'You will not go hungry in it [the Garden] or suffer from nakedness. You will not go thirsty in it or burn in the sun.' Ta Ha 118-119

11. Instruct your family to do salat, and be constant in it. We do not ask you for provision. We provide for you. And the best end result is gained by taqwa. Ta Ha 132

12. Those who make hijra in the Way of Allah and then are killed or die, Allah will provide for them handsomely. Truly Allah is the best Provider. Al-Hajj 58

13. ...so that Allah can reward them for the best of what they did and give them more from His unbounded favour. Allah provides for anyone He wills without reckoning. An-Nur 38

14. Allah expands the provision of any of His slaves He wills and restricts it. Allah has knowledge of all things. Al-'Ankabut 62

15. How many creatures do not carry their provision with them! Allah provides for them and He will for you. He is the All-Hearing, the All-Knowing. Al-'Ankabut 60

16. Do they not see that Allah expands provision for whoever He wills and also restricts it? There are certainly Signs in that for people who have iman. Ar-Rum 37

17. Say: 'My Lord expands the provision of anyone He wills or restricts it. But the majority of mankind do not know it.' Saba 36

18. Say: 'My Lord expands the provision of any of His slaves He wills or restricts it. But anything you expend will be replaced by Him. He is the Best of Providers.' Saba 39

19. Allah is very gentle with His slaves. He provides for anyone He wills. He is the Most Strong, the Almighty. Ash-Shura 19

20. Were Allah to expand the provision of His slaves, they would act as tyrants on the earth. But He sends down whatever He wills in a measured way. He is aware of and He sees His slaves. Ash-Shura 27

21. Your provision is in heaven – and what you are promised. Adh-Dhariyat 22

22. I do not require any provision from them and I do not require them to nourish Me. Truly Allah, He is the Provider, the Possessor of Strength, the Sure. Adh-Dhariyat-57-58

23. ... it is He Who enriches and Who satisfies. An-Najm 48

24. It is He who made the earth submissive to you, so walk its broad trails and eat what it provides. The Resurrection is to Him. Al-Mulk 15

25. Allah expands provision to anyone He wills and restricts it. They rejoice in the life of the dunya. Yet the life of the dunya, compared to the akhira, is only fleeting enjoyment. Ar-Ra'd 26

26. The Keys of the heavens and earth belong to Him. He expands the provision of anyone He wills or restricts it. He has knowledge of all things. Ash-Shura 12

27. Your Lord is He who propels the ships on the sea for you so that you may seek His bounty. He is indeed Most Merciful to you. Bani Isra'il 66

28. Do they not know that Allah expands the provision of anyone He wills and restricts it? Az-Zumar 52

29. Say: 'Who provides for you from the heavens and earth?' Say: 'Allah.' Saba 24

30. Mankind! remember Allah's blessing to you. Is there any creator other than Allah providing for you from heaven and earth? There is no god but Him. So how have you been perverted. Fatir 3

31. It is He who shows you His Signs and sends down provision to you out of heaven. But none pay heed save those who make tawba. So call upon Allah, making your deen sincerely His, even though the kafirun detest it. Al-Mumin 12-13

32. Allah is He who created you, then provides for you, then will cause you to die and then bring you back to life. Can any of your partner-gods do any of that? Glory be to Him and may He be exalted above anything they associate with Him! Ar-Rum 40

33. Say: 'Who provides for you out of heaven and earth? Who controls hearing and sight? Who brings forth the living from the dead and the dead from the living? Who directs the whole affair?' They will say, 'Allah.' Say, 'So will you not have taqwa?' Yunus 31

34. 'Allah expands the provision of any of His slaves He wills or restricts it. Al-Qasas 82

35. 'Allah provides for whoever He wills without any reckoning.' Al 'Imran 37

Testing, Trials and Calamities

1. We will test you with a certain amount of fear and hunger and loss of wealth and life and fruits. But give good news to the

steadfast: Those who, when disaster strikes them, say, 'We belong to Allah and to Him we will return.' Those are the people who will have blessings and mercy from their Lord; they are the ones who are guided. Al-Baqara 155-157

2. Or did you imagine that you were going to enter the Garden without Allah knowing those among you who had struggled and knowing the steadfast? Al 'Imran 142

3. But then you faltered, disputing the command, and disobeyed after He showed you what you love.* Among you are those who want the dunya and among you are those who want the akhira. Then He turned you from them in order to test you – but He has pardoned you. Allah shows favour to the muminun. Al 'Imran 152

4. The life of the dunya is just the enjoyment of delusion. You will be tested in your wealth and in yourselves and you will hear many abusive words from those given the Book before you and from those who are mushrikun. But if you are steadfast and have taqwa, that is the most resolute course to take. Al 'Imran 186-187

5. ...We tried them with good and evil so that hopefully they would return. Al-A'raf 168

6. Know that your wealth and children are a trial... Al-Anfal 28

7. Do not let their wealth and their children impress you. Allah merely wants to punish them by them in the dunya, and for them to expire while they are kafirun. At-Tawba 55

8. Musa said, 'My people! if you have iman in Allah, then put your trust in Him, if you are Muslims.' They said, 'We have put our trust in Allah. Our Lord, Do not make us a target for this wrongdoing people...' Yunus 84-85

9. But to those who made hijra after they were persecuted and then did jihad and remained steadfast, to them your Lord is All-Compassionate, Most Merciful. An-Nahl 110

10. We made everything on the earth adornment for it so that we could test them to see whose actions are the best. Al-Kahf 7

11. Do not direct your eyes longingly to what We have given certain of them to enjoy, the flower of the life of this world, so that We can test them by it. Your Lord's provision is better and longer lasting. Ta Ha 131

12. Your wealth and children are a trial. But with Allah there is an immense reward. At-Taghabun 15

13. Or did you suppose that you would be left without Allah knowing those of you who have done jihad... At-Tawba 16

14. It is He who appointed you khalifs on the earth and raised some of you above others in rank so He could test you regarding what He has given you. Al-An'am 166

15. What assailed you on the day the two armies met was by Allah's permission, so that He would know the muminun. Al 'Imran 166

16. And We cut them up on the earth into parties, some of them being righteous and others of them falling short of that, and We tried them with blessings and with misfortunes, that they might turn to Allah. Al-A'raf 168

17. We test you with both good and evil as a trial. And you will be returned to Us. Al-Anbiya 35

18. Do people imagine that they will be left to say, 'We have iman,' and will not be tested? Al-'Ankabut 2

19. We will test you until We know the true fighters among you and those who are steadfast and test what is reported of you. Muhammad 31

20. Which one of your Lord's blessings do you then dispute? An-Najm 55

21. And We sent down iron in which there lies great force and which has many uses for mankind, so that Allah might know those who help Him and His Messengers in the Unseen. Allah is All-Strong, Almighty. Al-Hadid 25

22. For all I know it might be a trial for you and you will have enjoyment for a time.' Al-Anbiya 111

23. ...so that He can make what Shaytan insinuates a trial for those with sickness in their hearts and for those whose hearts are hard – the wrongdoers are entrenched in hostility – Al-Hajj 53

24. When harm touches man he calls on Us. Then when We grant him a blessing from Us he says, 'I have only been given this because of my knowledge.' In fact it is a trial but most of them do not know it. Az-Zumar 49

25. You who have iman! seek help in steadfastness and salat. Allah is with the steadfast. Al-Baqara 153
26. ... and who are steadfast in poverty and illness and in battle. Those are the people who are true. They are the people who have taqwa. Al-Baqara 177
27. It is Allah Who gives life and causes to die. Al 'Imran 156
28. If Allah touches you with harm, none can remove it but Him. If He touches you with good, He has power over all things. Al-An'am 17
29. Say:'Who rescues you from the darkness of the land and sea? You call on Him humbly and secretly:"If you rescue us from this, we will truly be among the thankful."' Al-An'am 63
30. As for those who have iman and do right actions – We impose on no self any more than it can bear. Al-A'raf 42
31. When harm touches man, he calls on Us, lying on his side or sitting down or standing up. Then when We remove the harm from him he carries on as if he had never called on Us when the harm first touched him. In that way We make what they have done appear good to the profligate. Yunus 12
32. When We let people taste mercy after hardship has afflicted them, immediately they plot against Our Signs. Say: 'Allah is swifter at plotting.' Your plotting is recorded by Our Messengers. Yunus 21
33. We do not impose on any self any more than it can stand. With Us there is a Book which speaks the truth. They will not be wronged. Al-Muminun 62
34. When We give people a taste of mercy, they rejoice in it, but when something bad happens to them because of what they themselves have done, they immediately lose all hope. Ar-Rum 36
35. ...When We let a man taste mercy from Us he exults in it. But if something bad strikes him for what he has done he is ungrateful. Ash-Shura 48
36. No misfortune occurs except by Allah's permission. Whoever has iman in Allah – He will guide his heart. Allah has knowledge of all things. At-Taghabun 11
37. Be fearful of trials which will not afflict solely those among you who do wrong. Know that Allah is severe in retribution. Al-Anfal 25

Courtesy

1. You who have iman! do not enter houses other than your own until you have asked permission and greeted their inhabitants. That is better for you, so that hopefully you will pay heed. And if you find no one at home do not go in until permission has been granted you. And if you are told to go away then go away. That is purer for you. Allah knows what you do. There is nothing wrong in your entering houses where no one lives and where there is some service for you. Allah knows what you divulge and what you conceal. An-Nur 27-29

2. You who have iman! those you own as slaves and those of you who have not yet reached puberty should ask your permission to enter at three times: before the Dawn Prayer, when you have undressed at noon, and after the Salat al-'Isha' – three times of nakedness for you. There is nothing wrong for you or them at other times in moving around among yourselves from one to another. In this way Allah makes the Signs clear to you. Allah is All-Knowing, All-Wise. Once your children have reached puberty, they should ask your permission to enter as those before them also asked permission. In this way Allah makes His Signs clear to you. Allah is All-Knowing, All-Wise. An-Nur 56-57

3. As for women who are past child-bearing age and no longer have any hope of getting married, there is nothing wrong in their removing their outer clothes, provided they do not flaunt their adornments; but to refrain from doing so is better for them. Allah is All-Hearing, All-Knowing. An-Nur 58

4. There is no objection to the blind, no objection to the lame, no objection to the sick nor to yourselves if you eat in your own houses or your fathers' houses or your mothers' houses or your brothers' houses or your sisters' houses or the houses of your paternal uncles or paternal aunts or the houses of your maternal uncles or maternal aunts or places to which you own the keys or those of your friends. There is nothing wrong in your eating together or eating separately. And when you enter houses greet one another with a greeting from Allah, blessed and good. In this

way Allah makes the Signs clear to you so that hopefully you will use your intellect. An-Nur 59

5. You who have iman! do not raise your voices above the voice of the Prophet and do not be as loud when speaking to him as you are when speaking to one another, lest your actions should come to nothing without your realising it. Al-Hujurat 1

6. You who have iman! if a deviator brings you a report, scrutinize it carefully in case you attack people in ignorance and so come to greatly regret what you have done. Al-Hujurat 6

7. The muminun are brothers, so make peace between your brothers and have taqwa of Allah so that hopefully you will gain mercy. Al-Hujurat 10

8. You who have iman! people should not ridicule others who may be better than themselves; nor should any women ridicule other women who may be better than themselves. And do not find fault with one another or insult each other with derogatory nicknames. How evil it is to have a name for evil conduct after coming to iman! Those people who do not turn from it are wrongdoers. Al-Hujurat 11

9. You who have iman! avoid most suspicion. Indeed some suspicion is a crime. And do not spy and do not backbite one another. Would any of you like to eat his brother's dead flesh? No, you would hate it. And have taqwa of Allah. Allah is Ever-Returning, Most Merciful. Al-Hujurat 12

10. You who have iman! when you are told: 'Make room in the gathering,' then make room and Allah will make room for you! And when it is said, 'Get up', get up. Allah will raise in rank those of you who have iman and those who have been given knowledge. Allah is aware of what you do. Al-Mujadila 11

11. So come to houses by their doors and have taqwa of Allah, so that hopefully you will be successful. Al-Baqara 189

12. When you are greeted with a greeting, return the greeting or improve on it. Allah takes account of everything. An-Nisa 86

13. Do not say, 'You are not a mumin', to someone who greets you as a Muslim, simply out of desire for the goods of this world. An-Nisa 94

14. They will be given their reward twice over because they have been steadfast and because they ward off the bad with the good and give from what we have provided for them. When they hear worthless talk they turn away from it and say, 'We have our actions and you have your actions. Peace be upon you. We do not desire the company of the ignorant.' Al-Qasas 54-55

15. Ward off evil with what is better... Al-Muminun 96

16. A good action and a bad action are not the same. Repel the bad with something better and, if there is enmity between you and someone else, he will be like a bosom friend. None will obtain it but those who are truly steadfast. None will obtain it but those who have great good fortune. Fussilat 34-35

Accusations and Slander

1. When news of any matter reaches them they spread it about, whether it is of a reassuring or disquieting nature. If they had only referred it to the Messenger and those in command among them, those among them able to discern the truth about it would have had proper knowledge of it. An-Nisa 83

2. Have you authority to say this or are you saying about Allah what you do not know? Yunus 68

3. Do not pursue what you have no knowledge of. Hearing, sight and hearts will all be questioned. Bani Isra'il 36

4. But there are some people who trade in distracting tales to misguide people from Allah's Way knowing nothing about it and to make a mockery of it. Such people will have a humiliating punishment. Luqman 6

5. And those who abuse men and women who are muminun, when they have not merited it, bear the weight of slander and clear wrongdoing. Al-Ahzab 58

6. Do not mix up truth with falsehood and knowingly hide the truth. Al-Baqara 42

7. Say: 'Allah does not command indecency. Do you say things about Allah you do not know?' Al-A'raf 28

8. Why, when you heard it, did you not, as men and women of the muminun, instinctively think good thoughts and say, 'This is

obviously a lie'? Why did they not produce four witnesses to it? Since they did not bring four witnesses, in Allah's sight, they are liars. An-Nur 12-13

9. You were bandying it about on your tongues, your mouths uttering something about which you had no knowledge. You considered it to be a trivial matter, but, in Allah's sight, it is immense. Why, when you heard it, did you not say, 'We have no business speaking about this. Glory be to You! This is a terrible slander!'? An-Nur 15-16

10. Those who accuse women who are chaste, but who are careless and yet have iman, are cursed both in the dunya and the akhira, and they will have a terrible punishment. An-Nur 23

Promises, Trusts and Oaths

1. You who have iman! fulfil your contracts. Al-Ma'ida 1

2. It is only people of intelligence who pay heed: those who fulfil Allah's contract and do not break their agreement... Ar-Ra'd 20

3. Fulfil your contracts. Contracts will be asked about. Bani Isra'il 34

4. ...those who honour their trusts and contracts, those who stand by their testimony, those who safeguard their salat. Such people will be in Gardens, highly honoured. Al-Ma'arij 32-35

5. Allah does not take you to task for your inadvertent oaths, but He will take you to task for oaths you make intentionally. The expiation in that case is to feed ten poor people with the average amount you feed your family, or clothe them, or free a slave. Anyone without the means to do so should fast three days. That is the expiation for breaking oaths when you have sworn them. Keep your oaths. In this way Allah makes His Signs clear to you, so that hopefully you will be thankful. Al-Ma'ida 89

6. Do not sell Allah's contract for a paltry price. What is with Allah is better for you if you only knew. An-Nahl 95

7. No, the truth is, if people honour their contracts and have taqwa of Him, Allah loves those who have taqwa. Al 'Imran 76

8. But because of their breaking of their covenant, We have cursed them and made their hearts hard. Al-Ma'ida 13

9. Allah will not take you to task for inadvertent statements in your oaths, but He will take you to task for the intention your hearts have made. Allah is Ever-Forgiving, All-Forbearing. Al-Baqara 225

10. ...those who honour their contracts when they make them... Al-Baqara 177

11. No Prophet would ever be guilty of misappropriation. Those who misappropriate will arrive on the Day of Rising with what they have misappropriated. Then every self will be paid in full for what it earned. They will not be wronged. Al 'Imran 161

12. Do you not see those who have turned to people with whom Allah is angry? They belong neither to you nor to them. And they swear to falsehood and do so knowingly. Al-Mujadila 14

13. Be true to Allah's contract when you have agreed to it, and do not break your oaths once they are confirmed and you have made Allah your guarantee. Allah knows what you do. Do not be like a woman who spoils the thread she has spun by unravelling it after it is strong, by making your oaths a means of deceiving one another, merely because one community is bigger than another. Allah is only testing you by this... An-Nahl 91- 92

14. Do not make your oaths a means of deceiving one another or your foot will slip after it was firmly placed and you will taste evil for barring access to the Way of Allah and you will have a terrible punishment. An-Nahl 94

15. Those who pledge you [Muhammad] their allegiance pledge allegiance to Allah. Allah's hand is over their hands. He who breaks his pledge only breaks it against himself. But as for him who fulfils the contract he has made with Allah, We will pay him an immense reward. Al-Fath 10

16. O Prophet! Why do you make haram what Allah has made halal for you, seeking to please your wives? Allah is Ever-Forgiving, Most Merciful. Allah has made the expiation of your oaths obligatory for you. Allah is your Master – He is the All-Knowing, the All-Wise. At-Tahrim 2 [The expiation of oaths is described in No. 5 above]

17. Do not, by your oaths, make Allah a pretext to avoid good action and having taqwa and putting things right between people. Al-Baqara 224

18. We did not find many of them [the kuffar] worthy of their contract. We found most of them deviators. Al-A'raf 102

19. You who have iman! do not betray Allah and His Messenger, and do not knowingly betray your trusts. Al-Anfal 27

Shari'ah

Justice

1. Allah commands you to return to their owners the things you hold on trust and, when you judge between people, to judge with justice. How excellent is what Allah exhorts you to do! Allah is All-Hearing, All-Seeing. An-Nisa 58
2. You who have iman! be upholders of justice, bearing witness for Allah alone, even against yourselves or your parents and relatives. Whether they are rich or poor, Allah is well able to look after them. Do not follow your own desires and deviate from the truth. If you twist or turn away, Allah is aware of what you do. An-Nisa 135
3. But if you do judge, judge between them justly. Allah loves the just. Al-Ma'ida 42
4. Man is indeed wrongdoing, ungrateful. Ibrahim 34
5. Allah commands justice and doing good An-Nahl 90
6. If you want to retaliate, retaliate to the same degree as the injury done to you. But if you are patient, it is better to be patient. An-Nahl 126
7. You who have iman! show integrity for the sake of Allah, bearing witness with justice. Do not let hatred for a people incite you into not being just. Be just. That is closer to taqwa. Have taqwa of Allah. Allah is aware of what you do. Al-Ma'ida 8
8. ...that you are equitable when you speak – even if a near relative is concerned; and that you fulfil Allah's contract. That is what He instructs you to do, so that hopefully you will pay heed. Al-An'am 153
9. This is My Path and it is straight, so follow it. Do not follow other ways or you will become cut off from His Way. That is what He instructs you to do, so that hopefully you will have taqwa. Al-An'am 154
10. Say: 'My Lord has commanded justice.... Al-A'raf 29
11. We sent Our Messengers with the Clear Signs and sent down the Book and the Balance with them so that mankind might establish justice. Al-Hadid 25

Shari'ah

Permissible and Impermissible

1. Mankind! eat what is good and lawful on the earth. And do not follow in the footsteps of Shaytan. Al-Baqara 168
2. He has only forbidden you carrion, blood and pork and what has been consecrated to other than Allah. But anyone who is forced to eat it – without desiring it or going to excess in it – commits no crime. Allah is Ever-Forgiving, Most Merciful. Al-Baqara 173
3. Today all good things have been made halal for you. And the food of those given the Book is also halal for you and your food is halal for them. Al-Ma'ida 5
4. Haram for you are carrion, blood and pork, and what has been consecrated to other than Allah, and animals which have been strangled, and animals which have been killed by a blow, and animals which have fallen to their death, and animals which have been gored, and animals which wild beasts have eaten – except those you are able to slaughter properly – and animals which have been sacrificed on altars, and deciding things by means of divining arrows – that is deviance. … But if anyone is forced by hunger, not intending any wrongdoing, Allah is Ever-Forgiving, Most Merciful. Al-Ma'ida 3
5. You who have iman! do not make haram the good things Allah has made halal for you, and do not overstep the limits. Allah does not love people who overstep the limits. Al-Ma'ida 87
6. Eat the halal and good things Allah has provided for you, and have taqwa of Allah, Him in Whom you have iman. Al-Ma'ida 88
7. Eat that over which the name of Allah has been mentioned,if you have iman in His Signs. What is the matter with you that you do not eat hat over which the name of Allah has been mentioned,when He has made clear to you what He has made haram for you except when you are forced to eat it? Many people lead others astray through their whims and desires without having any knowledge. Your Lord knows best those who overstep the limits. Al-An'am 119-120
8. Do not eat anything over which the name of Allah has not been mentioned. To do so is sheer deviance. The shaytans inspire their friends to dispute with you. If you obeyed them you would then be mushrikun. Al-An'am 122

9. Say:'I do not find, in what has been revealed to me, any food it is haram to eat except for carrion, flowing blood, and pork – for that is unclean – or some deviance consecrated to other than Allah. But if anyone is forced to eat it, without desiring to or going to excess in it, your Lord is Ever-Forgiving, Most Merciful.' Al-An'am 146

10. So eat from what Allah has provided for you, halal and good, and be thankful for the blessing of Allah if it is Him you worship. An-Nahl 114

11. Eat of the good things We have provided for you but do not go to excess in it or My anger will be unleashed on you. Anyone who has My anger unleashed on him has plunged to his ruin. Ta Ha 81

12. [Allah i] ...provided you with good and wholesome things... Al-Mumin 64

13. Say: 'My Lord has forbidden indecency, both open and hidden, and wrong action, and unrightful tyranny, and associating anything with Allah for which He has sent down no authority, and saying things about Allah you do not know.' Al-A'raf 33

14. Say: 'Come and I will recite to you what your Lord has made haram for you': that you do not associate anything with Him; that you are good to your parents; that you do not kill your children because of poverty –We will provide for you and them; that you do not approach indecency –outward or inward; that you do not kill any person Allah has made inviolate –except with the right to do so. That is what He instructs you to do so that hopefully you will use your intellect. Al-An'am 152

15. Say: 'What do you think about the things Allah has sent down to you as provision which you have then designated as halal and haram?' Say: 'Has Allah given you authority to do this or are you inventing lies against Allah?' Yunus 59

16. He has forbidden you carrion, blood and pork and anything consecrated to other than Allah. But if someone is forced to eat it, without desiring to or going to excess in it, your Lord is Ever-Forgiving, Most Merciful. Do not say about what your lying tongues describe: 'This is halal and this is haram,' inventing lies against Allah. Those who invent lies against Allah are not

successful – a brief enjoyment, then they will have a painful punishment. An-Nahl 115-116

17. Say: 'Bad things and good things are not the same, even though the abundance of the bad things may seem attractive to you.' Have taqwa of Allah, people of intelligence, so that hopefully you will be successful. Al-Ma'ida 100

18. They will ask you what is halal for them. Say: 'All good things are halal for you, and also what is caught for you by hunting animals which you have trained as Allah has taught you. Eat what they catch for you, mentioning Allah's name over it.' And have taqwa of Allah. Allah is swift at reckoning. Al-Ma'ida 4

19. They will ask you about alcoholic drinks and gambling. Say, 'There is great wrong in both of them and also certain benefits for mankind. But the wrong in them is greater than the benefit.' Al-Baqara 219

20. You who have iman! wine and gambling, stone altars and divining arrows are filth from the handiwork of Shaytan. Avoid them completely so that hopefully you will be successful. Al-Ma'ida 90

21. Shaytan wants to stir up enmity and hatred between you by means of wine and gambling, and to debar you from remembrance of Allah and from salat. Will you not then give them up? Al-Ma'ida 91

22. Those who practise riba will not rise from the grave except as someone driven mad by Shaytan's touch. That is because they say, 'Trade is the same as riba.' But Allah has permitted trade and He has forbidden riba. Al-Baqara 275

23. You who have iman! do not feed on riba, multiplied and then remultiplied. Have taqwa of Allah so that hopefully you will be successful. Al 'Imran 130

24. Because of wrongdoing on the part of the Jews, We made haram for them some good things which had previously been halal for them; and because of their obstructing many people from the Way of Allah, and because of their practising riba when they were forbidden to do it, and because of their consuming people's wealth by wrongful means, We have prepared for the kafirun

among them a painful punishment. An—Nisa 149-50

25. What you give with usurious intent, aiming to get back a greater amount from people's wealth, does not become greater with Allah… Ar-Rum 39

26. It is prohibited to mistreat parents. Allah has ordered to treat parents nicely. Al-An'am 152

27. [Shaytan said] 'I will lead them astray and fill them with false hopes. I will command them and they will cut off cattle's ears. I will command them and they will change Allah's creation.' Anyone who takes Shaytan as his protector in place of Allah has clearly lost everything. An-Nisa 119

28. Abandon wrong action, outward and inward. Those who commit wrong action will be repaid for what they perpetrated. Al-An'am 121

29. Do not kill your children out of fear of being poor. We will provide for them and you. Killing them is a terrible mistake. Bani Isra'il 31

30. You who have iman! have taqwa of Allah and forgo any remaining riba if you are muminun. If you do not, know that it means war from Allah and His Messenger. But if you make tawba you may have your capital, without wronging and without being wronged. If someone is in difficult circumstances, there should be a deferral until things are easier. But making a free gift of it would be better for you if you only knew. Have fear of a Day when you will be returned to Allah. Then every self will be paid in full for what it earned. They will not be wronged. Al-Baqara 278-281

31. Why do their scholars and rabbis not prohibit them from evil speech and acquiring ill-gotten gains? What an evil thing they invent! Al-Ma'ida 63

Debts and writing them down

1. You who have iman! when you take on a debt for a specified period, write it down. A writer should write it down between you justly. No writer should refuse to write; as Allah has taught him, so he should write. The one incurring the debt should dictate and should have taqwa of Allah his Lord and not reduce it in any way.

If the person incurring the debt is incompetent or weak or unable to dictate, then his guardian should dictate for him justly. Two men among you should act as witnesses. But if there are not two men, then a man and two women with whom you are satisfied as witnesses; then if one of them forgets, the other can remind her. Witnesses should not refuse when they are called upon. Do not think it too trivial to write down, whether small or large, with the date that it falls due. Doing that is more just in Allah's sight and more helpful when bearing witness and more likely to eliminate any doubt – unless it is an immediate transaction hand to hand, taken and given without delay. There is nothing wrong in your not writing that down. Call witnesses when you trade. Neither writer nor witness should be put under pressure. If you do that, it is deviancy on your part. Have taqwa of Allah and Allah will give you knowledge. Allah has knowledge of all things. If you are on a journey and cannot find a writer, something can be left as a security. If you leave things on trust with one another the one who is trusted must deliver up his trust and have taqwa of Allah his Lord. Do not conceal testimony. If someone does conceal it, his heart commits a crime. Allah knows what you do. Al-Baqara 282-283

2. You who have iman! do not consume one another's property by false means, but only by means of mutually agreed trade. And do not kill yourselves. Allah is Most Merciful to you. An-Nisa 29

Retaliation

1. You who have iman! retaliation is prescribed for you in the case of people killed: free man for free man, slave for slave, female for female. But if someone is absolved by his brother, blood-money should be claimed with correctness and paid with good will. That is an easement and a mercy from your Lord. Al-Baqara 178

2. We prescribed for them in it: a life for a life, an eye for an eye, a nose for a nose, an ear for an ear, a tooth for a tooth, and retaliation for wounds. But if anyone forgoes that as a sadaqa, it will act as expiation for him. Al-Ma'ida 45

3. If you want to retaliate, retaliate to the same degree as the in-

jury done to you. But if you are patient, it is better to be patient. An-Nahl 126
4. If someone is wrongly killed We have given authority to his next of kin. But he should not be excessive in taking life... Bani Isra'il 33
5. And if anyone inflicts an injury the same as the one done to him and then is again oppressed, Allah will come to his aid. Al-Hajj 60
6. A mumin should never kill another mumin unless it is by mistake. Anyone who kills a mumin by mistake should free a mumin slave and pay blood-money to his family unless they forgo it as a sadaqa. If he is from a people who are your enemies and is a mumin, you should free a mumin slave. If he is from a people you have a treaty with, blood money should be paid to his family and you should free a mumin slave. Anyone who cannot find the means should fast two consecutive months. This is a concession from Allah. Allah is All-Knowing, All-Wise. An-Nisa 92
7. There is life for you in retaliation, people of intelligence, so that hopefully you will have taqwa. Al-Baqara 179
8. Sacred month in return for sacred month – sacred things are subject to retaliation. So if anyone oversteps the limits against you, overstep against him the same as he did to you. But have taqwa of Allah. Know that Allah is with those who have taqwa. Al-Baqara 194

Marriage

1. Do not marry women of the mushrikun until they have iman. A slavegirl who is one of the muminun is better for you than a woman of the mushrikun, even though she may attract you. And do not marry men of the mushrikun until they have iman. A slave who is one of the muminun is better for you than a man of the mushrikun, even though he may attract you. Such people call you to the Fire whereas Allah calls you, with His permission, to the Garden and forgiveness. He makes His Signs clear to people so that hopefully they will pay heed. Al-Baqara 221
2. A man who has fornicated may only marry a woman who has fornicated or a woman of the mushrikun. A woman who has

fornicated may only marry a man who has fornicated or a man of the mushrikun. Doing such a thing is haram for the muminun. An-Nur 3

3. Your women are fertile fields for you, so come to your fertile fields however you like. Send good ahead for yourselves and have taqwa of Allah. Know that you are going to meet Him. And give good news to the muminun. Al-Baqara 223

4. If a woman fears cruelty or aversion on her husband's part, there is nothing wrong in the couple becoming reconciled. Reconciliation is better. But people are prone to selfish greed. If you do good and have taqwa, Allah is aware of what you do. An-Nisa 128

Divorce

1. Those who swear to abstain from sexual relations with their wives can wait for a period of up to four months. If they then retract their oath, Allah is Ever-Forgiving, Most Merciful.
2. If they are determined to divorce, Allah is All-Hearing, All-Knowing.
3. Divorced women should wait by themselves for three menstrual cycles; and it is not lawful for them to conceal what Allah has created in their wombs if they have iman in Allah and the Last Day. Their husbands have the right to take them back within that time, if they desire to be reconciled. Women possess rights similar to those held over them to be honoured with fairness; but men have a degree above them. Allah is Almighty, All-Wise.
4. Divorce can be pronounced two times; in which case wives may be retained with correctness and courtesy or released with good will. It is not lawful for you to keep anything you have given them unless a couple fear that they will not remain within Allah's limits. If you fear that they will not remain within Allah's limits, there is nothing wrong in the wife ransoming herself with some of what she received. These are Allah's limits so do not overstep them. Those who overstep Allah's limits are wrongdoers.
5. But if a man divorces his wife a third time, she is not halal for him after that until she has married another husband. Then if he divorces her, there is nothing wrong in the original couple get-

ting back together provided they think they will remain within Allah's limits. These are Allah's limits which he has made clear to people who know.

6. When you divorce women and they reach the end of their 'idda, then either retain them with correctness and courtesy or release them with correctness and courtesy. Do not retain them by force, thus overstepping the limits. Anyone who does that has wronged himself. Do not make a mockery of Allah's Signs. Remember Allah's blessing to you and the Book and Wisdom He has sent down to you to admonish you. Have taqwa of Allah and know that Allah has knowledge of all things.

7. When you divorce women and they reach the end of their 'idda, do not prevent them from marrying their first husbands if they have mutually agreed to it with correctness and courtesy. This is an admonition for those of you who have iman in Allah and the Last Day. That is better and purer for you. Allah knows and you do not know.

8. Mothers should nurse their children for two full years – those who wish to complete the full term of nursing. It is the duty of the fathers to feed and clothe them with correctness and courtesy – no self is charged with more than it can bear. No mother should be put under pressure in respect of her child nor any father in respect of his child. The same duty is incumbent on the heir. If the couple both wish weaning to take place after mutual agreement and consultation, there is nothing wrong in their doing that. If you wish to find wet-nurses for your children, there is nothing wrong in your doing that provided you hand over to them what you have agreed to give with correctness and courtesy. Have taqwa of Allah and know that Allah sees what you do.

9. Those of you who die leaving wives behind: they should wait by themselves for four months and ten nights. When their 'idda comes to an end, you are not to blame for anything they do with themselves with correctness and courtesy. Allah is aware of what you do.

10. Nor is there anything wrong in any allusion to marriage you make to a woman, nor for any you keep to yourself. Allah knows that you will say things to them. But do not make secret arrange-

ments with them, rather only speak with correctness and courtesy. Do not finally decide on the marriage contract until the prescribed period has come to its end. Know that Allah knows what is in your selves, so beware of Him! And know that Allah is Ever-Forgiving, All-Forbearing. (The above ten sections: al-Baqara 227-233)

11. There is nothing wrong in your divorcing women before you have touched them or allotted a dowry to them. But give them a gift – he who is wealthy according to his means and he who is less well off according to his means – a gift to be given with correctness and courtesy: a duty for all good-doers.

12. If you divorce them before you have touched them but have already allotted them a dowry, they should have half the amount which you allotted, unless they forgo it or the one in charge of the marriage contract forgoes it. To forgo it is closer to taqwa. Do not forget to show generosity to one another. Allah sees what you do. (The above two sections: al-Baqara 234-5)

13. Those of you who die leaving wives behind should make a bequest to their wives of maintenance for a year without them having to leave their homes. But if they do leave you are not to blame for anything they do with themselves with correctness and courtesy. Allah is Almighty, All-Wise. Al-Baqara 238

14. Divorced women should receive maintenance given with correctness and courtesy: a duty for all who have taqwa. Al-Baqara 239

15. You who have iman! when you marry believing women and then divorce them before you have touched them, there is no 'idda for you to calculate for them, so give them a gift and let them go with kindness. Al-Ahzab 49

16. If you are afraid of not behaving justly towards orphans, then marry other permissible women, two, three or four. But if you are afraid of not treating them equally, then only one, or those you own as slaves. An-Nisa 3

17. That makes it more likely that you will not be unfair. Give women their dowry as an outright gift. But if they are happy to give you some of it, make use of it with pleasure and goodwill. An-Nisa 4

18. If any of your women commit fornication, four of you must

be witnesses against them. If they bear witness, detain them in their homes until death releases them or Allah ordains another procedure for their case. An-Nisa 15

19. If two men commit a like abomination, punish them. If they make tawba and reform, leave them alone. Allah is Ever-Returning, Most Merciful. An-Nisa 16

20. You who have iman! it is not halal for you to inherit women by force. Nor may you treat them harshly so that you can make off with part of what you have given them, unless they commit an act of flagrant indecency. Live together with them correctly and courteously. If you dislike them, it may well be that you dislike something in which Allah has placed a lot of good. An-Nisa 19.

21. If you desire to exchange one wife for another and have given your original wife a large amount, do not take any of it. An-Nisa 20

22. How could you take it when you have been intimate with one another and they have made a binding contract with you? An-Nisa 21

23. Haram for you are: your mothers and your daughters and your sisters, your maternal aunts and your paternal aunts, your brothers' daughters and your sisters' daughters, your foster mothers who have suckled you, your foster sisters by suckling, your wives' mothers, your stepdaughters who are under your protection: the daughters of your wives whom you have had sexual relations with (though if you have not had sexual relations with them there is nothing blameworthy for you in it then), the wives of your sons whom you have fathered, and marrying two sisters at the same time – except for what may have already taken place. Allah is Ever-Forgiving, Most Merciful. An-Nisa 23

24. And also married women, except for those you have taken in war as slaves. This is what Allah has prescribed for you. Apart from that He has made all other women halal for you provided you seek them with your wealth in marriage and not in fornication. An-Nisa 24

25. Men have charge of women because Allah has preferred the

one above the other and because they spend their wealth on them. Right-acting women are obedient, safeguarding their husband's interests in his absence as Allah has guarded them. If there are women whose disobedience you fear, you may admonish them, refuse to sleep with them, and then beat them. But if they obey you, do not look for a way to punish them. Allah is All-High, Most Great. An-Nisa 34

26. If you fear a breach between a couple, send an arbiter from his people and an arbiter from her people. If the couple desire to put things right, Allah will bring about a reconciliation between them. Allah is All-Knowing, All-Aware. An-Nisa 35

27. You will not be able to be completely fair between your wives, however hard you try. But do not be completely partial so as to leave a wife, as it were, suspended in mid-air. And if you make amends and have taqwa, Allah is Ever-Forgiving, Most Merciful. An-Nisa 128

28. And do not go near to fornication. It is an indecent act, an evil way. Bani Isra'il 32

29. A woman and a man who commit fornication: flog both of them with one hundred lashes and do not let compassion for either of them possess you where Allah's deen is concerned, if you have iman in Allah and the Last Day. A number of muminun should witness their punishment. An-Nur 2

30. Do not marry any women your fathers married – except for what may have already taken place. That is an indecent act, a loathsome thing and an evil path. An-Nisa 22

31. Marry off those among you who are unmarried and those of your slaves and slavegirls who are salihun. If they are poor, Allah will enrich them from His bounty. Allah is All-Encompassing, All-Knowing. An-Nur 32

32. So are chaste women from among the muminun and chaste women of those given the Book before you [halal for you in marriage], once you have given them their dowries in marriage, not in fornication or taking them as lovers. Al-Ma'ida 5

33. But those who make accusations against chaste women and then do not produce four witnesses: flog them with eighty lashes

and never again accept them as witnesses. Such people are deviators – except for those who after that make tawba and put things right. Allah is Ever-Forgiving, Most Merciful. Those who make an accusation against their wives and have no witnesses except themselves, such people should testify four times by Allah that they are telling the truth and a fifth time that Allah's curse will be upon them if they are lying. And the punishment is removed from her if she testifies four times by Allah that he is lying and a fifth time that Allah's anger will be upon her if he is telling the truth. Were it not for Allah's favour to you and His mercy and that Allah is Ever-Returning, All-Wise. An-Nur 4-10

34. Corrupt women are for corrupt men and corrupt men are for corrupt women, Good women are for good men and good men are for good women. The latter are innocent of what they say. They will have forgiveness and generous provision. An-Nur 26

35. Those who cannot find the means to marry should be abstinent until Allah enriches them from His bounty... An-Nur 33

36. Allah has not allotted to any man two hearts within his breast, nor has He made those of your wives you equate with your mothers[1] your actual mothers nor has He made your adopted sons your actual sons. These are just words coming out of your mouths. But Allah speaks the truth and He guides to the Way. Al-Ahzab 4

37. Those of you who divorce your wives by equating them with your mothers, they are not your mothers.[1] Your mothers are only those who gave birth to you. What you are saying is wrong and a slanderous lie. But Allah is Ever-Pardoning, Ever-Forgiving. Al-Mujadila 2

38. If there are women whose disobedience you fear, you may admonish them, refuse to sleep with them, and then beat them. But if they obey you, do not look for a way to punish them. Allah is All-High, Most Great. An-Nisa 34

39. O Prophet! When any of you divorce women, divorce them during their period of purity and calculate their 'idda carefully.

---

[1] This refers to a type of divorce in which men would equate their wives with their mothers, thus preventing any further relations with them.

And have taqwa of Allah, your Lord. Do not evict them from their homes, nor should they leave, unless they commit an outright indecency. Those are Allah's limits, and anyone who oversteps Allah's limits has wronged himself. You never know, it may well be that after that Allah will cause a new situation to develop. At-Talaq 1

40. Then when they have reached the end of their 'idda either retain them with correctness and courtesy or part from them with correctness and courtesy. Call two upright men from among yourselves as witnesses and they should carry out the witnessing for Allah. This is admonishment for all who have iman in Allah and the Last Day. Whoever has taqwa of Allah – He will give him a way out and provide for him from where he does not expect. Whoever puts his trust in Allah – He will be enough for him. Allah always achieves His aim. Allah has appointed a measure for all things. At-Talaq 2-3

41. In the case of those of your wives who are past the age of menstruation, if you have any doubt, their 'idda should be three months, and that also applies to those who have not yet menstruated. The time for women who are pregnant is when they give birth. Whoever has taqwa of Allah – He will make matters easy for him. At-Talaq 4

42. That is Allah's command which He has sent down to you. Whoever has taqwa of Allah – He will erase his bad actions from him and greatly increase his reward. At-Talaq 5

43. Let them live where you live, according to your means. Do not put pressure on them, so as to harass them. If they are pregnant, maintain them until they give birth. If they are suckling for you, give them their wages and consult together with correctness and courtesy. But if you make things difficult for one another, another woman should do the suckling for you. At-Talaq 6

44. Those who divorce their wives by equating them with their mothers, and then wish to go back on what they said, must set free a slave before the two of them may touch one another. This is what you are enjoined to do. Allah is aware of what you do. Anyone who cannot find the means must fast for two consecutive

months before the two of them may touch one another again. And anyone who is unable to do that must feed sixty poor people. That is to affirm your iman in Allah and His Messenger. These are Allah's limits. The kafirun will have a painful punishment. Al-Mujadila 3-4

45. If a couple do separate, Allah will enrich each of them from His boundless wealth. Allah is All-Encompassing, All-Wise. An-Nisa 129

Inheritance

1. Men receive a share of what their parents and relatives leave and women receive a share of what their parents and relatives leave, a fixed share, no matter whether it is a little or a lot. An-Nisa 7

2. Allah instructs you regarding your children: A male receives the same as the share of two females. If there are more than two daughters they receive two-thirds of what you leave. If she is one on her own she receives a half. Each of your parents receives a sixth of what you leave if you have children. If you are childless and your heirs are your parents your mother receives a third. If you have brothers or sisters your mother receives a sixth, after any bequest you make or any debts. With regard to your fathers and your sons, you do not know which of them is going to benefit you more. These are obligatory shares from Allah. Allah is All-Knowing, All-Wise. An-Nisa 11

3. We have appointed heirs for everything that parents and relatives leave. If you have a bond with people, give them their share. Allah is a witness of all things. An-Nisa 33

4. ...nor has He made your adopted sons your actual sons[2]. These are just words coming out of your mouths. But Allah speaks the truth and He guides to the Way. Call them after their fathers. That is closer to justice in Allah's sight. And if you do not know who their fathers were then they are your brothers in the deen and people under your patronage. You are not to blame for any honest mistake you make but only

---

[2] Thus they cannot inherit any of the fixed shares.

for what your hearts premeditate. Allah is Ever-Forgiving, Most Merciful. Al-Ahzab 4-5

5. You devour inheritance with voracious appetites and you have an insatiable love of wealth. Al-Fajr 19-20

6. You receive half of what your wives leave if they are childless. If they have children you receive a quarter of what they leave after any bequest they make or any debts. They receive a quarter of what you leave if you are childless. If you have children they receive an eighth of what you leave after any bequest you make or any debts. If a man or woman has no direct heirs, but has a brother or sister, each of them receives a sixth. If there are more than that they share in a third after any bequest you make or any debts, making sure that no one's rights are prejudiced. This is an instruction from Allah. Allah is All-Knowing, All-Forbearing. An-Nisa 12

7. You who have iman! it is not halal for you to inherit women by force. Nor may you treat them harshly so that you can make off with part of what you have given them... An-Nisa 19

8. They will ask you for a fatwa. Say: 'Allah gives you a fatwa about people who die without direct heirs: If a man dies childless but has a sister she receives half of what he leaves, and he is her heir if she dies childless. If there are two sisters they receive two-thirds of what he leaves. If there are brothers and sisters the males receive the share of two females. Allah makes things clear to you so you will not go astray. Allah has knowledge of all things.' An-Nisa 176

Weights and Measures

1. ...that you give full measure and full weight with justice – We impose on no self any more than it can bear. Al-An'am 153

2. Give full measure when you measure and weigh with a level balance. That is better and gives the best result. Bani Isra'il 35

3. Give full measure. Do not skimp. Weigh with a level balance. Do not diminish people's goods and do not go about the earth, corrupting it. Ash-Shu'ara 181-3

4. He erected heaven and established the balance, so that you would not transgress the balance. Give just weight – do not skimp in the balance. Ar-Rahman 7-9

5. Give full measure and full weight. Do not diminish people's goods. Do not cause corruption in the land after it has been put right. That is better for you if you are muminun. *Al-A'raf 85*
6. My people! Give full measure and full weight with justice; do not diminish people's goods; and do not go about the earth, corrupting it. What endures with Allah is better for you if you are muminun. I am not set over you as your keeper.' *Hud 84-86*
7. Woe to the stinters! Those who, when they take a measure from people, exact full measure, but when they give them a measure or weight, hand over less than is due. Do such people not realise that they will be raised up on a Terrible Day, the Day mankind will stand before the Lord of all the worlds? *Al-Mutaffifin 1-6*

Riba – Usury

1. Those who practise riba will not rise from the grave except as someone driven mad by Shaytan's touch. That is because they say, 'Trade is the same as riba.' But Allah has permitted trade and He has forbidden riba. Whoever is given a warning by his Lord and then desists, can keep what he received in the past and his affair is Allah's concern. But all who return to it will be the Companions of the Fire, remaining in it timelessly, for ever. Allah obliterates riba but makes sadaqa grow in value! Allah does not love any persistently ungrateful wrongdoer. *Al-Baqara 274-5*
2. You who have iman! have taqwa of Allah and forgo any remaining riba if you are muminun. If you do not, know that it means war from Allah and His Messenger. But if you make tawba you may have your capital, without wronging and without being wronged. *Al-Baqara 277-8*
3. You who have iman! do not feed on riba, multiplied and then remultiplied. Have taqwa of Allah so that hopefully you will be successful. *Al 'Imran 130*
4. Because of wrongdoing on the part of the Jews, We made haram for them some good things which had previously been halal for them; and because of their obstructing many people from the Way of Allah, and because of their practising riba when they were forbidden to do it, and because of their consuming people's wealth

by wrongful means, We have prepared for the kafirun among them a painful punishment. An-Nisa 159

Miscellanous

Dress

1. Children of Adam! We have sent down clothing to you to conceal your private parts, and fine apparel, but the garment of taqwa – that is best! That is one of Allah's Signs, so that hopefully you will pay heed. Al-A'raf 26
2. Allah has made shaded places for you in what He has created and He has made shelters for you in the mountains and He has made shirts for you to protect you from the heat and shirts to protect you from each other's violence. In that way He perfects His blessing on you so that hopefully you will become Muslims. An-Nahl 81
3. Say to the muminun that they should lower their eyes and guard their private parts. That is purer for them. Allah is aware of what they do. Say to the mumin women that they should lower their eyes and guard their private parts and not display their adornments – except for what normally shows – and draw their head-coverings across their breasts. They should only display their adornments to their husbands or their fathers or their husbands' fathers, or their sons or their husbands' sons or their brothers or their brothers' sons or their sisters' sons or other women or those they own as slaves or their male attendants who have no sexual desire or children who still have no awareness of women's private parts. Nor should they stamp their feet so that their hidden ornaments are known. Turn to Allah every one of you, muminun, so that hopefully you will have success. An-Nur 30-31
4. [Wives of the Prophet] Remain in your houses and do not display your beauty as it was previously displayed in the Time of Ignorance. Al-Ahzab 33
5. They incur no blame in respect of their fathers or their sons or their brothers or their brothers' or sisters' sons, or their women or any slaves they own. Have taqwa of Allah. Allah is witness of all things. Al-Ahzab 55
6. O Prophet! Tell your wives and daughters and the women of the muminun to draw their outer garments closely round themselves.

This makes it more likely that they will be recognised and not be harmed. Allah is Ever-Forgiving, Most Merciful. Al-Ahzab 59

Travel

1. Have they not travelled in the land and seen the final fate of those before them? They were far greater than them in strength. Allah cannot be withstood in any way, either in the heavens or on earth. He is All-Knowing, All-Powerful. Fatir 43
2. How many wrongdoing cities We destroyed, and now all their roofs and walls are fallen in; how many abandoned wells and stuccoed palaces! Have they not travelled about the earth and do they not have hearts to understand with or ears to hear with? It is not their eyes which are blind but the hearts in their breasts which are blind. Al-Hajj 45-46
3. Have they not travelled in the earth and seen the final fate of those before them? They had greater strength than them and cultivated the land and inhabited it in far greater numbers than they do. Their Messengers also came to them with the Clear Signs. Allah would never have wronged them; but they wronged themselves. Ar-Rum 9
4. Have they not travelled in the land and seen the final fate of those before them? They were more numerous than them and greater in strength and left more and deeper traces on earth, but what they earned was of no use to them. Al-Mumin 82
5. Are they not guided by the many generations We destroyed before them, among whose ruined homes they walk around? There are certainly Signs in that. So will they not listen? As-Sajda 26
6. How many generations before them We destroyed who had greater force than them and scoured many lands! Did they find any way of escape? There is a reminder in that for anyone who has a heart, or who listens well, having seen the evidence. Qaf 36-37
7. Say: 'Travel about the earth and see the final fate of the deniers.' Al-An'am 11
8. Say: 'Travel about the earth and see the final fate of those before. Most of them were mushrikun.' Ar-Rum 42

Bequests

1. It is prescribed for you, when death approaches one of you and if he has some goods to leave, to make a will in favour of his parents and relatives, correctly and fairly: a duty for all those who have taqwa. Then if anyone alters it after hearing it, the crime is on the part of those who alter it. Allah is All-Hearing, All-Knowing. Al-Baqara 180-181
2. But if someone fears bias or wrongdoing on the part of the person making the will, and puts things right between the people involved, in that case he has not committed any crime. Allah is Ever-Forgiving, Most Merciful. Al-Baqara 182
3. Those of you who die leaving wives behind should make a bequest to their wives of maintenance for a year without them having to leave their homes. But if they do leave you are not to blame for anything they do with themselves with correctness and courtesy. Allah is Almighty, All-Wise. Al-Baqara 238 (Abrogated by the ayat on inheritance.)

The Ummah and Islam

1. In this way We have made you a middlemost community. Al-Baqara 143
2. This nation of yours is one nation and I am your Lord, so worship Me. Al-Anbiya 92
3. We have appointed for every nation a rite that they observe, so let them not dispute with you about the matter. Call the people to your Lord. You are guided straight. Al-Hajj 67
4. The deen with Allah is Islam. Al 'Imran 19
5. You are the best nation ever to be produced before mankind. You enjoin the right, forbid the wrong and have iman in Allah. Al 'Imran 110
6. Say: 'I am commanded to be the first of the Muslims,...' Al-An'am 14
7. Do not worship anyone but Allah! Hud 2
8. If they become Muslim, they have been guided. Al 'Imran 20
9. Allah has chosen this deen for you, so do not die except as Muslims. Al-Baqara 132

Miscellaneous

10. There is no compulsion where the deen is concerned. Al-Baqara 256
11. We know best what they say. You are not a dictator over them. So remind, with the Qur'an, whoever fears My Threat. Qaf 45
12. Today I have perfected your deen for you and completed My blessing upon you and I am pleased with Islam as a deen for you. Al-Ma'ida 3

Du'a — Supplications

إِيَّاكَ نَعْبُدُ وَإِيَّاكَ نَسْتَعِينُ ﴿٥﴾ اهدِنَــــا الصِّرَاطَ الْمُسْتَقِيمَ ﴿٦﴾ صِرَاطَ الَّذِينَ أَنْعَمْتَ عَلَيْهِمْ غَيْرِ الْمَغْضُوبِ عَلَيْهِمْ وَلَا الضَّالِّينَ ﴿٧﴾

1. Guide us on the Straight Path, the Path of those whom You have blessed, not of those with anger on them, nor of the misguided. Al-Fatiha 5-7

رَبَّنَا وَاجْعَلْنَا مُسْلِمَيْنِ لَكَ وَمِن ذُرِّيَّتِنَا أُمَّةً مُّسْلِمَةً لَّكَ وَأَرِنَا مَنَاسِكَنَا وَتُبْ عَلَيْنَا إِنَّكَ أَنتَ التَّوَّابُ الرَّحِيمُ ﴿١٢٨﴾

2. 'Our Lord, make us both Muslims submitted to You, and our descendants a Muslim community submitted to You. Show us our rites of worship and turn towards Us. You are the Ever-Returning, the Most Merciful.' Al-Baqara 128

رَبَّنَا لَا تُؤَاخِذْنَا إِن نَّسِينَا أَوْ أَخْطَأْنَا رَبَّنَا وَلَا تَحْمِلْ عَلَيْنَا إِصْرًا كَمَا حَمَلْتَهُ عَلَى الَّذِينَ مِن قَبْلِنَا رَبَّنَا وَلَا تُحَمِّلْنَا مَا لَا طَاقَةَ لَنَا بِهِ وَاعْفُ عَنَّا وَاغْفِرْ لَنَا وَارْحَمْنَا أَنتَ مَوْلَانَا فَانصُرْنَا عَلَى الْقَوْمِ الْكَافِرِينَ ﴿٢٨٦﴾

3. 'Our Lord, do not take us to task if we forget or make a mistake! Our Lord, do not place on us a load like the one You placed on those before us! Our Lord, do not place on us a load we have not the strength to bear! And pardon us; and forgive us; and have mercy on us. You are our Master so help us against the people of the kafirun.' Al-Baqara 286

رَبَّنَا لَا تُزِغْ قُلُوبَنَا بَعْدَ إِذْ هَدَيْتَنَا وَهَبْ لَنَا مِن لَّدُنكَ رَحْمَةً إِنَّكَ أَنتَ الْوَهَّابُ ﴿٨﴾

4. 'Our Lord, do not make our hearts swerve aside after You have guided us. And give us mercy from You. You are the Ever-Giving.' Al 'Imran 8

رَبَّنَا اغْفِرْ لَنَا ذُنُوبَنَا وَإِسْرَافَنَا فِي أَمْرِنَا وَثَبِّتْ أَقْدَامَنَا وَانصُرْنَا عَلَى الْقَوْمِ الْكَافِرِينَ ﴿١٤٧﴾

5. 'Our Lord, forgive us our wrong actions and any excesses we went to in what we did and make our feet firm and help us against these kafir people.' Al 'Imran 147

رَبَّنَا مَا خَلَقْتَ هَذَا بَاطِلاً سُبْحَانَكَ فَقِنَا عَذَابَ النَّارِ ﴿١٩١﴾ رَبَّنَا إِنَّكَ مَن تُدْخِلِ النَّارَ فَقَدْ أَخْزَيْتَهُ وَمَا لِلظَّالِمِينَ مِنْ أَنصَارٍ ﴿١٩٢﴾ رَبَّنَا إِنَّنَا سَمِعْنَا مُنَادِياً يُنَادِي لِلإِيمَانِ أَنْ آمِنُوا بِرَبِّكُمْ فَآمَنَّا رَبَّنَا فَاغْفِرْ لَنَا ذُنُوبَنَا وَكَفِّرْ عَنَّا سَيِّئَاتِنَا وَتَوَفَّنَا مَعَ الأَبْرَارِ ﴿١٩٣﴾ رَبَّنَا وَآتِنَا مَا وَعَدتَّنَا عَلَى رُسُلِكَ وَلاَ تُخْزِنَا يَوْمَ الْقِيَامَةِ إِنَّكَ لاَ تُخْلِفُ الْمِيعَادَ ﴿١٩٤﴾

6. 'Our Lord, You have not created this for nothing. Glory be to You! So safeguard us from the punishment of the Fire. Our Lord, those You cast into the Fire, You have indeed disgraced. The wrongdoers will have no helpers. Our Lord, we heard a caller calling us to iman: "Have iman in your Lord!" and we had iman. Our Lord, forgive us our wrong actions, erase our bad actions from us and take us back to You with those who are truly good. Our Lord, give us what You promised us through Your Messengers, and do not disgrace us on the Day of Rising. You do not break Your promise.' Al 'Imran 191-194

رَبَّنَا ظَلَمْنَا أَنفُسَنَا وَإِن لَّمْ تَغْفِرْ لَنَا وَتَرْحَمْنَا لَنَكُونَنَّ مِنَ الْخَاسِرِينَ ﴿٢٣﴾

7. [Adam and Hawwa said] 'Our Lord, we have wronged ourselves. If you do not forgive us and have mercy on us, we will be among the lost.' Al-A'raf 23

8. Call on your Lord humbly and secretly. He does not love those who overstep the limits. Do not corrupt the earth after it has been put right. Call on Him fearfully and eagerly. Allah's mercy is close to the good-doers. Al-A'raf 54-55

تُضِلُّ بِهَا مَن تَشَاءُ وَتَهْدِي مَن تَشَاءُ أَنتَ وَلِيُّنَا فَاغْفِرْ لَنَا وَارْحَمْنَا وَأَنتَ خَيْرُ الْغَافِرِينَ ﴿١٥٥﴾ وَاكْتُبْ لَنَا فِي هَذِهِ الدُّنْيَا حَسَنَةً وَفِي الآخِرَةِ إِنَّا هُدْنَا إِلَيْكَ

9. [Musa said] 'You misguide [by this trial] those You will and guide those You will. You are our Protector so forgive us and have mercy on us. You are the Best of Forgivers. Prescribe good for us in this dunya and in the akhira. We have truly turned to You.' Al-A'raf 155-156

Du'a – Supplications

$$\text{رَبِّ قَدْ آتَيْتَنِي مِنَ الْمُلْكِ وَعَلَّمْتَنِي مِن تَأْوِيلِ الأَحَادِيثِ فَاطِرَ السَّمَاوَاتِ وَالأَرْضِ}$$
$$\text{أَنتَ وَلِيِّي فِي الدُّنْيَا وَالآخِرَةِ تَوَفَّنِي مُسْلِماً وَأَلْحِقْنِي بِالصَّالِحِينَ ﴿١٠١﴾}$$

10. [Yusuf said] 'My Lord, You have granted power to me on earth and taught me the true meaning of events. Originator of the heavens and earth, You are my Friend in this world and the Next. So take me as a Muslim at my death and join me to the people who are salihun.' Yusuf 101

$$\text{رَبِّ اجْعَلْنِي مُقِيمَ الصَّلاَةِ وَمِن ذُرِّيَّتِي رَبَّنَا وَتَقَبَّلْ دُعَاءِ ﴿٤٠﴾ رَبَّنَا اغْفِرْ لِي}$$
$$\text{وَلِوَالِدَيَّ وَلِلْمُؤْمِنِينَ يَوْمَ يَقُومُ الْحِسَابُ ﴿٤١﴾}$$

11. [Ibrahim said] 'My Lord! Make me and my descendants people who establish salat. My Lord! Accept my prayer. Our Lord! Forgive me and my parents and the muminun on the Day the Reckoning takes place.' Ibrahim 40-41

$$\text{وَقُل رَّبِّ أَدْخِلْنِي مُدْخَلَ صِدْقٍ وَأَخْرِجْنِي مُخْرَجَ صِدْقٍ وَاجْعَل لِّي مِن لَّدُنكَ سُلْطَاناً نَّصِيراً ﴿٨٠﴾}$$

12. Say: 'My Lord, make my entry sincere and make my leaving sincere and grant me supporting authority direct from Your Presence.' Al-Isra or Bani Isra'il 80

$$\text{رَبَّنَا آتِنَا مِن لَّدُنكَ رَحْمَةً وَهَيِّئْ لَنَا مِنْ أَمْرِنَا رَشَداً ﴿١٠﴾}$$

13. 'Our Lord, give us mercy directly from You and open the way for us to right guidance in our situation.' Al-Kahf 10

$$\text{قَالَ رَبِّ اشْرَحْ لِي صَدْرِي ﴿٢٥﴾ وَيَسِّرْ لِي أَمْرِي ﴿٢٦﴾ وَاحْلُلْ عُقْدَةً مِّن لِّسَانِي ﴿٢٧﴾ يَفْقَهُوا قَوْلِي ﴿٢٨﴾}$$

14. He said, 'O Lord, expand my breast for me and make my task easy for me. Loosen the knot in my tongue so that they will understand my words.' Ta Ha 25-28

$$\text{وَقُل رَّبِّ زِدْنِي عِلْماً} \; ﴿١١٤﴾$$

15. Say: 'My Lord, increase me in knowledge.' Ta Ha 111

$$\text{وَقُل رَّبِّ أَنزِلْنِي مُنزَلاً مُّبَارَكاً وَأَنتَ خَيْرُ الْمُنزِلِينَ} \; ﴿٢٩﴾$$

16. And say: 'My Lord, land me in a blessed landing-place. You are the best Bringer to Land.' Al-Muminun 29

$$\text{إِنَّهُ كَانَ فَرِيقٌ مِّنْ عِبَادِي يَقُولُونَ رَبَّنَا آمَنَّا فَاغْفِرْ لَنَا وَارْحَمْنَا وَأَنتَ خَيْرُ الرَّاحِمِينَ} \; ﴿١٠٩﴾$$

17. There was a group of My slaves who said, 'Our Lord, we have iman, so forgive us and have mercy on us. You are the Best of the Merciful.' Al-Muminun 110

$$\text{رَبَّنَا اصْرِفْ عَنَّا عَذَابَ جَهَنَّمَ إِنَّ عَذَابَهَا كَانَ غَرَاماً} \; ﴿٦٥﴾$$

18. [The slaves of the All-Merciful say] 'Our Lord, avert from us the punishment of Hell, its punishment is inescapable pain.' Al-Furqan 65

$$\text{رَبَّنَا هَبْ لَنَا مِنْ أَزْوَاجِنَا وَذُرِّيَّاتِنَا قُرَّةَ أَعْيُنٍ وَاجْعَلْنَا لِلْمُتَّقِينَ إِمَاماً} \; ﴿٧٤﴾$$

19. [The slaves of the All-Merciful say] 'Our Lord, give us joy in our wives and children and make us a good example for those who have taqwa'. Al-Furqan 74

$$\text{رَبِّ هَبْ لِي حُكْماً وَأَلْحِقْنِي بِالصَّالِحِينَ} \; ﴿٨٣﴾ \; \text{وَاجْعَل لِّي لِسَانَ صِدْقٍ فِي الْآخِرِينَ} \; ﴿٨٤﴾ \; \text{وَاجْعَلْنِي مِن وَرَثَةِ جَنَّةِ النَّعِيمِ} \; ﴿٨٥﴾$$

20. [Ibrahim said] 'My Lord, give me right judgement and unite me with the salihun; and make me highly esteemed among the later peoples; and make me one of the inheritors of the Garden of Delight.' Ash-Shu'ara 83-85

$$\text{وَلَا تُخْزِنِي يَوْمَ يُبْعَثُونَ} \; ﴿٨٧﴾ \; \text{يَوْمَ لَا يَنفَعُ مَالٌ وَلَا بَنُونَ} \; ﴿٨٨﴾ \; \text{إِلَّا مَنْ أَتَى اللَّهَ بِقَلْبٍ سَلِيمٍ} \; ﴿٨٩﴾$$

21. [Ibrahim said] '... and do not disgrace me on the Day they are raised up, the Day when neither wealth nor sons will be of any use – except to those who come to Allah with sound and flawless hearts.' Ash-Shu'ara 87-89

Du'a – Supplications

$$\text{رَبِّ أَوْزِعْنِي أَنْ أَشْكُرَ نِعْمَتَكَ الَّتِي أَنْعَمْتَ عَلَيَّ وَعَلَى وَالِدَيَّ وَأَنْ أَعْمَلَ صَالِحاً تَرْضَاهُ وَأَصْلِحْ لِي فِي ذُرِّيَّتِي إِنِّي تُبْتُ إِلَيْكَ وَإِنِّي مِنَ الْمُسْلِمِينَ ﴿ ١٥ ﴾}$$

22. ...'My Lord, keep me thankful for the blessing You bestowed on me and on my parents, and keep me acting rightly, pleasing You. And make my descendants salihun. I have made tawba to You and I am truly one of the Muslims.' Al-Ahqaf 14

$$\text{وَالَّذِينَ جَاؤُوا مِن بَعْدِهِمْ يَقُولُونَ رَبَّنَا اغْفِرْ لَنَا وَلِإِخْوَانِنَا الَّذِينَ سَبَقُونَا بِالْإِيمَانِ وَلَا تَجْعَلْ فِي قُلُوبِنَا غِلًّا لِّلَّذِينَ آمَنُوا رَبَّنَا إِنَّكَ رَؤُوفٌ رَّحِيمٌ ﴿ ١٠ ﴾}$$

23. Those who have come after them say, 'Our Lord, forgive us and our brothers who preceded us in iman and do not put any rancour in our hearts towards those who have iman. Our Lord, You are All-Gentle, Most Merciful.' Al-Hashr 10

$$\text{رَبَّنَا عَلَيْكَ تَوَكَّلْنَا وَإِلَيْكَ أَنَبْنَا وَإِلَيْكَ الْمَصِيرُ ﴿ ٤ ﴾ رَبَّنَا لَا تَجْعَلْنَا فِتْنَةً لِّلَّذِينَ كَفَرُوا وَاغْفِرْ لَنَا رَبَّنَا إِنَّكَ أَنتَ الْعَزِيزُ الْحَكِيمُ ﴿ ٥ ﴾}$$

24. ...'Our Lord, we have put our trust in You, and have made tawba to You. You are our final destination. Our Lord, do not make us a target for those who are kafir and forgive us. Our Lord, You are the Almighty, the All-Wise.' Al-Mumtahana 4-5

$$\text{رَبِّ اغْفِرْ لِي وَلِوَالِدَيَّ وَلِمَن دَخَلَ بَيْتِيَ مُؤْمِناً وَلِلْمُؤْمِنِينَ وَالْمُؤْمِنَاتِ وَلَا تَزِدِ الظَّالِمِينَ إِلَّا تَبَاراً ﴿ ٢٨ ﴾}$$

25. [Nuh said] 'My Lord, forgive me and my parents and all who enter my house as muminun, and all the men and women of the muminun. But do not increase the wrongdoers except in ruin!' Nuh 28

$$\text{رَبَّنَا أَفْرِغْ عَلَيْنَا صَبْراً وَتَوَفَّنَا مُسْلِمِينَ ﴿ ١٢٦ ﴾}$$

26. [They said] 'Our Lord, pour down steadfastness upon us and take us back to You as Muslims.' Al-A'raf 126

$$\text{فَقَالُوا عَلَى اللهِ تَوَكَّلْنَا رَبَّنَا لَا تَجْعَلْنَا فِتْنَةً لِّلْقَوْمِ الظَّالِمِينَ ﴿ ٨٥ ﴾}$$

27. They said, 'We have put our trust in Allah. Our Lord, Do not make us a target for this wrongdoing people.' Yunus 85

أَنِّي مَسَّنِيَ الضُّرُّ وَأَنتَ أَرْحَمُ الرَّاحِمِينَ ﴿ ٨٣ ﴾

28. [Ayyub said] 'Great harm has afflicted me and You are the Most Merciful of the merciful.' Al-Anbiya 82

فَنَادَىٰ فِي الظُّلُمَاتِ أَن لَّا إِلَٰهَ إِلَّا أَنتَ سُبْحَانَكَ إِنِّي كُنتُ مِنَ الظَّالِمِينَ ﴿ ٨٧ ﴾ فَاسْتَجَبْنَا لَهُ وَنَجَّيْنَاهُ مِنَ الْغَمِّ وَكَذَٰلِكَ نُنجِي الْمُؤْمِنِينَ ﴿ ٨٨ ﴾ وَزَكَرِيَّا إِذْ نَادَىٰ رَبَّهُ رَبِّ لَا تَذَرْنِي فَرْدًا وَأَنتَ خَيْرُ الْوَارِثِينَ ﴿ ٨٩ ﴾

29. ... [Yunus - Dhu'n-Nun] called out in the pitch darkness: 'There is no god but You! Glory be to You! Truly I have been one of the wrongdoers.' We responded to him and rescued him from his grief. That is how We rescue the muminun. And Zakariyya when he called out to his Lord, 'My Lord, do not leave me on my own, though You are the Best of Inheritors.' Al-Anbiya 86-88

وَقُل رَّبِّ اغْفِرْ وَارْحَمْ وَأَنتَ خَيْرُ الرَّاحِمِينَ ﴿ ١١٨ ﴾

30. Say: 'My Lord, forgive and be merciful! You are the Best of the Merciful.' Al-Muminun 119

قُلْ أَعُوذُ بِرَبِّ الْفَلَقِ ﴿ ١ ﴾ مِن شَرِّ مَا خَلَقَ ﴿ ٢ ﴾ وَمِن شَرِّ غَاسِقٍ إِذَا وَقَبَ ﴿ ٣ ﴾ وَمِن شَرِّ النَّفَّاثَاتِ فِي الْعُقَدِ ﴿ ٤ ﴾ وَمِن شَرِّ حَاسِدٍ إِذَا حَسَدَ ﴿ ٥ ﴾

31. Say: I seek refuge with the Lord of Daybreak, from the evil of what He has created and from the evil of the darkness when it gathers and from the evil of women who blow on knots and from the evil of an envier when he envies. Al-Falaq 1-5

قُلْ أَعُوذُ بِرَبِّ النَّاسِ ﴿ ١ ﴾ مَلِكِ النَّاسِ ﴿ ٢ ﴾ إِلَٰهِ النَّاسِ ﴿ ٣ ﴾ مِن شَرِّ الْوَسْوَاسِ الْخَنَّاسِ ﴿ ٤ ﴾ الَّذِي يُوَسْوِسُ فِي صُدُورِ النَّاسِ ﴿ ٥ ﴾ مِنَ الْجِنَّةِ وَالنَّاسِ ﴿ ٦ ﴾

32. Say: I seek refuge with the Lord of mankind, the King of mankind, the God of mankind, from the evil of the insidious whisperer who whispers in people's breasts and comes from the jinn and from mankind. An-Nas 1-6

رَبَّنَا آتِنَا فِي الدُّنْيَا حَسَنَةً وَفِي الْآخِرَةِ حَسَنَةً وَقِنَا عَذَابَ النَّارِ ﴿ ٢٠١ ﴾

33. 'Our Lord, give us good in the dunya, and good in the akhira, and safeguard us from the punishment of the Fire.' Al-Baqara 199

Du'a – Supplications

﴿ ٢٥٠ ﴾ رَبَّنَا أَفْرِغْ عَلَيْنَا صَبْراً وَثَبِّتْ أَقْدَامَنَا وَانصُرْنَا عَلَى الْقَوْمِ الْكَافِرِينَ

34. [Those with Talut-Saul said] 'Our Lord, pour down steadfastness upon us, and make our feet firm, and help us against the kafir people.' Al-Baqara 248

﴿ ٣٨ ﴾ رَبِّ هَبْ لِي مِن لَّدُنْكَ ذُرِّيَّةً طَيِّبَةً إِنَّكَ سَمِيعُ الدُّعَاءِ

35. [Zakariyya said] 'O Lord, grant me by Your favour an upright child. You are the Hearer of Prayer.' Al 'Imran 38

﴿ ١٥١ ﴾ رَبِّ اغْفِرْ لِي وَلأَخِي وَأَدْخِلْنَا فِي رَحْمَتِكَ وَأَنتَ أَرْحَمُ الرَّاحِمِينَ

36. [Musa said] 'My Lord! Forgive me and my brother and cause us to enter into your mercy, and you are the most Merciful of the Merciful ones.' Al-A'raf 151

﴿ ٣٥ ﴾ قَالَ رَبِّ اغْفِرْ لِي

37. He [Sulayman] said, 'My Lord, forgive me…' Sad 34

﴿ ٤١ ﴾ وَاذْكُرْ عَبْدَنَا أَيُّوبَ إِذْ نَادَى رَبَّهُ أَنِّي مَسَّنِيَ الشَّيْطَانُ بِنُصْبٍ وَعَذَابٍ

38. Remember Our slave Ayyub when he called on his Lord: 'Shaytan has afflicted me with exhaustion and suffering.' (To be repeated in illness) Sad 40

﴿ ١٦ ﴾ رَبَّنَا إِنَّنَا آمَنَّا فَاغْفِرْ لَنَا ذُنُوبَنَا وَقِنَا عَذَابَ النَّارِ

39. 'Our Lord, we have iman, so forgive us our wrong actions and safeguard us from the punishment of the Fire.' Al 'Imran 16

Supplications after reading the Noble Qur'an

O Allah! Change my fear in my grave into love.
O Allah! Have mercy on me in the name of the Great Qur'an, and make it for me a Guide and Light and Guidance and Mercy.
O Allah! Make me remember what of I have forgotten; make me know of it that which I have become ignorant of; and make me recite it in the hours of the night and the day; and make it an argument for me O Sustainer of all the worlds. Ameen!

Glossary of Terms

akhira: not a substantive noun but an adjective, 'the later', indicating the hereafter or the next life: the events after death including the Rising, the reckoning and entrance into the Garden or the Fire.

deen: from a root that has the sense of debt and credit transaction – *dayn* – it is the life lived in awareness of the debt owed the Creator, and thus religion in the broadest sense. However, it is deeper in meaning than religion since it includes all the acts of one's living including buying and selling, renting and trading, marriage and divorce, etc., and not just the acts of worship.

dunya: not a substantive noun but an adjective, 'the lower'. It is this world as one's experience of ambition, desire, status, one's experience of wealth or poverty, etc.

establish salat: as well as the act of prayer, it comprises everything necessary to bring about the communal performance of prayer, and cannot be reduced to the private piety of individuals' performance of prayer.

fatwa: a judgement on a matter.

Hajj: the major pilgrimage to Makkah which is obligatory on every Muslim man and woman once in a lifetime if possible.

iman: signifies believing a thing or in a thing. Its primary meaning is the becoming true to the trust with respect to which Allah has confided in one, by a firm believing with the heart; not by profession of belief with the tongue only without the assent of the heart. It consists in iman in Allah, His angels, His books, His Messengers, the Last Day, the Garden and the Fire, and that the Decree of good and evil is from Him.

Islam: it means to submit or surrender, and this is both to Allah and to His Messenger ﷺ. The practical form of that is the five pillars of Islam: the witnessing that there is no god but Allah and that Muhammad is the

Messenger of Allah, the establishment of the five daily prayers, the payment of the Zakat, the fasting from dawn to sunset each day of the month of Ramadan and the Hajj-pilgrimage to Makkah once in a lifetime for those who are able to do so.

kafir, pl. kafirun, kuffar: from *kafara* – he veiled, concealed, hid or covered something, meaning 'he covered over the blessings of Allah'. Second, 'he was ungrateful or unthankful'. Third, it means 'he denied'. It also has the common meaning of 'he disbelieved'.

khalifa: a deputy or 'one who stands in during the absence of the King.' This is man's role in the creation if he steps in the feetsteps of the prophets.

mushrikun: from *shirk*, associating a partner with Allah. The term 'idolators' gives the sense that it is the worship of the idol that is significant, but close examination would reveal that it is the act of self-will on the part of the idolator in his choosing his own gods that is repugnant.

sadaqa: from the root 'he told the truth'. Very often in the Qur'an it means Zakat. However, it often means giving to someone in need, either as an optional act or as compensation for some failing or shortcoming in an act of worship, or for a wrong action.

salihun: the right-acting, the people who do right, also said to be those who are in the right place at the right time. They are one of the four categories of those 'whom Allah has blessed': the prophets, the utterly true, the witness/martyrs and the right-acting.

self, soul – *nafs*: Soul is not the best translation as it implies a spiritual entity separate from the body, a cartesian dualism of which Islam is free.

shaytan pl. shayatin: one of a large group of beings comprising both invisible beings – Jinn – and members of the human race whose wrong action has led them to attempting to mislead others. Sometimes by it Iblis, the first of the shaytans, is meant.

Glossary of Terms

Sign – *ayah*: a verse of the Qur'an, a sign of the Divine in His creation, and a miracle.

Sura a chapter of Qur'an.

taqwa: from a root meaning to protect and guard oneself, taqwa encompasses the awareness of Allah that drives one to obey Him and avoid disobeying Him, and certainly contains some element of fear.

The House: the name for the Ka'bah in Makkah.

The Maqam of Ibrahim: the position in front of the door of the Ka'bah at which Ibrahim ﷺ prayed, and at which the Muslims pray in the rites performed there.

Truth – *haqq*: although we have chosen 'truth' as its translation, this misses an essential element in this word. That is because truth has become in our minds those statements which are true, whereas the *haqq* is that which really *is*, and is thus also one of the Divine names as well as a name of the Qur'an.

'Umra: the lesser pilgrimage. This may be performed at any part of the day or night at any time of the year, and takes a number of hours.

Zakat: the obligatory tax on held wealth taken by the amir from the independently wealthy and distributed among the eight categories due it, including the poor and the bereft. It acts as a purification of the wealth, and irresistibly suggests the image of pruning, that act which is so essential for the well-being of the fruit-bearing tree.